BRIAN REYNOLDS

The Times and Life of
the Northamptonshire Sportsman

Ian Addis
Mick Dean
Brian Slough

Kind regards
Ian Addis

DIAMETRIC PUBLICATIONS
2000

Brian Reynolds: The Times and Life of the Northamptonshire Sportsman

ISBN 0 9533482 6 1

First published in 2000 by
Diametric Publications, 45 Grosvenor Road, Kettering, Northamptonshire

Jacket design by Robert Mercer.

Printed & bound in the United Kingdom by Woolnough Bookbinding Ltd.,
Irthlingborough, Northamptonshire.

Introduction

Brian Reynolds was born in Kettering. He has never lived anywhere else. He played cricket for his home County for over twenty years. He then coached Northamptonshire for twenty-five years. There are others who have spent a lifetime in cricket but Brian Reynolds' loyalty to his native County is unbeatable. He also played football with distinction for Kettering Town.

In the Yorkshire Pennine town of Holmfirth, three fictional old men fix wheels to a bath and push it down the hill. In the Northamptonshire boot and shoe town of Kettering, three old men have tried to produce a worthy tribute to the town's most successful and revered sportsman.

Brian Reynolds made a profound impact on the authors. Two were born, bred and currently live in Kettering. The third has been a resident of Kettering for just thirty-five years. There are differences of opinion amongst the trio; in what follows, the joins may be obvious. But not as obvious, it is hoped, as the admiration all three have for their subject.

Acknowledgements

Our gratitude is due to many people who have assisted us with information and encouragement.

Without the local press, this offering would have been much poorer. The support of Ian Davidson, Sports Editor of the Northamptonshire Evening Telegraph and Liz McBride, the Librarian, has been essential. Also crucial has been the help of Andrew Radd who is undoubtedly too modest to accept the fact that he knows everything about, and everyone in, Northamptonshire cricket.

We acknowledge the help of former cricketers, former footballers, golfers, residents of Kettering, and those involved in the later years of Brian's work. In particular we must mention (alphabetically) Eddie Armstrong, Ray Bailey, Bill Barron, David Buckby, Bob Darlow, Mr and Mrs Joe Deer, Bill Draper, John and Peter Draper, Jim Harker, David Heggie, Don Mabelson, Gordon Rogers and David Steele.

We have spoken to many people on our ramblings round the County Ground and have valued all contributions and suggestions. Our sincere apologies to anyone who has been inadvertently omitted.

We have also received the considerable assistance and pleasurable hospitality of the Reynolds family, Angela, Sue and Ian, as well as the man himself.

Most of the artefacts come from the personal collections of Brian and the authors. We are grateful to the Northamptonshire Newspapers for permission to use their photographs and other material.

The Prologues

"There is a story to unfold,
A tale, fit for the telling"

Anon

Avondale Colts
Ian Addis

Edgbaston 1954
Mick Dean

Promise and fulfilment
Brian Slough

The Team of Dreams

AVONDALE COLTS FC

Back (l to r): Keith Bishton, Gordon Rogers, Vic Abbott, Barry Goldsworthy, Bernard Reed.

Middle (l to r): Arnold Sadler, Willie Easton, Dennis Franklin, Gordon Lee, Brian Skipper, Harold Towns, Bob Darlow, Cyril Fletton.

Front (l to r): Brian Whitwick, Reg Ainsworth, Don Turner, Bill Ashby, Brian Reynolds.

IAN ADDIS'S TALE

My father and I sat on opposite sides of the table in the Flettons' kitchen in Orchard Crescent. Mr Fletton, or 'Old Fleck' as my mother always called him, stood at the stove, fork in hand, frying herrings. We had only called to book his services as a chimney sweep but he'd insisted that we stay and share his supper.

My father was delighted to accept but I had no appetite. A glance at the fish lying side by side in the blackened pan, eyes gleaming, Old Fleck's hands ingrained with a lifetime's soot, and the rising cloud of acrid smoke were enough to put me off my food for a week.

The door into the living room was open and there, lovingly arranged on the wooden clothes-horse in front of the fire, hung a complete set of football jerseys. I recognised them at once - the distinctive yellow and green quartered colours of the Avondale Colts, pride of the Kettering and District Youth League, shirts fit for heroes.

The manager and architect of the team's success, Old Fleck's eldest son, Cyril, sat in a well-worn armchair alongside the fireplace, immersed in the sports pages of the Daily Herald, oblivious to my admiring gaze. I pictured the players' faces, familiar from countless winter Saturday afternoons spent at the Glebe Farm playing field just a short walk from my Holly Road home.

Barely six years old, I was yet to graduate to Rockingham Road, the Poppies and the Birmingham League. And, in those pre-television days, my knowledge of the lofty heights of the English First Division was entirely gleaned from the pages of the Saturday 'Pink Un'. Brian Skipper, Gordon Rogers, Bob Darlow, Harry Towns and a fresh-faced youngster called Brian Reynolds. These were my Lawtons, Matthews, Mannions and Carters.

On one of the rare occasions that my father had joined me on the touchline, he pointed out the Colts stocky, fleet-footed winger, and remarked, "That lad will play for England. But at cricket, not football."

Throughout the twenty or more years that he followed Brian's career, my father's opinion never wavered, even when he was later forced to amend 'will' to 'should have'.

On the evidence of that evening at the Flettons, he was a far better judge of a cricketer than he was of a fish supper.

The Team of '54

Northamptonshire at Edgbaston, May 1954

Back (l to r): Brian Reynolds, Keith Andrew, Alan Liddell, Syd Starkie, Freddie Jakeman, George Tribe.

Front (l to r): Jock Livingston, AL 'Dick' Wells, Dennis Brookes, Norman Oldfield, Vince Broderick.

MICK DEAN'S TALE

In 1954, a five-year old who had already demonstrated a talent for remembering useless information - he could write the names of all the Pakistani tourists - was taken to Edgbaston by his father whenever Warwickshire were at home on a Saturday.

All I remember of my first visit - towards the end of the 1953 season - is being amused by the constant to-and-froing of the players on a day of many showers. On my second visit I can recall vividly Yorkshire's Frank Lowson having a stump sent cartwheeling by Tom Pritchard to end play for the day. My memory of my third visit is of a vociferous crowd, whose barracking and sarcastic comments greatly amused this infant.

The object of the crowd's displeasure, most commonly manifested by slow-handclapping, was 'Reckless' Reynolds, as the local paper dubbed him. I still remember being impressed by the way the Northamptonshire man ignored it all; I don't remember finding it at all boring, though looking back at the statistics - Northants all out for 258 in 163 overs - it is understandable why some spectators thought it less than entertaining. At tea, Northants were 124 for four with opener Reynolds undefeated on 39 after 260 minutes.

My admiration for the Northamptonshire man increased the following year when another batsman provoked the slow-handclap at Edgbaston. Trevor Bailey's response was different; he refused to continue batting until the noise abated. "Because he's an amateur - and knows that he's famous," explained father.

When exiled to a foreign land - Scotland - my England team that was selected for 'roll-the-pencil' Ashes series during double French lessons always included LN Devereux (my club's professional) and B Reynolds.

A week after I moved to Kettering I was delighted to discover there was a Championship match taking place in the town, walked down to the Northampton Road ground and found that it was Brian's benefit match. I was almost disappointed to discover that BL Reynolds was not always the dour stonewaller I had imagined him to be.

I looked up Wisden's account of that 1954 match which Warwickshire won by two wickets with six minutes to spare. "Northamptonshire batted slowly on the opening day, but their tactics seemed justified when Warwickshire finished 80 runs behind on first innings." Northamptonshire lost, despite Brian laying a solid foundation.

As an outsider, I am sometimes inclined to dismiss Northamptonshire as a 'so far but no farther' County - and not just at cricket. As happened at Edgbaston in 1954, the promising start so often tails away. If that generalisation has any truth, Brian Reynolds is not a typical Northamptonshire man.

BRIAN SLOUGH

Some years ago, a theatre director of my acquaintance suggested to the actors playing Dogberry and Verges in his production of 'Much Ado About Nothing' that they should spend the day at the County Ground. Not to watch the cricket, mind you, but the performance of two of the gatemen, whom they could use as role models. The actor playing Dogberry had never previously been to a county match. As he sat among the spectators at the football ground end, one of Dogberry's malapropisms kept entering his head: "To babble and to talk is most tolerable and not to be endured." By lunch time he was convinced that those around him were only there for the chat; the cricket seemed incidental.

Most county grounds are rife with gossip and much ado about nothing, not least at Northampton, with its ready access for the boundary stroller. Rumour is a keen traveller, especially in calamities, when any babble is believed and Northants has had more than its fair share of them.

At such times, talk harks back to the received wisdom of the 'golden days' and the nostalgic comfort of players who inhabited them. The arrival of FR Brown (what other hero has such a prosaic name?). 1954 to 1957, when the County were seventh, seventh, fourth and then second in the Championship, with Brookes, Livingston, Tribe, Tyson and Andrew. 1965 and second again, with the contrasting figures of Milburn and Steele. It is somehow appropriate, however, that the linchpin throughout that time was a local hero, without whom no team is complete: Brian Leonard Reynolds.

My dictionary of names has the following entries: "Brian, Celtic: strength. Leonard, Teutonic: lionstrong." Perhaps there is more force in names than most men dream of?

In the 1951 Playfair Annual, Gordon Ross wrote of the debutant: "And, for the future, there is also the promise of Reynolds (batsman)." "Promising" is one of those safety-first adjectives in which commentators take refuge when assessing young players. In the 'Who's Who' section of that Playfair, for example, it was also applied to Alan Mason (Yorkshire), David R Davies (Glamorgan) and Russell Wood (Gloucestershire). None of these worthies, for whatever reason, made Who's Who in 1952. Promise, they say, can inhibit performance, though Mason's best figures were five for 56 against (whisper it softly) Northamptonshire. The editor (a certain Peter West) also judged Statham and Trueman as "promising". Peter May was deemed "very promising" and Colin Cowdrey - born in 1932 like Brian Reynolds - "outstanding". Early Playfairs always had a soft spot for southern public schoolboys, sometimes justifiably.

Another compiler of Who's Who, Geoffrey Chaucer, believed that promise is a form of debt. If so, then Brian repaid his with interest and a hefty bonus. Some statistics are instructive. He appeared in 426 first-class matches for Northamptonshire (only Dennis Brookes and Jack Timms played more). His 18,640 runs (bettered again, at the time of Brian's retirement, only by Brookes and Timms) in 732 innings, contained twenty-one centuries. In ten separate seasons he recorded over 1,000 runs, what used to be seen as the batsman's benchmark.

He held 299 catches, 45 of them while keeping wicket. Such details, however, are but pointers to the story, rather like saying that Brian Johnston, born in Little Berkhamsted on 24 June 1912, was a writer and broadcaster.

For starters, it could be said of Brian Reynolds, as a 'Daily Telegraph' editorial once did of Brian Johnston, that he carried his love of cricket and the wider applications of that sporting ethos, through life. That is a greater tribute than 18,640 runs. Cricket, like religion, can codify and illumine much of life. When Brian began his professional career, cricket still claimed for itself a civilising mission: a means to impart the moral values of co-operation and working for others. At that time, I was involved in a coaching course at Lilleshall. It was headed by Michael Walford (a triple Oxford blue, Somerset cricketer and Olympic hockey captain), George Geary of Leicestershire and the incomparable HS Altham. It was suggested to participants, as Altham did to newcomers at Winchester College, that if they were to find themselves, then it was necessary to lose themselves in something bigger. Brian has lost himself in Northamptonshire cricket, in the County Club itself, and a myriad other outlets beyond.

Apart from a short gap at the end of his first-class playing career, he has served Northamptonshire County Cricket Club for almost fifty years in a variety of roles: player; senior professional; coach; Second Eleven captain; Cricket Development Officer and scout. He said to me once that he would do almost anything for Northamptonshire, apart from keeping the score in one of those little wooden huts. The arrival of computers has not changed his mind.

That kind (or any kind) of commitment is unusual nowadays and seems likely to become increasingly rare. Indeed, Brian's length of service, and his range of employment within one Club, are probably unique. Today's players appear to switch counties (countries in a few cases) as readily as their sponsored cars, fast reflecting the transfer system in football. A list of the Northamptonshire playing staff in 1998, for instance, shows that twelve of the twenty-nine either arrived from another first-class county or were to move to one in the future. That is not a criticism; some of that twelve were released and the mortgage needs to be paid.

It is difficult to think Brian would ever have played for another county. That oft-quoted sentiment, which John Arlott wrote about him, bears repetition: "In his own mind he is not only a cricketer, he is a Northamptonshire cricketer." The same might be said of David Capel. Not only the traditionalists among us relaxed and approved when he accepted a coaching post with his home county, in preference to playing elsewhere. Brian was also pleased. Football-phobes argue that a burgeoning transfer market will be an inevitable consequence of the two-division Championship and one dayers, with unfortunate outcomes for supposedly weaker counties. ECB gurus see it as a means to raise standards and stimulate public interest, as with football. Back page scandal sells not only papers, but seats in the stand. We shall see, as Mark Nicholas likes to say. Either way, you can't buck the market, even in cricket.

Today's player movement merely reflects the wider world, where short-term contracts and periodic career shifts are now the norm, even encouraged. Cricket is predominantly a business and therefore subject to the same machinations and values as any other. It is axiomatic that this invasion by the business 'ethic' is breaking down the boundaries of idealism and the sometimes dishonourable realities from which cricket was designed to provide an escape. "Sledging" (even the sound of the word is ugly), pressurising umpires, and dishonest appeals are but three obvious reflections of society's ruthless realities. Is it romantic naïveté to suggest they rarely surfaced in Brian's playing days?

Sir Pelham Warner, who once despaired that cricket should ever become a circus, would be alarmed at the effects of commercialism on the game's participants and its essential dignity. To take but one example: trivial perhaps, or symptomatic of something darker. 1950 team photos show players in pristine whites, sparkling buckskin boots, and unadulterated club blazers. Today's garish one-day kit is a predictable outcome of allowing sponsors' logos on conventional clothing, but when these logos dominate county crests, the symbolic implications should not be ignored.

Yet we live in a society dominated by the production and consumption of images, to an extent where not even cricket can remain immune from circus-style spectacle, our growing form of cultural expression. No wonder the Championship seems anachronistic to anyone under fifty. The infiltration is unavoidable; its extent is apparent if you imagine a Brookes, Brown or Reynolds walking to the crease accompanied by Bruce Springsteen or, come to think of it, Vera Lynn.

The danger is that the game itself seems threatened by its accompanying apparatus of promotion-hype, to a point where it can appear incidental to the expensive preparation required to stage it. The irony is that in the case of the Championship it is likely that no amount of hype will save it. In a radio interview in January 2000, after his return from England's tour to South Africa, Michael Atherton said he saw no purpose in the Championship and its days were numbered. Brian will recall that when he became a professional two million spectators watched Championship games. By 1966, the number had dropped to 513,578.

That decline, its seemingly remorseless continuation, the ramifications and reasons for it, are paramount in Brian's career. During fifty years in the game, he has seen or experienced just about every facet of it. At the conclusion of his widely acclaimed book, 'Betrayal', Graeme Wright thought the struggle for cricket's soul was being lost, principally because of self-interest. He contrasts that betrayal with those people who are trying to keep that soul alive, teaching youngsters the game, "in the hope that, as well as a love of the game, they will be imbued with something of the philosophy of the game: its unique place in the nation's life, its nobility of spirit, its code of chivalry and respect." Reading that reminded me of Harry Altham's words at Lilleshall.

'Betrayal' was written in 1993, when Brian Reynolds was one of those 'people' Wright lauded, in his position as Cricket Development Officer (did anyone in 1950 ever dream such a role would even be necessary?). That same year he organised, in exemplary fashion, a Kwik-cricket festival for a range of Primary schools throughout Northamptonshire. True, it was part of his remit, but it was a splendid occasion, when there was no doubting he was keeping the soul alive of the game he loves.

Brian Leonard Reynolds, 57 The Oval

"The past it is a magic word,
Too beautiful to lose.
It looks back like a lovely face,
Who can forget the past?"

John Clare,
'Childhood'

Headlands

The thirty-five shilling bat

Lo-Lo and Pants

A home fit for heroes

"My mother never needed to bother where I was. She knew I'd come home when it was dark."

Fate decreed that Brian Reynolds should be born and raised in The Oval. Not Kennington's, of course, but Kettering's – a ring of council-built houses on what was, during the nineteen thirties, the south-west edge of the town. Nevertheless, the Headlands playing field, within throwing distance of Brian's front door, provided the lads from the estate with their own Test Match and Cup Final arena. Throughout the holidays, and every evening after school, they would assemble and pick sides, football or cricket, depending on the season. "My mother never needed to bother where I was. She knew I'd come home when it was dark."

Many of the boys would grace local sports teams in later years, most notably Derek Plews, familiarly known as 'Ginner', and his brother Len, an accomplished footballer and cricketer who married a Jehovah's Witness and never played again; John and Peter Draper, cricketing members of the Montagu Street furniture dynasty; champion cyclist Bernard 'Onker' Smith and Town League stalwarts 'Nip' Collier, Mick Beasley, Dick Hilliard and John Hill. Everyone was welcome. Older boys mingled happily with youngsters, but there were no concessions for age. "It was very much the school of hard knocks. You soon became streetwise in those games."

However, as contemporaries are quick to point out, by the age of eight or nine, Brian was more than holding his own at cricket with players almost twice his age. The team that had him on its side had a distinct advantage. He didn't just swing and hope, like most did, but played straight. And as he grew up, the qualities that characterised his approach to the professional game, became more and more evident. When he eventually owned a cricket bat, purchased from the Sports and Rubber Company in the High Street for the princely sum of thirty four shillings and tenpence, or £1.75 in today's money, it was guarded most jealously, loaned to no-one and treasured like a craftsman's tool of the trade.

He was always ready to take advice, particularly from the more senior players. Among the older generation of boys whose example inspired the young Reynolds was Don Collins, step-brother to Oval neighbours Nip and Trevor Collier, and a good medium pace bowler who was later killed in action along with fellow Kettering soldiers, Bill Walters and Ivor Gunn, while serving with the British forces in Italy during the Second World War.

The rough, bumpy outfield where the wicket was set up provided a far from ideal batting surface, especially as they played with a hard ball and no pads. In later years they trespassed on wickets carefully prepared by groundsman Bernard Loasby for Town League matches. "We always chose pitches as far away as possible from the gate in Highfield Road and kept one eye open for Mr Loasby. Someone would shout, 'Here's Uncle Lo-Lo' and we'd scatter. But we'd be back again the minute he'd gone."

In those days, the Headlands sports field boasted football, rugby and cricket pitches, and an impressive wooden grandstand complete with tiers of seats. There were also three double sets of cricket practice nets, which were booked out to Town League teams on summer evenings. The closest Brian came to formal instruction was when acting as ball retriever for the Old Centralians team, during their regular net practices at the ground. Sitting on a shooting stick behind the net, and studying every ball through pebble-lensed spectacles, schoolteacher RG Braithwaite, familiarly known as 'Pants', would proffer sound advice to both batsman and bowler, while from a distance, the young Reynolds watched, listened and learned.

When Leonard Reynolds married Ethel Toseland in 1923, there was no question of their moving into their own house. Nor could they live with in-laws. Ethel's mother and father were both dead and Len's parents had converted the front room of their house in Windmill Avenue into a shop to provide a living for a sister who suffered from tuberculosis and couldn't manage factory work. The newly-weds spent the first few years of married life in the front room of the Drapers' family home in Naseby Road. When Brian's elder brother, Jack, was born in September 1925, the two families continued to live under the same roof until the Reynolds moved into their newly-built council house at 57 The Oval, eighteen months later. Like their counterparts off Windmill Avenue, these 'homes fit for heroes', modest, but with neat front gardens, were in marked contrast to the Victorian red-bricked terraced rows that proliferate around Kettering's town centre.

Born in 1899, Len Reynolds had enlisted as an under-age volunteer in the Middlesex Regiment during the First World War. The effects of being gassed, and then taken prisoner, took their toll in later life when he suffered badly from bronchial problems and emphysema.

On his return from the Army, he rejoined lastmakers, Mobbs and Lewis, working as a moulder at their Carrington Street foundry. The work was both hard and dangerous. On one occasion a huge vat overturned and Len found himself surrounded by a river of molten metal. While leaping over the stream in a desperate bid to escape serious injury, his trailing foot was badly scalded and for several weeks it seemed likely that it would require amputation. Unsurprisingly, the accident had a salutary effect upon the young man who decided that there must be less hazardous ways of making a living.

He rented a small factory unit in Water Street and together with a partner, Bill Crofts, bought up scrap brass, melted it down and manufactured machine parts. For a time the enterprise prospered but, when a travelling salesman approached offering the pair an opportunity to safeguard the business through the purchase of a large industrial smelting cupola on the 'never-never', Len opted out. The late twenties were no time to get into debt and family responsibilities wore heavily. Long periods of unemployment followed.

During this time, as Jack Reynolds clearly recalls, desperate measures were required to make ends meet. "My father used to buy rabbits at the market for threepence, bring them home, skin them, sell the meat for sixpence and then get a few more pennies for the skins from Sculthorpe's butcher's shop in Northall Street."

A decidedly more savoury occupation, with something of a sporting dimension, made good use of Len's driving talents. "In those days, as I remember, you could sign on the dole for three days and work for two. Dad used to keep himself busy at the beginning of the week and then spend Fridays and Saturdays at the Evening Telegraph in Dryland Street. He cleaned the vans and the bosses' cars, delivered copies of 'The Kettering Leader' around the local newsagents, and on winter Saturday evenings took bundles of 'The Football Telegraph' to Wellingborough. It was always a race between the Kettering 'Pink Un' and the Northampton 'Green Un' to be the first on the streets of Wellingborough with the football results. Dad often took me with him on those journeys and I remember the excitement as we hurried along the A509. There was no time to stop on the way. As we approached Isham and then Harrowden, dad would say, "Get the bundle ready, open the window", and out it would go. There was no one-way system in Wellingborough in those days and we drove straight down to the Market Square. If there was a policeman on point-duty, dad would wave a couple of Pink Uns at him as a bribe to stop the traffic and let us through. When we got back to the Evening Telegraph offices the editor, Frank Hutchen, would enquire anxiously, 'Did you beat 'em?' There was no fooling him. If we had, it was worth half a crown. If we hadn't, there just was a black look saying, 'Well, do better next time!'"

During the Second World War, Len Reynolds drove articulated lorries by day and was a reserve policeman by night. The lorries were loaded with Wellington bomber wings at the Sywell factory where they were manufactured and delivered to Kettering's old bus depot on the corner of Havelock Street and Rockingham Road for completion. After the war he worked as an odd-job man at the Munn and Felton shoe factory in Clarence Road but failing health eventually led to lengthy periods of absence and he died in Kettering General Hospital of bronchial pneumonia in January 1962. A member of the generation of working class men seldom seen in public without a flat cap, he is remembered affectionately by both his sons as 'something of a rough diamond.'

John Draper, who lived opposite the Reynolds family at number 54 The Oval, describes him as "a considerate fair-minded man, possessing a wisdom of purity that stood alongside the hard experiences of his life. He was a homespun philosopher who had little time for life's artificialities, was never deceived by salesmen, politicians or the like, and kept to simple truths about the realities of life. As he was wont to say, 'the big fishes eat the little ones'."

Ethel Reynolds had grown up in Wood Street, Kettering. One of six sisters, her parents had owned a florists in Newland Street, but both had died when comparatively young. When first married, Ethel worked in the closing room at Timpson's shoe factory in Bath Road, but left on the arrival of baby Jack and never returned. Three of her sisters moved away from Kettering; Jessica made her home in Hall Green, Birmingham and Doris and Olive moved to Matlock, though Olive later moved close to Jessica in the Birmingham suburb of Acocks Green. Winifred married Cyril Dalby, shoeroom foreman at East's factory in Northall Street and settled in the Broadway while the unmarried Beatrice lived in a flat in Hampden Crescent before moving to a bungalow in Martin Road.

Reynolds seven for 2

Stamford Road v Central School, 1946

"So old in youth and so untimely sad"

HE Bates,
'We who now wait'

The Workhouse and chickens

Family Tragedy

The Hallelujah Chorus

A Bowling Prodigy

"I suppose the tragedy helped me to stand on my own two feet and make my own way in life."

The world into which Brian Reynolds was born, on June 10th 1932, was a very harsh place. Economic depression ravaged Kettering's staple industry, the boot and shoe trade, throughout the thirties. So many of the town's skilled men were unemployed that it was claimed that Mr Hawthorn, factory manager at William Timpson's in Bath Road, had merely "to go outside, raise his arms, and fifty would appear clamouring for work." Young men fortunate enough to hold down a job often failed to apply for their entitled 'man's wage' on reaching the age of twenty-one, for fear of being given their 'cards'. Poverty was rife, and for many the spectre of the workhouse, known as the Union and located in the building in London Road currently occupied by St Mary's Hospital, was no imaginary fear.

Most men from the estate worked in the fickle boot and shoe industry. Some, like the neighbour who performed menial jobs for stallholders late into the night at the town's Saturday market, supplemented their frugal incomes through casual work. Brian's family, in common with others, kept chickens in their small back garden, while many worked allotments, or garden-fields as they were known, on a large area of land to the east of Highfield Road.

Today the houses around The Oval look much as they did seventy years ago. However, closer inspection reveals tell-tale changes. The front gardens are somewhat scruffier, cars occupy grass verges, satellite dishes cling to outside walls and double-glazed PVC units have replaced the original metal-framed windows. Inside, conditions are decidedly less primitive. The trappings of modern life: central heating, refrigerators, washing machines, vacuum cleaners, fitted kitchens, shower units, televisions and telephones are now *de rigeur*. Yet few who grew up without these 'luxuries' would consider themselves deprived. For many, drudgery simply went with the territory. But for some, like Jack and Brian Reynolds, it nurtured the small, determined worm of ambition.

Jack Reynolds left school in 1939 at the age of fourteen. On his mother's advice he sought work at Timpson's shoe factory which, 'offered a job for life and a pension.' He was given work inserting toe puffs at a weekly rate of 10/6d.

Following the outbreak of war, as more and more young men were called up for active service, vacancies occurred in higher grade jobs. 'Stiffener boys' were paid £2 a week, but when youngsters like Jack took on the extra responsibility they continued to be paid at the old rate. Imbued with his father's sense of fair play, Jack encouraged the other four boys in his team to seek a meeting with the foreman, Mr Tompkins, who referred the matter to the afore-mentioned Mr Hawthorn, the formidable factory manager. "When we insisted on receiving the going rate for the job, he gave us a week's notice. Two days before we were supposed to finish, he called us into his office, read us the riot act and told us that if we didn't carry on at 10/6d, he'd make sure we didn't get a job anywhere else in the town. Two of us stuck by our principles and left. The other three stayed on."

The war brought new employment opportunities to the town and Jack found work at Holborn's Engineering Works in Morley Street. The firm, which made gearings for Rolls Royce Merlin engines, had been bombed out of their Coventry factory. The sixteen year old was paid £3/5/0d a week for twelve hour, night and day shifts.

Towards the end of 1942, the Reynolds family was dealt a terrible blow. At about eight o'clock on the morning of Saturday 29th November Jack returned from night shift, said "Good morning" to his mother who was about to polish the lino on the living room floor, and went straight upstairs to bed. Some time later he was awakened by the next door neighbour, Mrs Pack, who was banging furiously on his bedroom door.

"Apparently my mother had gone on an errand to Corby's general store on the corner of Argyll Street and St Michael's Road, collapsed in the shop and was lying unconscious in their living room waiting for the doctor and an ambulance to arrive. My father was out on his lorry and Brian, who was only ten at the time, was probably playing with his pals on the Headlands sportsfield. I got dressed quickly and hurried along to Corby's. Some time after I got to the shop my dad arrived and the decision was made to take my mother home instead of to hospital. She was carried upstairs and made comfortable in the front bedroom. We were told that she had suffered a massive stroke and even if she regained consciousness there was no hope of a recovery. She lingered on for over a week but died the following Sunday, 6th December, aged just forty-seven."

The effect upon Len Reynolds and his two sons was shattering. "Our parents had been devoted to each other and to us. We were all knocked for six. The neighbours, particularly the Packs, Colliers, Colemans, and especially Alf and Phyllis Butlin, were all very supportive. They kept an eye on Brian, taking him into their homes if ever dad or I wasn't about."

Jack applied for deferment from military service but was called up the following year, joining the Royal Inniskilling Dragoons as a wireless operator and gunner. He landed at Ostend shortly after D-Day, crossed the Rhine and accompanied his regiment all the way to Berlin. When hostilities ceased, Jack joined the regimental dance band, putting his musical talents to good use.

As a child he had enjoyed family Christmases at his Uncle Albert's Barnwell Street home. Cousin Claude played cornet in the Fuller Mission Brass Band and when young Jack blew into his instrument and succeeded in making a reasonably melodic sound it was suggested he might have the aptitude to become a bandsman. However, his father laid down the law. "If you take up an instrument, you've got to treat it seriously. Practice, practice and more practice."

An instrument was purchased from Richardson's Music Store in Dalkeith Place and the young musician never looked back. Within a few years he was playing solo cornet with the Fuller Mission Band and, before joining the Army, played trumpet in his cousin Les Dalby's locally renowned 'Broadway Bandits'. Concert tours with the service band enlivened the immediate post-war days but it was 1947 before Jack was demobbed and returned to The Oval.

With his brother away in the forces and his father out at work for much of the time Brian often had to fend for himself. Typically, he puts a positive slant on his experiences. "Looking back, I suppose the tragedy helped me to stand on my own two feet and make my own way in life."

Like other children on the estate, from the age of four Brian attended Hawthorn Road Mixed Infant and Junior School, which was then under the headship of Captain Hudson. When classes gathered in the hall for morning assembly, the Headmaster always sat beneath a huge landscape painting which adorned the wall above. The work of eminent Kettering artist, George Harrison, the picture assumed great significance, dominating Brian's recollections of early school life. Revisiting what is now Hawthorn Primary School almost sixty years later in his role as Northamptonshire's Cricket Development Officer, he was delighted to learn that the picture had survived, albeit relegated from its prime position to a less conspicuous location in the school's attic.

An appreciation of art continued into his secondary years at Stamford Road School, but received something of a blow when his representation of a church and lichgate received short shrift from teacher, Mr Capps. "I'd taken hours over it. I thought it was a smashing job but he found fault with just about everything. Perhaps it wasn't very good, but the criticism hurt."

Not, however, as much as a comment by another member of staff. "His name was Sid Painter. I can't remember just what I'd done to upset him, but he said that I'd end up as one of those people standing on the street corner up to no good, or always lining up at the Labour Exchange out of work. I never forgot it and was determined to prove him wrong. I saw his son in town the other day. He looked identical to his father, and those words came straight back into my mind. I don't think teachers always realise the significance some children attach to their words."

"We had a school choir, led by the music teacher, Sid Knapman. Our signature tune was 'The Hallelujah Chorus', but other offerings escape my memory. However, I'll never forget the time Sid lined the whole class up, thirty or so, in a big square around the classroom, and caned us all for messing about when he came into the room."

Brian had little interest in academic subjects and sought solace in his beloved sport. Fortunately there was cricket and PE teacher, Arthur Weatherall.

Bowling "Prodigy"

DESCRIBED by his sports master as a "future county player," 16-year-old Brian Reynolds, son of Mr. and the late Mrs. L. T. Reynolds, of 57, The Oval, Kettering, wants to take up cricket professionally and is an "expert" bowler.

"He was my mentor, a marvellous man, who loved sport and gave us all tremendous encouragement. Under his tuition, we won the Clarke Cup for cricket. I've always thought that if the teacher, or Head, is keen on sport the opportunities for the children will be there. They recognise its importance and make time despite the many other demands."

The appreciation was mutual. In an 'Evening Telegraph' article from June 1946, Mr Weatherall demonstrated a shrewd assessment of Brian's cricketing potential when he said of the fourteen year old, "for a schoolboy he shows great ability at batting and he can also bowl off-breaks, leg-breaks and fast straight balls. He has excellent prospects and if he carries on as he is doing he has every chance of becoming a county cricketer." Described by the press as a 'bowling prodigy', those fast straight balls accounted for some remarkable statistics against local school teams. Over a space of three weeks he took twenty-one wickets for a total of 17 runs. With their star bowler recording seven for 2 against the Central School, seven for 8 against the Grammar School and seven for 7 against the Parish Church School, it is no surprise that Stamford Road School's Manor side topped the league.

At the traditional presentation tea, held at the Parish Church School in the Horsemarket, Brian received the cup from Alderman Mrs CW Clarke, the widow of its donor and a well known local magistrate. Her address, which was reported at length in the local newspaper, contained a strong message, much of it decidedly anachronistic by today's standards. "I hope you boys will make good use of your spare time. Not like one lad I saw recently who was swinging on a road sign. This is the type of behaviour we are trying to avoid, but before I got there to admonish him he had gone." However, when she urged the boys to be good citizens and to take a pride in their town and in working for it, her words struck a chord with at least one member of her youthful audience. It furthered Brian's resolve to make the best of his talents, to serve his community with honour, and to become a professional cricketer. As he told the reporter, "I have been interested in cricket almost since I could walk and I should like to take it up as a career."

It gave him great satisfaction some years later when, as an established Northamptonshire player, he was invited to attend the function as a celebrated guest. Brian presented the cup to Grammar School captain, Peter Larcombe, in the presence of both Alderman Mrs Clarke and the long-serving chairman of Kettering and District Schools Cricket Association, a certain RG Braithwaite.

Strangely, Brian's own cricketing talent appears to owe little to pedigree. Len Reynolds had been a useful boxer in his younger days, appearing in local promoter Tom Hefford's celebrated shows. Brother Jack was a left-arm bowler and represented Kettering Boys at football but played little sport on leaving school.

Brian's secondary education had begun in 1943 and, in common with many other pupils of the time, was interrupted by war-time contingencies. Attendance was only part-time and classes were often held in the Fuller Church Sunday School rooms, some distance from the Montagu Street building. There was certainly little opportunity to take leaving examinations and Brian's formal education ended three years later when, at the age of fourteen, he began work for Mr Thompson, a newsagent and wholesale tobacconist in the Horsemarket. "I'd worked at the shop as a newspaper boy for some time and when I was offered the full-time job it was too good to refuse. I used to make up the orders in the back room and then deliver them to shops and pubs around the town."

The presentation of the Clarke Cup in 1956. From the left:

Ray Lilley, teacher at Gladstone Street, Rothwell;
Keith Buckby, Kettering Grammar School under 13 captain with the Thornton Shield;
Pat Thornton, well-known and much-respected Kettering jeweller;
Brian Reynolds;
Alderman Mrs CW Clarke;
John Cowell, Grammar School history master and later deputy head.
Peter Larcombe, Kettering Grammar School under 15 captain (later a stalwart of Kettering Town CC) with the Clarke Cup;
RG Braithwaite.

Reynolds b Armstrong 11

Kettering Town v Kaycee, North Park, Kettering, 1949

1944 - 1949

"If ever world were blessed, now it is."

Laurie Lee,
'April Rise'

Trent Bridge

Kettering Town CC and FC

The Festival of Britain

On trial at Wantage Road

"When I first arrived at the club, the only kit I possessed was a white shirt."

NOTTS. COUNTY CRICKET CLUB

ENGLAND v. AUSTRALIA

TRENT BRIDGE GROUND, June 10th, 11th 12th, 14th & 15th, 1948

Batsman's No.	ENGLAND	1st Innings		2nd Innings
1	Hutton, L.	b Miller	3	
2	Washbrook, C.	c Brown b Lindwall	36	
3	W. J. Edrich	Bld Johnston	18	
4	Compton, D.	Bld Miller	19	
5	Hardstaff, J.	Ct Miller b Johnston	0	
6	Barnett, C. J.	Bld Johnston	8	
7	N. W. D. Yardley (Cp)	L.B.W. Toshack	3	
8	Evans, T. G. (Wk)	Ct Morris b Johnston	12	
9	Laker, J. C.	Ct Tallon b Miller	63	
10	Bedser, A. V.	Ct Brown b Johnston	22	
11	Young, J.	not out	1	
		Extras	10	Extras
		Total	195	Total

Wkts. 1st Inn	1	2	3	4	5	6	7	8	9	10	2nd Inn	1	2	3	4	5	6	7	8	9	10
fell	9	15	46	46	48	60	74	74	163												

Bowler's No.	AUSTRALIA	1st Innings	2nd Innings
1	D. G. Bradman (Cpt(		
2	S. G. Barnes		
3	A. Morris		
4	A. L. Hassett		
5	K. R. Miller		
6	I. W. Johnson		
7	W. A. Brown		
8	R. Lindwall		
9	D. Tallon (wk)		
10	W. A. Johnston		
11	E. R. Toshack		
		Extras	Extras
		Total	Total

Wkts. 1st Inn	1	2	3	4	5	6	7	8	9	10	2nd Inn	1	2	3	4	5	6	7	8	9	10
fell																					

ANALYSIS

AUSTRALIA Bowling		overs	mds	runs	wkts		overs	mdns	runs	wkts

ENGLAND Bowling										

Umpires: Messrs. F. Chester & E. Cook   Commence: Friday 11.30

ENGLAND WON THE TOSS   Luncheon 1.30   Stumps drawn 6.30

Sport continued to provide a much needed outlet. "I'd cycled over to Northampton a few times during the war to watch cricket. There was no Championship at that time, but I remember watching a County side play an Australian Services team at the old Spinney Hill ground off the Kettering Road.[1]"

After the war there were several trips to Wantage Road but his growing love of the game was crowned by a trip to Nottingham in the summer of 1948. "It was my sixteenth birthday and my father asked what I wanted for a present. I said I'd like to go to see England play Australia in the First Test at Trent Bridge. We travelled by train but when we got to the ground it was drizzling and I was worried that there'd be no play. We queued outside waiting for the gates to open. Everyone had to pay to get in. There were no advance ticket sales in those days. At last there was a decision to open the gates, we went inside, and I had my first view of a Test Match ground. I can still see the heavy roller being taken around the square in ever increasing circles. I suppose that, besides rolling the pitch, it was getting rid of the water. I discovered in later years that the surface of the outfield was as impeccable as it looked that morning. You could always run and pick a ball up at Trent Bridge with absolute confidence."

Among the many artefacts accumulated during a lifetime in the game, Brian treasures a scorecard from that momentous occasion – June 10th 1948. He watched as England were dismissed for a paltry first innings total of 165 but, with play restricted by the late start, Australia's openers Barnes and Morris safely negotiated the day's few overs remaining and he never saw his boyhood hero, the great Bradman, bat.[2]

The previous spring Brian had been invited for a trial at Kettering Town Cricket Club on the recommendation of Arthur Weatherall, himself a member at Northampton Road. The schoolmaster, a card-carrying member of the Communist Party, no doubt enjoyed introducing the promising boy from 'the wrong side of the tracks', although his protégé couldn't have made a less impressive start with the bat. "We were in the nets alongside the old pavilion. Gordon Sharman, a factory manager at Gravestock's, rolled me over first ball - but nobody got one past the bat after that."

---

1 During the war matches were played at the Northampton Brewery Company's Ground at Spinney Hill. The Australian match that Brian saw took place on July 16 1944 when Northamptonshire lost to the Royal Australian Air Force by 69 runs in a one-day game. Bowled out for 122, the Australian airmen skittled Northants for 53. DR Christofani top-scored and took four wickets for the Aussies. Jack Webster and Reg Partridge took three wickets each for Northamptonshire. Christofani never played Test cricket though he featured with some success in the unofficial 'Tests' of 1945, scoring 110* and taking five for 55 at Old Trafford.

2 Second day spectators did see the great man. Bradman scored 138, one more than Lindsay Hassett as the Aussies totalled 509. England batted better in the second innings, though Ray Lindwall was unable to bowl. Denis Compton scored a marvellous 184 and Len Hutton made 74. Australia's target was 98; they won by eight wickets.
Next on the 'Invincibles' agenda was Northampton but Bradman didn't play. Hassett scored another hundred as the County lost by an innings and 64 runs. Bert Nutter was the nearest Northants had to a hero, taking five for 57. He shared the new ball with Ramesh Divecha, later to play five Tests for India, who was making his only appearance for Northants.

It must have been something of a culture shock. "When I first arrived at the club, the only kit I possessed was a white shirt, but someone kindly found me boots and a pair of flannels." As evidenced by the newspaper photograph *below*, even the flannels were missing when he took the field for a full scale, pre-season practice match.

Town Players Go Into Action

There is a wonderful incongruity about the group, the figure in dark trousers, exuberant, face alight with excitement, contrasting beautifully with the dignified, rather aristocratic bearing of former county player, HJH Lamb[3], the club's distinguished opening batsman. Cravats abound and WRF Chamberlain[4], Lamb's opening partner sports a splendidly idiosyncratic, public school cap. Yet, despite the glaring differences in social background, Brian's unassuming personality and precocious skill provided a passport to acceptance and an early chance to make his mark.

---

3 Henry John Hey Lamb was a stalwart of Kettering Town CC and a former captain of Northamptonshire. Born in Kettering in 1912, he was a Cambridge graduate but not a blue. He played one match for Northamptonshire in 1934, being selected to play at Kettering against Warwickshire when Reg Partridge's nine for 66 produced a rare Northants victory. In 1936 whilst working as an articled clerk in his father's law firm he was called up to be captain - it was a season in which Northamptonshire had five captains. In total he played in 38 matches scoring 1085 runs at 16.95 and took 23 catches and made one stumping. His highest score, 91*, was against Essex. His last first-class appearance was in 1938. For nearly thirty years he was president of Kettering Town CC. He died in 1993; Lamb & Holmes remains a leading firm of solicitors in Kettering.
4 Frank Chamberlain played six times for Northamptonshire in 1946. He was mooted as a candidate for the captaincy in 1947 but was 'unavailable'. In later years he found time to make a significant contribution to management, attaining the position of chairman of both Northamptonshire CCC and the Test and County Cricket Board.

Progress was rapid. He was selected for Kettering's second team, the Wanderers, to play against Leicester Ivanhoe on May 10th 1947 but to his huge disappointment the game was rained off.

Three weeks later, and still ten days short of his fifteenth birthday, he hit 59 against Kibworth Town. By July he had won a place in the Kettering side that met a Reg Partridge XI in the Wollaston-born County player's benefit match at Northampton Road. Among those appearing for the visitors were several players who would eventually become team-mates at Northampton's County Ground, including Dennis Brookes, Vince Broderick and Ken Fiddling.

WANDERERS XI 1947

Standing (l to r): H. D. Moore, R. Northern, N. S. Smith, J. M. Gibbings, R. Aveling, G. Beeney, C. Mandeville (Scorer).
Sitting (l to r): P. Thompson, F. R. Toseland, K. G. Dix (Captain), J. Tebbutt, B. Reynolds.

From 'A Century of Cricket at Kettering'.

"Everyone was very good to me, particularly Joe Deer and Frank Toseland, who carted us around to matches in his little Austin 10. The journeys to matches were often more memorable than the games themselves. I remember one day, when we were out Oundle way, Frank was driving with the window down when a pheasant suddenly flew up from a nearby field and hit the top of the car immediately above the window with an almighty crash. An inch or so lower and it would have struck him full in the face."

Frank Toseland's daughter, now Mrs Joe Deer, recalls Brian's early days at the Town ground. "My father was club secretary at the time and took a great interest in the rather scruffy boy with the boundless enthusiasm and talent to match. I can picture them still, my father bowling, Brian batting, a study in concentration."

The winter months were spent, as ever, playing football, although the Glebe playing field had replaced the Headlands as a home pitch. Brian's first club was Avondale Colts, the nursery side which produced many stalwarts of local football and became invincible at youth level under the management of the genial Cyril Fletton, a drayman for the Kettering Industrial Co-operative Society.

The Glebe provided several pitches which extended to the avenue of trees planted by an eighteenth century Montagu of Boughton. Its primitive changing facilities were located in the peculiar building, part working farm, part dressing-rooms, where players shared the circular, metal bath once used for dipping sheep. Brian eventually graduated to Mrs Morris's Bible Class, a well established Amateur League club also based at the Glebe, before making the move to the more exalted setting of Rockingham Road – home of Kettering Town FC. He soon won a place in the Poppies reserve side as a flying winger, appearing regularly in the club's United Counties League team during the late forties.

Kettering Town reserves, 1949

Back (l to r): Rex Smith, Teddy Tart, Ron Bayliss, Ken Walker, Jim Woodward, Ken Laxton, Don Mabelson, Albert Frost.
Front (l to r): Dickens, Brian Reynolds, Bill Dean, Pat Connelly, Pat Maguire.

However, cricket remained Brian's first love. By 1948 he had won an occasional place in Kettering Town's first team and was developing something of a reputation as an attacking batsman. "Mike Warrington, who was one of Northampton Saints' star fast bowlers in those days, had been told to look out for me. He was determined to put this young upstart in his place and made sure the first ball to me was extra quick. Apparently I ran down the wicket and smashed the ball straight back past him for four."

By the following season Brian was a permanent fixture in the first team, recording over 500 runs and hitting his highest score to date - an unbeaten 99! August 1949 proved a most fruitful month. On the evening of Thursday 4th, the Town side defeated works team Kaycee in the final of the Kettering Knock-Out competition, played at the North Park ground. Brian contributed eleven runs to his side's total of 101 before being bowled by Eddie Armstrong, one of the clothing company's two 'guests', i.e. non-employees. Eddie later became a long-standing member of the County Supporters Club.

KETTERING TOWN

J Shapiera	c Faulkner	b Sculthorpe	1	Armstrong	9	0	59	2
LW Curtis	run out		49	Sculthorpe	9	0	38	1
WJB Smith	run out		9					
BL Reynolds		b Armstrong	11					
EF Towell	c and	b Armstrong	11					
RP Bird	not out		12					
GH Draper	not out		4					
GB Sharman								
KG Dix								
J Tebbutt								
A Meunier								
Extras			4					
TOTAL		(five wkts)	**101**					

KAYCEE

A Chapman		b Smith	7	Smith	9	0	27	4
L Grant	c Bird	b Smith	0	Sharman	9	0	22	3
F Faulkner	c Bird	b Sharman	2					
A Johnson		b Sharman	11					
E Armstrong	run out		10					
S Miller		b Smith	1					
H Rawson	c Meunier	b Sharman	9					
J Hollis		b Smith	1					
H Sculthorpe	not out		4					
B Brown	not out		4					
C Whiteford								
Extras			2					
TOTAL		(eight wkts)	**51**					

KETTERING TOWN won by 50 runs

The match was fully covered in the Evening Telegraph with a detailed report and photographs. The headline "FIRST K.O. CUP WIN SINCE 1936" referred to the fact that it had been thirteen years since the Town Club had won this cup. The opening sentence informed readers that "when skipper Faulkner caught Shapiera behind the wicket with only two runs to the credit of Kettering Town CC last night, hope rose high among Kaycee CC supporters at North Park".

The Kaycee supporters numbered more than a handful. In this era the Knock-out final attracted a substantial number of spectators who, in places, would stand several deep. The North Park was one of the venues for Town League matches, along with the Glebe and the Northampton Road 'Rec'. On these Council owned grounds, several matches would take place each Saturday, the outfields overlapping, especially at the 'Rec' where the Town League games took place on the opposite side of the Ise from the Town ground.

Some of the matches were in the Kettering & District League, founded in 1897, and generally regarded, but not by many of those who played in the Town League, as superior. The grounds and the leagues provided opportunities for the working men of Kettering to enjoy a game of cricket after their Saturday morning work in teams based on factory, social club or group of friends. Some factories had their own grounds, Kaycee, for example, at this time playing at Lewis Road on land which eventually formed part of the site of Kettering High School.

Neither league now exists, victims of the desire to improve facilities. Now Kettering people have to travel, to Weekley or Rushton or Burton Latimer or Isham, to play their cricket. Players will not tolerate the Rec - fielders mingling with the next game, no sixes, a dressing room (with one cold tap) to share with the opposition, whatever the local dogs have deposited and a long walk to the Talbot. Instead today's players have sightscreens, showers and a private bar. Quality of surroundings up, quantity of players down. No more can the young lads wander down to the local piece of grass and watch cricketers practising or playing.

But in 1949 town cricket was still a sport for both participating and spectating. Back at the North Park, Reynolds had perished with barely a mention, "went at 31". At "the half-way stage of the 18 over innings there were only 35 on the board". However after Towell had gone, Curtis dominated proceedings. He was, the paper informed us, "very unlucky to miss his half-century when he was seeing the ball perfectly. He threw away his wicket when dodging about to see if two byes could be stretched to three." The Town then produced "a lively wind-up to the innings, RP Bird whacking 12 runs out of the last over." Note that there were no bowling restrictions. Both sides employed just two bowlers; both number elevens neither batted nor bowled.

The Kaycee reply never threatened to reach the target. After eight overs they were 11 for three "in light which was barely good enough for soccer". The enthusiastic but well-mannered crowd gave "a special clap to Rawson, who had to use a runner in consequence of a calf muscle strained when fielding" before they watched Alderman Dyson presenting the cup and miniatures at the pavilion.

Three weeks after receiving his miniature, Brian attended trials at the County Ground, Northampton, on the recommendation of Kettering's veteran captain, Edgar Towell. He joined approximately eighty other hopefuls including Gordon Inwood, Dave Roberts and fellow Town batsman, Joe Shapiera.

The local press featured several testimonials to his potential, most notably from Gordon Sharman, the bowler who had knocked over his stumps on Brian's first appearance at the Town ground. "He is a natural born sportsman, virtually uncoached and a cricketer of outstanding ability."

Brian's appetite for county cricket had no doubt been whetted by Worcestershire's visit to Kettering for a championship match against Northamptonshire back in July. The first day's play, which took place during the town's factory holiday fortnight, attracted a crowd of 6,250 spectators. It lasted only two days and the visitors won by an innings to provide memories of the thirties.

The weekend after his County Ground trial, confidence no doubt boosted by an invitation to return to Northampton the following April, Brian scored 65 not out at Rothwell on the Saturday and an undefeated 60 for a Kettering Sunday XI against a Town League Select side the following day.

Brian still acknowledges his huge debt to Edgar Towell[5]. "He really took me under his wing. Not only did he help my cricket, but he also found me a job in his footwear factory in Stamford Road where I was taught hand-sewing by one of the 'old school', a chap called Joe Buckby who lived in Hallwood Road. He could make a shoe all the way through, even to stitching the upper, sole and heel on, and he passed his knowledge on to me. Under his tuition I graduated to doing the whole job myself. I soaked the toe-puff and stiffener and inserted them into the upper, tacked the upper on to the last and moulded it into shape and then sewed the welt round ready for the shoe to be soled. It was certainly a great sense of achievement when the shoes turned out well."

So proficiently did Brian master this skill that in 1951 he was invited to demonstrate his expertise on Towell's exhibition stand at the Festival of Britain. His presence in the Power and Production Pavilion at the South Bank Exhibition attracted the attention of journalist, Victoria Chappelle, assistant features editor with the Overseas Press Services Division of the government's Central Office of Information. An interview with the young craftsman provided the substance of an article, quoted below, in which Brian reiterates his twin ambitions and expresses his appreciation of assistance received from Edgar Towell.

Few of the onlookers at the display of shoemaking, as they watch the nimble fingers of 19-year-old Brian Reynolds pull the waxed threads in and out of the welt of a handmade shoe, realise that his mind is probably on English cricket. Already he has twice played for Northamptonshire in the First Eleven – he has his Second Eleven Cap – and his ambition is not only to become a good craftsman but to

---

5   Edgar Fremantle Towell was born in Kettering in 1901. He made his debut for Northamptonshire in 1923 and played the last of his 70 matches in 1934. A left-handed bat, he scored 1,199 runs at an average of 12.75 (highest score 66) and took 102 wickets at an average cost of 33.12 (best four for 42) with his medium pace. His innings of 66 (he scored one other half-century) was at Kettering in 1933. The opponents were Essex whose opening bowlers, Morris Nichols and Peter Smith, both played Test cricket. It was Smith who bowled Towell for 66, a score exceeded by Vallance Jupp's 95 and Fred Bakewell's 123 as Northamptonshire totalled 539. Towell was not required in the second innings as Northants triumphed by seven wickets as they reached their target of 33 in 20 minutes with four minutes to spare. He died in 1972.

become a professional cricketer as well. He dreams of cricket in the summer, and plays football in the winter to keep him fit.

At the moment Brian is a National Serviceman, but when he heard that his firm – JW Towell and Son Ltd., of Kettering, England – was short of craftsmen, he offered to give up a week of his leave to help at the Exhibition. He owes a great deal to the firm, he says, for Mr EF Towell, who once played cricket for Northamptonshire, noticed his possibilities as a cricketer when he took him on as an apprentice shoemaker. "He thinks I could do something at cricket," says Brian. "Anyway, he has certainly helped me along. And I like this shoemaking job. You're always learning."

DEMONSTRATION

OF HAND MADE FOOTWEAR

by B. REYNOLDS,

of J. W. TOWELL & SON, LTD.

Only five of the original trialists were recalled to Northampton the following spring: R Langley, D Brewster, MEJC Norman, DG Greasley and BL Reynolds. Of these just Doug Greasley, a Yorkshireman with a residential qualification, and Brian were offered a season's contract, along with New Zealander, Peter Arnold. Mick Norman, though, was taken on to the staff a year later.

"I can't remember the terms. Just that it seemed like a fortune at the time." It's very clear that money was of secondary importance. The first part of Brian's ambition had been realised. He now had to win a place in the Northamptonshire side.

> **B Reynolds lbw b Heane 30**
>
> Scunthorpe, 1950

1950

"They pass as pass the April rains
And memory alone remains"

JL Carr
'Chepstow'

The County Ground

Batting-on

A Cambridge Hundred

Call-ups

"We were net bowlers."

When the young Reynolds turned up at Wantage Road at the start of the 1950 season, the County Ground was, to state the obvious, rather different from what a tyro would find fifty years later.

The Abington Avenue end of the ground was the home of Northampton Town Football Club, the 'Cobblers', then performing in the Football League's Third Division South. The main, i.e. only, stand was next to, and parallel with, Abington Avenue; it ran the full length of the pitch. Behind both goals was terracing which did not extend the full width of the pitch. This was particularly noticeable at the eastern, Kop, end where the bowling green intruded. The western end, the Hotel end, was then open but was covered shortly after and became the major source of shelter on rain-affected cricket days. Since 1950 the floodlights have come and gone, inaugurated in October 1960 with a visit from Arsenal.

During the football season, wooden boards were placed along the southern touchline across the outfield; in the summer a row of movable seats was placed around the boundary at the football end. The rest of the football pitch was used as a car park, a feature seized on by the press when the Cobblers won promotion to the First Division in 1965 and Arsenal, Aston Villa, Chelsea, Leeds United, Liverpool, Manchester United, Newcastle United and Tottenham Hotspur were amongst the clubs who played on the car park (though it was Fulham who attracted the largest ever County Ground attendance - 24,523 - in April 1966).

The cricket end of the ground might have been described as ramshackle, had there been sufficient buildings to warrant that accolade. Apart from the pavilion, the shell of which provided the basis of the much larger Spencer Pavilion (completed in 1991), there was only the small West Stand and the even smaller Ladies Stand which was in front of the tennis courts, now the area for parking sponsored cars.

Northampton was not the only ground that was some way short of basic. Leicester's Grace Road, a not very glorified school playing field, was generally regarded as the poorest headquarters ground in the Championship. Essex didn't even have a ground of their own; instead they played their home matches on eight different grounds, having a week at each.

Membership of a County Club was then something of a status symbol. Ordinary membership was £2 10s per annum, though this was reduced to £2 if you lived outside a 20 mile radius of Northampton Guildhall. Five guineas bought you a Vice President's ticket which, amongst other privileges, allowed the VP to "bring his car into the Ground and Enclosure without charge", but "when using one of the twenty spaces between the Score Box and Pavilion a charge of Five Shillings per day will be made". It must have been a good view: to park your car for a day cost 10% of the annual ordinary membership fee.

It was only slightly different elsewhere. At egalitarian, but not proletarian, Edgbaston ("the Membership List remains closed"), for example, the annual subscription of £2 2s entitled the member to a number of privileges including, "the right to purchase for £1 a Motor Car Ticket admitting vehicle and driver in uniform on all match days to the Members' Car Park". Another privilege was "the right to negotiate with any Senior Professional for individual coaching lessons at the nets for the member or his son"

Names and addresses were published in the Northamptonshire Year Book (a tradition which continued for several years). Whilst the most notable 1950 entry is perhaps in the Vice-Presidents section - HE Bates, The Granary, Little Chart, Ashford, Kent - it is noticeable how many prominent club cricketers were County members. At this time County Clubs all had playing members. Only a few actually played but many took advantage of the practice facilities. At Northampton, "from May 1st Ground Bowlers will be made available as under, subject to there being no match in progress". The 'as under' featured Monday to Thursday from 10.30 to 12.00, Tuesday and Friday from 2.30 to 4.30 and Monday, Tuesday, Wednesday and Friday from 6.00 to 8.30. A separate net was set aside for junior members on Monday to Wednesday evenings.

Asked what he did during his first year on the staff, Brian replied, "We were net bowlers."

There were, of course games to play, and the newcomers played in both the Second Eleven and the Club and Ground side, a mixture of amateurs and young professionals. There was no Second Eleven Championship in 1950 (it did not start until 1959) but there were eight competitive two-day fixtures in the Minor Counties Championship plus five friendly matches.   .

The Club & Ground side flew the flag around the county in one day games. One traditional game was against the Kettering & District League who, in 1950, were bowled out for 111. The C&G won by ten wickets, scoring 165 without loss. Another instance of batting-on occurred in the match at Finedon Dolben. Brian suspects that the playing conditions changed during the game: it began as a one innings match and finished as two (and a bit more). Finedon, having been skittled for 28, gained a first innings lead when they bowled the County side out for 21. Second time around, Dolben's eleven were all out for 53. Needing 61 to win, Peter Arnold made 56 and Doug Greasley 106 not out, as the Club & Ground closed on 192 for two!

"You were always looking to get in the first team but it was a bit different then, knowing that National Service would come along," recalls Brian. "There were good players in the first team but I wasn't there just to be a net bowler."

The first team had been galvanised at the start of the 1949 season by the appointment of Freddie Brown, the amateur recruited and paid (by Timken) to bring professionalism to Northamptonshire. In Brown's initial season Northants had risen from 17th (and last) to 6th in the County Championship.

Brown completed the double of 1,000 runs and 100 wickets, though didn't quite achieve this in Championship matches (993 and 93). There were four other principal bowlers: Bob Clarke, fast to medium left-arm (87 Championship wickets), Gordon Garlick (73), a former Lancashire off-spinner, Bert Nutter (59), a former Lancashire seamer, and Vince Broderick (59), a Lancashire-born slow left-armer.

The batting was dominated by Norman Oldfield (2,114 Championship runs) and Dennis Brookes (1,806). Both played one Test for England. Brookes, from the West Riding of Yorkshire, played in the first Test at Bridgetown in 1948 but broke a finger during the match, thus ending both his Caribbean tour and his England career. Oldfield played against the West Indies at the Oval in 1939, a fortnight before the outbreak of war. Then with Lancashire, his first innings 80 remains the highest score by an Englishman who played in only one Test.

They were supported by Fred Jakeman (963), a Yorkshireman in his first season of Championship cricket (at the age of 29), Bill Barron (823) from Durham, and Eddie Davis (760), one of the brothers from Brackley. The elder Davis, Percival, scored 304 in eight matches, a similar record to Yorkshireman Des Barrick. Broderick (730) and Clarke (588) justified the title of all-rounders. Behind the stumps was Ken Fiddling who had played several times for Yorkshire before joining Northants in 1947.

Northern accents soon became familiar to Bronk. And there was a new accent in 1950, that of Leonard 'Jock' Livingston, the left-hander from Sydney who had sought a professional career in England when Neil Harvey was selected ahead of him for the 1948 tour of England. Livingston had spent the previous winter touring India with the Commonwealth team. At Delhi, in the first unofficial Test, he had scored 123 in an opening partnership of 226 with Oldfield (151). Also in the side was George Tribe. It's not often there are three Northamptonshire players in a Test match; only a churlish pedant would point out that, at the time, only one had played for Northants and that it wasn't actually a Test match.

Missing in 1950 was Jack Timms, Silverstone-born, who had played for his native County since 1925. In his last innings he scored 40 at Rushden in July 1949 against Sussex. A Northants stalwart during the darkest years, it is quite possible that nobody has ever been on the losing side in more County Championship matches than Jack.

A few amateurs made a handful of appearances in the side, though no-one other than Jack Webster (11 wickets in six games) played more than three times. Perhaps the most interesting was Doctor Carlos Bertram Clarke. He was a Barbadian who played in all three Tests on the West Indies' 1939 tour of England. He last played for Northants in 1949. His next first-class match was ten years later when he made his debut for Essex at the age of forty-one. In 1983, he was awarded the OBE for services to the West Indian community in London.

In 1950 there was only one form of cricket played by County first teams: three-day cricket. And there was only one competition - the County Championship. There were two matches a week: Saturday, Monday and Tuesday, and Wednesday to Friday. There was no professional Sunday cricket - it was against the law to charge admission on the Sabbath - and the season ran, almost precisely, from May 1st to August 31st. All Counties played twenty-eight (two more than in 1949) Championship matches. Twelve Counties were met both home and away, two at home only and two away only. Every County had a match against the touring side (Lancashire, Surrey and Yorkshire had two) who always came for the entire season: in 1950 the West Indians began with a two-day friendly at Eastbourne on April 24th and finished at Carlisle on September 14th, beating Carlisle and Westmorland in a one-day game.

The first Minor Counties match of 1950 was against Worcestershire II. It began on May 10 at Bromsgrove School; Northants won by an innings and 66 runs. The Reynolds debut was not the stuff of dreams. He did not bat (he was due to come in next when the declaration was made at 274 for three), did not bowl and caught no-one. Barrick and Percy Davis both reached three figures and Barrick took six for 39 in the second innings. The home side included two future Test players, Jack Flavell and Martin Horton.

The next game was nearly a month later: the opposition was Lincolnshire, the venue Scunthorpe. Not exactly one of England's sporting hot-spots, though, in the summer of 1950, the town was awash with excitement at the prospect of the forthcoming football season. The local football club, Scunthorpe and Lindsey United, were leaving the Midland League and joining the big boys - Accrington Stanley, Barrow, Bradford Park Avenue, Gateshead, New Brighton, Southport as well as Bradford City, Stockport County and Tranmere Rovers - in the Football League's Third Division North.

There was less excitement in the steel works on Wednesday June 7th when Northants II arrived in town. Brian batted at four and was soon at the crease as Eddie Davis went for 5 and Doug Greasley for 2. He scored 30, helping top-scorer Barrick (71) stabilise the innings. He was three days short of his eighteenth birthday at the time; the man who trapped him lbw was five months past his forty-sixth birthday. George Heane, who scored 132 and took five for 61 in the first innings of this match, had been captain of Nottinghamshire before the war and returned to play his final four games for Notts in 1951. In the second innings, Brian made 22, the second highest in a total of 131. Lincolnshire needed 46 to win; they got them for two.

At Edgbaston, Warwickshire's coach, Derief Taylor, did Brian twice; Jack Bannister, who took the new ball in partnership with Roly Thompson, provided the first instance of 'caught Reynolds' in the Northants scorebook. In the return match at Northampton, Brian was caught in the second innings by WE Houghton. Eric Houghton was not a great cricketer but he is remembered with considerable affection at Villa Park where he both played and managed, as he did at Notts County; he played soccer seven times for England in the early thirties. A friendly against Leicestershire II at Market Harborough at the end of June found Maurice Hallam in the opposition; they enjoyed remarkably similar careers and their paths crossed many times.

Then Fenner's. "To be honest, I can't remember much about it. I know I was pleased, and it was not out!" Brian's recollection of his first Northamptonshire century, 104* against Cambridgeshire, may be a little vague but that's hardly surprising given that the rain-affected match, personal achievements aside, was not of the greatest significance. Categorised as 'no result', the match that included Brian's maiden century for his County was not included in the calculation of points per game which decided the placings in the Minor Counties table. Northants finished 20th; Cornwall were 32nd and last. Wisden noted that, "Northamptonshire Second Eleven began soundly, but fell away. The side showed strength in batting and fielding, but weakness lay in the attack. B Reynolds, aged 17, displayed excellent form with the bat."

CAMBRIDGESHIRE v NORTHAMPTONSHIRE II

Fenner's, July 20 and 21, 1950

NORTHAMPTONSHIRE II

PC Davis		lbw b Gambrell	3	Hoyles	40	4	140	3
DG Greasley	c Medhurst	b Hoyles	5	Gambrell	31	1	122	3
E Davis		b Hoyles	6	Royston	12	2	46	0
V Broderick	c Gambrell	b Medhurst	36	Medhurst	10	0	67	1
FS Jakeman		b Gambrell	90	Rogers	4	0	25	0
DW Barrick		b Gambrell	110					
BL Reynolds	not out		104					
RW Clarke		b Hoyles	39					
HW Wright	not out		7					
D Constable								
S Gigner								
		b7, l2, n1	10					
		(seven wkts dec)	**410**					

CAMBRIDGESHIRE

CJ Harrison	not out		57	Clarke	10	2	30	1
MA Crouch		b Clarke	11	Gigner	8	1	12	0
HWF Taylor	not out		33	Broderick	16	7	23	0
JG Rogers				Barrick	10	3	30	0
H Medhurst				Greasley	6	2	5	0
JT Coombes								
R Gautrey								
J Hoyles								
J Gambrell								
CMB Sessions								
SR Royston								
		b5	5					
		(one wicket)	**106**					

NO RESULT

"I suppose it did cross my mind that a hundred would do my chances of first team selection no harm. But I was also thinking about my call-up to National Service", is Brian's recollection of events fifty years ago. Within two months of the century at Fenner's he had been called-up to the Northamptonshire Regiment. But within one month of the Cambridge hundred he was called-up to the Northamptonshire Championship side.

> ## B. Reynolds   run out   22
> Northampton, August 1950

1950

Who that well his work beginneth
The rather a good end he winneth.

John Gower,
'Confessio Amantis'

Twelfth-man at Headingley

First team debut

Brothers

A divided Championship?

"We wanted, above all, to be professional cricketers"

There's an anthology waiting to be compiled. Its provisional title, 'My First Time', has a section on cricketing debuts. Several, such as David Steele's first Test at Lord's, select themselves. Others are more esoteric, a matter of individual interest or memory. MEJC Norman's 17 against the Indian tourists in 1952; Peter Mills's 68 for Northants against Sri Lanka in 1981 (having already scored 111 against them for the Combined Universities); or Gareth Smith's 1986 dismissal of Sunil Gavaskar with his second ball. Surprisingly often with Northants, the first match is the last, which raises interesting questions in itself. In my beginning is my inevitable end, as Eliot almost said. Two instances shared not only justified chagrin at playing just once but, like Brian, Kettering connections. Most notably, Peter Pickering, who kept goal for Kettering in the Southern League when Brian was playing and also held the fort in Northants' 1953 victory against Lancashire at Old Trafford, after the County had struggled to muster a team. This remarkable match receives the detailed attention it deserves in Stephen Chalke's book 'Runs in the Memory'. It runs in Brian's memory, as a ball from Statham "felled him like a log", as Frank Tyson put it. In less testing circumstances Reginald Wooster took five for 54 in his single appearance and then settled for club cricket at home in Kettering. His home, incidentally, no more than a Malachy mishit from where Pickering kept goal. There's no record of Lord Lilford's feelings after his brief 1911 sojourn; in any case, he had more profitable ways to occupy his time. Likewise, someone called SP Coverdale in 1987.

Brian's debut was against Sussex, August 16,17,18, 1950, at Northampton. A cursory glance at the scorecard might suggest to the unknowing local supporter that the only unusual item was "L Livingston c Webb b James 0". Livingston, from New South Wales, had left Lancashire League cricket to join Northants. In this, his first season, he was the County's principal run-getter (1805, average 46.28).

A week before the Sussex game Brian had gone to Leeds as twelfth-man for the first team. That Yorkshire side (third behind joint champions Lancashire and Surrey) included Johnny Wardle, Norman Yardley, Willie Watson, Frank Lowson and the supreme Hutton. Household names; in 1950 cricketers still achieved such status. Before the universal acquisition of television sets, you either watched them live or in brief glimpses on Pathé News at the Odeon. Brian's dominant recollection of that trip involved Northants' household name in the hotel on arrival. All the players were given their allotted room numbers apart from the young twelfth-man. Diffidently, he mentioned the omission to the skipper, only to be told: "You're in the room next to mine. You'll be in bed by ten o'clock and I shall check that you are." He was, and FR Brown did.

To Brian, of course, the eventual debut was special. "The skipper told me I was playing. I got my chance because Bill Barron was playing for the Cobblers at Ipswich." The Northamptonshire Evening Telegraph's introduction to the first day's play prosaically states, "Barron, having taken up football duties, was an absentee from the team and B Reynolds, of Kettering, who has shaped well in club cricket this season and who joined the ground staff, had his first chance in the county side. He is only eighteen but has shown considerable promise." The anonymous reporter also noted the "ominous looking clouds" (presciently as it turned out) and (less so) scoring "so slow that the cricket was almost tedious."

NORTHAMPTONSHIRE v SUSSEX at Northampton on August 16, 17, 18 1950

Toss - Sussex
SUSSEX

John Langridge	c Jakeman	b Nutter	24			
DV Smith		b Clarke	24			
GHG Doggart		b Nutter	12			
G Cox	not out		141			
C Oakes		b Garlick	128			
JY Oakes	not out		10	1	not out	5
+RT Webb				2	not out	3
KPA Mathews						
*Jas Langridge						
DJ Wood						
AE James						
		b4, l6, n1	11		b1	1
		(4 wkts dec)	350		(0 wkt)	9

Nutter	38	10	81	2					
Webster	23	5	69	0		3	1	2	0
Clarke	24	6	66	1					
Garlick	33.2	9	88	1					
Broderick	8	2	35	0					
Barrick						2	0	6	0

NORTHAMPTONSHIRE

*D Brookes	c Jn Langridge	b James	31
N Oldfield	c Webb	b Wood	84
+L Livingston	c Webb	b James	0
F Jakeman	c Doggart	b C Oakes	58
D Barrick		b J Oakes	36
BL Reynolds		run out	22
AE Nutter		lbw b J Oakes	1
V Broderick	c James	b J Oakes	42
J Webster		lbw b C Oakes	0
RW Clarke	not out		3
RG Garlick		b C Oakes	0
		b18, l3, w1	22
			299

Wood	22	7	56	1
James	24	9	41	2
J Oakes	30	8	67	3
Jas Langridge	12	3	35	0
C Oakes	24.3	5	54	3
Doggart	2	0	15	0
Cox	9	6	9	0

Umpires: HL Parkin, A Skelding   **MATCH DRAWN**

Brian batted at six, in a drawn game curtailed by rain, scoring 22 before being run out by Vince Broderick (not for the last time). He remembers it clearly (as you do). "Brod pushed it in front of the wicket on the leg side and called for one. First game, so I set off like the proverbial, only to be told 'No, go back.' I ran there and back, but was out by a good yard." Brod's version is not known. Suffice to say, the next time Brian was run out was two seasons later, while opening the batting against Cambridge University. His fellow opener was Vincent Broderick.

The Sussex innings contained a fourth wicket partnership of 256 by George Cox and Charles Oakes. At the declaration Cox remained unbeaten on 141. Brian remembers him as "a bad starter. It seemed like noughts and hundreds with George." A thought given added credence in Alan Ross's poem 'A Cricketer in Retirement: George Cox',

"Never one for half measures, as generous
With ducks as half-centuries"

Cox made 448 appearances for his home county and Christopher Martin-Jenkins thought it strange that he and John Langridge never played for England.

Brian holds John Langridge in high esteem: one anecdote suggests why. When Keith Andrew became wicket keeper for Northants, Brian was asked to take over at first slip, where he had never previously fielded. He sought the assistance of John who, by then, was umpiring. "John was one of the best" (confirmed by his career record of 779 catches) "and a great help to me." The lucidity and detail in which John's advice is recalled is testimony to its efficacy. His concluding tip, "Don't talk, concentrate", runs counter to much modern practice, where close catchers find it good to talk. John had lived through a world war, where careless talk was costly.

That story also illustrates two other characteristics about Brian and most of his contemporaries: the willingness of established professionals to listen and learn from experienced players; and the camaraderie of the county circuit, lauded as one of its strengths. Perhaps it still exists. It certainly contributed to the quality of life, providing some compensation for the salary scales. Mind you, his time as a National Serviceman was even less financially rewarding, and with no compensating lifestyle. The train fare home from his Colchester base was more than a week's pay.

Another facet of the game's close-knit family (literally so) was apparent in Brian's first game, "that familiar pattern of families Sussex is rich in." Sussex played John and James Langridge, Charles and James Oakes. In Robertson-Glasgow's words: "Sussex cricket is something of a family affair. The scoresheets have been full of brothers Gilligan, Langridge, Parks; of father and son George Cox. And if you ask a small boy his name at a Horsham cricket match he will probably answer 'Oakes'". The West Stand's chattering classes have been known to conjecture over a Gallone's ice-cream why cricket, more than any other sport, has nurtured so many brothers. Or is that another myth? Sussex may top the poll, but Northamptonshire has had its fair share. Percy and Eddie Davis, Peter and Jim Watts, and Alec and Graeme Swann have all represented the Club during Brian's career.

Like John Gower's bad verse, so with a cricket match, there's usually a subtext. In retrospect, this debut game highlights contentious changes to the present first-class structure. One in particular springs from the late August date. Northamptonshire finished the 1950 season in tenth place; Sussex were thirteenth. In 1999, the last under the old format, Sussex were eleventh, Northants thirteenth. Northants' record for the twenty-eight Championship matches in 1950 reads: won 6, lost 4, drawn 15, and 'no decision' 3. It was said that they suffered because of the wet summer and damp pitches.

Most pundits regarded Northamptonshire's season as a major disappointment, especially after the progress in 1949. Expectations had been high, evident in this pre-season comment in the local paper: "Applications for season tickets are brisk, particularly for ground tickets. In view of increased admission charges, this ticket for £1 for all matches is remarkable value." After June 16, however, there was only one outright win. Brian's debut was the twenty-fifth game of the summer and, with three to follow, was a typical late-season, mid-table fixture. Indeed, to modern zoilists it epitomised the mind-numbing pointlessness which their two-division Championship was designed to remove.

Plus ça change, plus c'est la même chose. Two division advocates are as old as the Pennines. One such was TJ Matthews, secretary of Lancashire in 1912 and whistleblower. He informed the world that three years earlier Yorkshire had canvassed all the counties in support of an elaborate scheme of classification, as unworkable as it was unsatisfactory, because it divided the counties into two divisions of equal merit. He also believed his was "an age of competition. The old easy-going days have gone."

In 1913, Northamptonshire's AJ 'Pat' Darnell was a centre of a storm. He put a scheme to the MCC which required the bottom two Counties to apply for re-election (which would have seen Northamptonshire become a minor county round about the time Brian Reynolds was born). This upset Lancashire who called a secret meeting of the eleven 'leading' Counties. It also upset another Lord, Hawke of Yorkshire. Northamptonshire "were taking too much of a lead" and that would never do.

Ring any bells, my Lord (McLaurin)? Commissioned reports on the structure of County Cricket proliferate like those on the railways. By 1983 some twenty methods had been used to decide the order of precedence alone. For Dr Beeching now read Lord McLaurin. In an interview in December 1997, appointed to effect change, he described the Championship as the foundation of the whole game. "If you don't have a decent County Championship," he said, "then you're not going to get cricketers capable of playing five-day Tests." Nothing exceptional in that, until you consider the hidden agenda. In that same interview Tim Lamb, the Chief Executive of the England and Wales Cricket Board (and sometime Northants seamer), said he was encouraged by the number of counties who were saying that the prime raison d'être of the Championship was to develop players to play Test cricket. Yet again in cricket, plus ça change. They might have been surprised to learn that sixty years earlier Percy Fender was writing something similar: "the counties are really the mainspring of the game in the manner in which they provide the training ground for the advanced player on his way to the highest honours."

At which point similarities in the thinking of the Lord, the Honourable, and Percy end. Most poignantly in the context of carping attacks on the supposed cosy cabal of the Championship, Fender believed it was "a forcing house" in the English game, "for it offers to the individual player an opportunity for intensive practice of the game in competitive conditions." He was so certain of the Championship's "intensive" character that he repeats the epithet several times during the course of the article. At one moment, in a phrase reminiscent of Milton (John not Arthur) he writes of its being "an enormous hive of intensive cultivation."

That opinion directly opposes those modern administrators and players who, convinced of its mediocrity, proposed a two-division Championship to promote unflagging competition throughout the season. They spoke so often of the 'comfort zone' in which players operated, that it became a received opinion. Essentially, runs their credo, two divisions equals fiercer competition, stimulates higher standards, closer approximation to Test cricket and bigger crowds. That view should be set against the backcloth of another Lamb statement: "It's not healthy that certain counties are now depending on the central Board for as much as 70 per cent of their annual income."

Does it follow, therefore, that were Brian's debut game played fifty years later, both Sussex and Northamptonshire would be competing more intensely in order to avoid second division status? Were standards lower in Test and County cricket in 1950? Were George Cox's 141 runs meaningless? Were the crowds short-changed? Or is today's viewpoint another of cricket's mythical facts, just as Marie Antoinette never said, "Let them eat cake."

There was little talk of re-organisation early in Brian's career, though there appeared to be plenty to criticise in English cricket. In the 1947 News Chronicle Cricket annual, Crawford White wrote, "England must play her young men. That is the urgent, striking lesson of the dismal tour of Australia just concluded." White listed a number of developments he wanted to see in 1947. He hoped, "that players shall adopt a dynamic attitude towards the game whether batting, bowling or fielding." He also wanted "more natural wickets to give bowlers greater encouragement and stimulate better stroke play amongst batsmen" as well as "provision of decent tea and better beer".

By 1949 little had happened to change White's tune. "England has two seasons in which to complete her cricket recovery and build up a winning team for the visit to Australia. Main objectives during this breathing space must be (1) to discover fast bowlers and (2) to retrieve lost standards in all our cricket." Move on another two years and White concludes his editorial by despairing that, "our cricket is being left behind and is not keeping pace with modern ideas".

Brian has no doubts that the cricket was properly competitive in 1950, and for the right reasons. "We always tried hard to win, even when we weren't doing very well. We played for the love of the game. We wanted, above all, to be professional cricketers. Money wasn't the be-all and end-all."

To express pride in one's profession often seems alien to these cynical times. Today's outlook brings to mind Shaw's dictum that professions are conspiracies against the laity. In cricketing terms some observers believe the modern professional is indifferent to the punters, until it's benefit time. They need energizing, from relegation or money, to give of their best. Similarly, professional administrators must examine how their own performance has conspired against the paying laity. How do you explain a fixture list in which four-day games are scheduled to end on Saturdays?

It isn't quite that simple, of course not. One complicating factor is attendances and their effect. On Whit Monday 1947, 30,000 watched Middlesex play Sussex; 50,000 in just two days saw Glamorgan play the tourists at Swansea. Tour matches now attract scant regard and attendances to match. In 1926 the Roses match at Old Trafford was watched on August Bank Holiday Monday by 38,600. Now, it's likely to be nearer 3,860. Meanwhile, at the other Old Trafford games are a 60,000 sellout. Most youngsters, talented at cricket and soccer, invariably opt for the glory game, with its lure of money, glamour and spectator idolatry. There is no 'comfort zone' before 60,000 and accompanying media frenzy. Contrast that with the relative privacy of a county cricket ground on a damp afternoon in August. It is then that professional pride is paramount.

In 1946 the five survivors of the seven Foster brothers, who all played for Worcestershire (Fostershire) before the First World War, wrote a letter to 'The Times' simply to make the point that the game was far more important than the relative position of the counties in the Championship table. It is difficult to conceive of today's professionals doing that. It's equally improbable that the newspaper would publish it if they did. - Were a professional footballer to voice the idea, he would be pilloried for bringing the game into disrepute.

Perhaps the Foster brothers would not have felt it romantic to remind professional cricketers of the Hippocratic Oath. Perhaps it should be posted on dressing room walls, instead of the motivational slogans so beloved of some modern coaches. "I will be loyal to the profession and just and generous to its members. I will lead my life and practise my art in uprightness and honour." A doctor won't blush at that, nor should a cricketer. That idealism informed Brian Reynolds' thinking when he said, "We wanted, above all, to be professional cricketers."

George Orwell would have understood that sentiment, though he hated games. Come to think of it, many did not enjoy '1984' and it was rather an arid year for Northants. He wrote some sense about cricket: "It gives expression to a well-marked trait in the English character, the tendency to value 'form' or 'style' more highly than success. In the eyes of any true cricket lover, it is possible for an innings of ten runs to be better (i.e. more elegant) than an innings of a hundred runs." Ten runs is hyperbolic, otherwise he's right. 'Style' is what sticks in the mind long after the results of most games are forgotten, even if they were to bring about promotion or relegation.

The first time Norman Oldfield's name cropped up in conversation, Brian's instant recall was those delicate latecuts. "He could pick up a bat in May, after seven or eight months, and time a late-cut to perfection." Mention his name now and the mind's eye immediately replays, not games won or lost, not those later recollections, but an exquisite late-cut.

It could well be that someone watching Northamptonshire play Sussex in August 1950 was equally captivated by a 'Buddy' latecut (it must have occurred in his innings of 84), perhaps a Reynolds coverdrive. Or, in one spectator's words, the "cultured strokes in front of the wicket" during George Cox jnr's unbeaten 141, or maybe his fielding:

45

" I come upon
A scorecard yellow as old flannels and suddenly
I see him, smilingly prowling the covers
In soft shoes, shirt rolled to the forearms,
Light as a yacht swaying at its moorings,
Receptive to breezes."

Cricket's 'style' is one reason why poets are inspired by it. It's not the game's structure that matters, but the way it is played.

Brian's second match was at Edgbaston, immediately following the Sussex game. The weather was kinder than it had been during the Sussex match, though it was rain on the third day that saved Northamptonshire from likely defeat. Warwickshire rattled up 378 and bowled Northants out for 121. Eric Hollies took nine for 56, the second best analysis of his career. Brian went for 5, stumped by Dick Spooner; Vince Broderick was the odd man out, bowled by Abdul Hafeez Kardar, the Indian Test cricketer who later became the first captain of Pakistan. In the second innings Northamptonshire were 258 for five, just one run in front, when the rain came: Reynolds not out 2.

The next match was at Lord's; Northants made two changes. In came Clarke and Fiddling - out went Eddie Davis and Reynolds. So, it was back to the seconds for the final two games, Both were at Northampton, both were drawn. There was nothing to please Brian. Against Cambridgeshire he made 3 and 0* and conceded 23 runs in his two overs before the Cambridgeshire declaration. The season finished with another 3 in the only innings against Lincolnshire.

Brian finished in fifth place in the Northamptonshire Minor Counties batting averages with 28.22 and is credited with being 86th in the official Minor Counties Cricket Association averages. That information is courtesy of the 1951 Northamptonshire Year Book. Whether it can be trusted is perhaps a little dubious given that wicket-keeper Dennis Constable played in all but one match and does not get a mention in the averages in either the Year Book or Wisden.

There were no more first-team appearances for Bronk until July 1952.

22412017 Private Reynolds

1951 - 1952

"I know the disciplines of war"
Fluellen in 'Henry V',
Shakespeare

Up the Poppies

Defending the Realm

A Day at the Races

The Maunsell Cup

"He is always correct in his attitude towards his seniors and is most popular with his comrades."

The record books suggest that Maurice Dunkley is the outstanding Kettering-born footballer who played cricket. His credentials are impressive. Not only did the diminutive winger assist Manchester City to a Second Division Championship success in 1946-47, but he also appeared thirty-six times for Northamptonshire between 1937-39.

Some years ago, while enjoying a round of golf at their Kettering club, Brian Reynolds asked Maurice how modern-day footballers compared with those from his time. The older man didn't mince his words. "We could kick a ball with either foot, pass, head, tackle and shoot. The only thing they can do better today, is run!."

There can be no doubt that Brian Reynolds is the outstanding Kettering-born cricketer who played football.

The summer of 1950 was a watershed in the history of 'the Poppies', Kettering Town Football Club. During the first post-war season, the club had entered teams in the Leicestershire Senior, the United Counties and the Kettering Amateur Leagues. Admission to the Birmingham League was sought, successfully, for the 1946-47 season However, after just four campaigns, including a championship triumph in 1947-48, the club decided a further step-up, to the Southern League, was desirable. The club had left the Southern League in 1930, one of many victims of the economic problems of the day.

To back the application, there was a major reorganisation within the club. A limited company was formed, shares were offered to supporters and a new chairman, Mr FJ Pascoe was appointed. To all intents and purposes the club was now sponsored by British Timken, the Duston-based bearing manufacturers of whom Pascoe (later Sir John) was a director. Describing his favourite recreation as, "the encouragement of all forms of sporting activity", Mr Pascoe was also actively involved in the post-war revival of Northamptonshire County Cricket Club, having told them, "You find the players, I'll find them jobs."

The application was successful, Kettering and Llanelly being elected to the two vacancies caused by Colchester United and Gillingham filling the two additional places in the expanded Third Division South of the Football League. Pascoe brought with him a new manager, Bob Calder, formerly of Queen's Park, who instigated the influx of a number of good-class Scottish players and, as with the cricket, a job at Duston was always available for any new signing. One subsequent beneficiary of this liaison was Bill Barron, Cobblers (and then Kettering Town) full-back and Northamptonshire batsman.

Cricketing footballers were nothing new at Rockingham Road. Brian Reynolds had made numerous appearances for Kettering's reserves under the former regime. In April 1950 he had been given his first outing in the Poppies first-team, playing a Birmingham League fixture against the now-forgotten Leicestershire side, Whitwick Colliery. Coincidentally, Brian replaced wing-half Bob Clarke, Northamptonshire's Finedon-born pace bowler, whose ligament injury would delay his start to the new cricket season.

At inside-forward that afternoon was Maurice Tompkin, the Leicestershire cricketer, who had befriended Brian and whose invitations to accompany him for evening net practices at Leicester's indoor cricket school had been gratefully accepted. How valuable those sessions proved to be in preparing the young batsman for his trial at Wantage Road later that month.

Brian was destined to make a solitary appearance for the Poppies first team in their inaugural Southern League season. Just twenty-five days after playing his second and final County game of the 1950 cricket campaign, he lined up at outside-left for the match against Headington (now Oxford) United at the Manor Ground. A crowd of 4,900 saw Brian help his side to a 3–2 victory, but within days the stocky winger had swapped his red and white jersey for khaki battledress. As the 'Evening Telegraph' reported on September 19th, "Kettering Town Football Club and Northamptonshire County Cricket Club are the losers of the services of one of their most promising players who joins the Forces this week."

National Service beckoned and Brian became Private Reynolds 22412017. He was posted to Colchester and quickly became established in the garrison football team. The side was led by an enthusiastic officer named Captain Alden who, when plans were made to reform the regiment and decamp to Minden in West Germany, resolved to take all the garrison's sportsmen along with him. The prospect of an overseas posting didn't please the young conscript, who knew that his cricketing interests would be better served by remaining as close to his native county as possible in order that he could "impress the powers-that-be" at the County Ground. While leaving the pitch after a regimental football match, Brian put his case to a sympathetic Captain Alden, who promised to do all he could to help.

But first there was more basic training to be completed with a 3 inch mortar platoon on a firing range in Thetford Forest. "We often used live ammunition. You dropped the bombs in the top, fired and, if all went well, watched them explode in the distance. But sometimes there was a 'misfire' and the live bomb would come shooting out the bottom of the mortar. They were primed to explode on impact and you had to grab them before they hit the ground. Talk about sharpening up reflexes – it was the best catching practice I ever had!"

Captain Alden was as good as his word and a short time later Brian was transferred to Headquarters in Colchester as batman to WO1 Willey, the Garrison Education Officer. "I had a little room, complete with stove, at the back of the Nissen hut, which housed a library and other resource material."

His service career continued with a move to Bury St Edmunds. There, Private Reynolds was assigned as batman to the Commanding Officer, Major Barratt. The C.O. was based in the brick-built comfort of the Suffolk depot; 22412017 Reynolds was billeted three-quarters of a mile down the road in a wooden hut.

The proximity of the Newmarket race-course was a real temptation to Brian who, along with several of his pals, decided one morning to hitch-hike the short distance from the camp. The illicit day at the races lasted just a couple of hours - there was a glimpse of Sir Gordon Richards - before the group was pulled up by military policemen, returned to barracks and placed under company orders. To his acute embarrassment, Brian found himself appearing before Major Barratt, but he needn't have worried unduly. The Commanding Officer, who obviously approved of the way his batman fulfilled his duties, merely looked quizzically at the recalcitrant before enquiring, "If you wanted to go to the races, why didn't you say something?"

Shortly afterwards, the re-opening of Wootton Barracks, on the outskirts of Northampton, was announced. On learning that the Commanding Officer designate, Major Ennalls, was looking for staff, Lieutenant Colonel Alleyne St.George Coldwell, secretary at the County Cricket Club, was influential in getting Brian a transfer. He was appointed batman to the camp's adjutant, Captain HA Bone and, in addition to his normal responsibilities, which included washing and polishing the Captain's car, (seen here at Wootton with Batman Reynolds on the left) Brian would occasionally baby-sit for the Bone family at their Spinney Hill home. By this time he had acquired a new means of transport, a Calthorpe 250cc motor-bike, with its gear-change handle famously located on the petrol tank.

The depot football team regularly competed against local sides including the County Police. In one game, Brian's reputation as a danger-man had obviously preceded him and his opposite number took the notion of marking far too literally. "The player, whose name was Martin Sykes, followed me all over the pitch trying to kick me, but I was a bit too quick in those days. Inspector Sykes, as he became, and I met up again at Kettering Golf Club, joining forces to win the foursomes championship in 1975."

With Kettering just a short motor-cycle ride away from the Wootton barracks, Brian resumed his association with the Poppies during the 1951-52 football season, making nineteen appearances and scoring ten goals. It was a time when local sides enjoyed remarkable support. 5,385 spectators filled the Sir Halley Stewart ground in Spalding for an FA Cup first qualifying round match, Brian scoring twice in the Poppies' 7–1 victory. He was chosen for the next tie, the drawn game against rivals Corby Town at Occupation Road which attracted the phenomenal attendance of 9,767, but was missing for the replay and would not return to first-team action until the following February. (Kettering went on to reach the First Round Proper before bowing out 3–0 to Bristol Rovers of the Third Division South on a quagmire of a pitch at Eastville).

By the beginning of April, Brian had re-established himself in the Southern League side, helping the club to a creditable seventh place in the table. However, the undoubted highlight of the season was the winning of the prestigious Maunsell Cup. A Reynolds goal accounted for Peterborough United in the semi-final and, on an unforgettable May Day evening before an ecstatic Rockingham Road crowd of 8,082, the Poppies annihilated a full Cobblers side 4–0 in the final. Brian, described in the brochure specially produced to commemorate the event as, "by way of being a Northamptonshire county cricketer", scored the third goal, diving to head home a cross from winger, HJ Potts, an Amateur Cup winner with Pegasus and himself an accomplished batsman.

```
┌─────────────────────────────────────────────────────────────────┐
│                                                                   │
│  Right              KETTERING                        Left         │
│                                                                   │
│                     (1) Pickering                                 │
│          (2) Johnson                    (3) Tart                  │
│          (4) Scott        (5) Waddell   (6) McAuley               │
│     (7) H. J. Potts  (8) Stenhouse  (9) Gallacher  (10) Whent  (11) Reynolds │
│                                                                   │
│          Referee :        ADVERTISING      Linesmen:              │
│         A. E. Court     RIGHTS ACQUIRED    R. Cooper              │
│       (Burton Latimer)   BY SPORTS       (Burton Latimer)         │
│                         PUBLICATIONS   A. Sanders (Rushden)       │
│                                                                   │
│   (11) Fowler   (10) Ramscar   (9) O'Donnell  (8) English  (7) Staroscik │
│          (6) Hughes       (5) Candlin      (4) Davie              │
│               (3) Southam       (2) Collins                       │
│                     (1) Feehan                                    │
│                                                                   │
│  Left            NORTHAMPTON                        Right         │
│  ───────────────────────────────────────────────────────────     │
│     Saturday, May 3rd, v. Chelmsford.   K.O. 3.0  p.m.            │
│                                                                   │
└─────────────────────────────────────────────────────────────────┘
```

The teams, as printed in the programme for the Maunsell Cup final on May 1st, 1952. Kettering were unchanged; for the Cobblers, Joe Payne played at inside-right and Jack English moved to the right-wing, in place of Feliks Staroscik, the Silesian signed from Third Lanark. Jimmy Stenhouse, Jackie Whent, Bronk and Jackie Gallacher were the scorers. Chairman Pascoe was absent: "As his side was soaring, so too was Mr Pascoe. He was strato-cruising back from a business trip to the United States."

Regular team-mates during the season included goalkeeper Peter Pickering, destined to make a memorable appearance for Northants against Lancashire the following August, and county stalwart and former Northampton Town full-back, Bill Barron. He was a member of that rare breed of sportsmen, now extinct[1], who were good enough to earn a living playing cricket in the summer and football in the winter.

Born in County Durham and a former miner, Bill had joined Northampton Town from Charlton Athletic in 1938. However, within a year his promising career had been interrupted by war. During RAF service he was fortunate to spend much of his time at Cardington, near Bedford but, like so many sportsmen of his generation, he looks back somewhat wistfully to what he considers his 'lost' years. "I was twenty-two when the war started and twenty-eight when it ended – the best years of your playing life."

---

1 Tony Cottey of Glamorgan, Sussex and Swansea City (three appearances in 1984-85) may well be the last to play in both the County Championship and the Football League. The last to successfully combine the two as full-time careers was perhaps Phil Neale of Worcestershire and Lincoln City.

On the resumption of League football after the war, Bill made the left-back spot his own, making 172 first team appearances for the Cobblers between 1946 and 1951 before accepting Pascoe's offer to move to the Poppies. During those immediate post-war years, the County Ground provided a backdrop to his dual roles as he successfully combined his two professions. He had joined the Northamptonshire staff in 1946, winning his county cap during that first season after scoring a Championship best 151 against Surrey at the Oval. Twice, in his six seasons at Wantage Road, he exceeded 1000 runs for the season and he made six centuries. His highest score was 161* at Fenner's in 1948 against a Cambridge eleven that included John Dewes, Hubert Doggart and Doug Insole and was skippered by Oundle's JM Mills.

The monetary rewards were poor, but Bill has no regrets about his sporting life. His prowess led directly to a job in the sales office at British Timken, which he held for thirty years until his retirement in 1981. "It sounds idealistic but we really did play for enjoyment in our day. Today it's all 'what can I get out of it?'"

While another team-mate of Brian's, Ray Bailey, holds the distinction of being the last player to play for both Northants and the Cobblers – he made one appearance against Doncaster Rovers in October 1971 while on loan from Gillingham – Bill Barron was unquestionably the most durable. Although they played numerous times in the same Kettering Town football side, Brian and Bill never appeared together in the Northamptonshire first eleven. While Brian was making his Championship debut against Sussex in August 1950, Bill was preparing for the opening game of the Cobblers' Third Division South campaign at Ipswich. And by the time the youngster had returned from National Service to stake a claim for a first-team place, the veteran had retired from the county scene.

The Maunsell Cup triumph was undoubtedly the highlight of the 1951-52 season, but another game, in another Northamptonshire competition, also stands out clearly in Brian's memory. It was a Senior Cup semi-final between Kettering Town reserves and Desborough Town at the latter's Waterworks Field. In the opposing ranks was none other than former Poppies player, and infant occupant of that shared council house in Naseby Road, Bill Draper. When Brian subjected Bill to a rather robust challenge, Bill's mother emerged from the grandstand, ran on to the pitch brandishing an umbrella and had to be restrained from attacking the young winger by a vigilant official.

Bill DRAPER

Brian's 'Service with the Colours' officially ended on October 8th, 1952, the date his service record states that he was discharged on termination of Whole-time National Service. His military conduct is described as "very good" and his testimonial, completed "with a view to civil employment", makes essential reading.

"During his service with the colours he has carried out his duties in an extremely satisfactory manner. He is intelligent, capable and tackles his work with energy and initiative. He is smart in appearance and has a very pleasing personality. He is always correct in his attitude towards his seniors and is most popular with his comrades. He is an all-round sportsman and has played in representative soccer and cricket, in and for the command. He intends to make his career as a professional in both these sports and undoubtedly has a future in this sphere."

There are many reminiscences of National Service which suggest a pointlessness. But some conscripts did see active service - and not just the relative sinecure of occupying Germany. Over a number of years a series of skirmishes brought loss of life to British troops: Aden, Cyprus, Palestine, for example. Here is not the place to ponder on the possible pointlessness of losing to 'terrorists' and then negotiating with them as they became the recognised representatives of the country they had fought for. Brian has the pragmatic approach of the majority of British squaddies; "I'm just glad they never sent me to Malaya."

Discharge from whole-time National Service was not quite the end of one's military career. On the day after discharge, October 9th, 1952, Brian was "deemed to have been enlisted for Part-time National Service into the East Anglian Brigade - Supplementary Reserve and posted to Depot - Northamptonshire Regiment". He remained in the Supplementary Reserve until March 1956.

"Being in the Territorials meant that you had to go on occasional manoeuvres. I was allocated to the Corby detachment and I remember one weekend we were on Salisbury Plain. It was absolutely hosing it down that night," recalls Pte. Reynolds. "I'd just completed digging a trench when the Company Commander, a bank manager from Bourne, announced that, as the enemy were coming this way, we were moving on. I was instructed to fill in the trench, which I did. We then moved to another part of the plain. 'Dig a trench here,' ordered the bank manager. 'You must be bloody joking. I've just filled one in,' I replied."

Young Reynolds didn't have time to wonder whether his refusal to obey an order would be construed as mutinous. Bourne man replied instantly. "If I dig a bit, will you?"

Even discharge from the Territorials on March 20th, 1956 was not the end of his connection with the Army. He was then allocated to the Army General Reserve and was only finally discharged from Reserve Liability on February 28th, 1964. "I can't remember anything ever happening."

Did National Service instil discipline? "Perhaps, but many of us already led disciplined lives. Sometimes there wasn't enough to do. I wanted to play football or cricket all day."

Books that have helped me!

GCB del.

Much prized by Brian is this pseudo-Victorian hand-drawn card, received from the regimental padre, GC Beach, on the occasion of his discharge and containing the message, "May you find the best things within your reach". The qualities identified - self-help and high aims - are more than appropriate.

Mr. F. R. Brown

"Foremost captain of his time
And, as the greatest only are,
In his simplicity sublime."

Alfred Tennyson

Off the rocks

The tonic of gin

Lettuces

Purposeful cricket

"He wouldn't ask you to do anything he couldn't do himself and he could do the lot."

A cricket team's attitude on the field, and the entertainment it provides, is directly connected to the captain. It is irrelevant how many kinds of new-style cricket administrators introduce, how its structure or the laws are changed, without the backing of the captains, they are wasting their time. When Brian Reynolds entered county cricket those were truths universally acknowledged. Alas, it's no longer that straightforward. The drip-drip influx of managers, 'specialist' coaches, directors of cricket, et al, has seen to that. The authoritarian, charismatic Frederick Richard Brown replaced by consensus management. For 'simplicity sublime' now read 'alickadoos gobbledegook'.

In 1949, when Brian was having end of season trials, the new Northamptonshire captain had already changed attitudes, on and off the field. That year the County finished sixth, the best position for thirty-six years. Brown stayed until 1953 and had a profound effect on Northamptonshire cricket, including Brian. After his departure, Wisden summed up his impact in a rare moment of metaphor, talking of Brown's pulling Northants off the rocks of adversity and welding them into a formidable combination. It is often forgotten that he played one hundred and two matches in those five seasons, missing over forty through Test duties, playing and selectorial, plus a shoulder injury in 1951. He appeared only twelve times in 1951, seventeen in 1953. Significantly, those were the worst final positions of his reign: 13th and 11th.

Matthew Engel and Andrew Radd's authoritative history of Northamptonshire CCC notes Vince Broderick's opinion that the team's resurgence owed more to Brown's playing ability than his captaincy. Brian, an avowed FR admirer, eulogises over both contributions, while recognising their complementary effect. He emphasises, in a tone that betokens respect, how "Freddie Brown wouldn't ask you to do anything he couldn't do himself and he could do the lot." As Walter Scott said, "We love a captain to obey," who is "ever the first to scale a tower." It is a truism of cricket that a captain needs to create a happy blend of self-interest and team-interest, and exemplify it himself. Brian is certain that Brown exemplified that truth.

He illustrates this conspicuous all-round talent by a game against Glamorgan at Neath in 1953, when circumstances necessitated the skipper's bowling "inners, outers, offers, and finally, leggers." At the age of forty-two he bowled forty-nine overs in the Glamorgan innings (twenty-five maidens, five for 83). His sparring partner, Broderick, also contributed forty-three overs (four for 59), but he was ten years younger. When they came off the field for lunch, the sweating skipper was asked what he would like to drink. "Fetch me a large gin and tonic or I'll never get through the afternoon." He didn't add, "And the same for Brod." That anecdote says much about changing times (and the restorative powers of gin).

There are similar stories when he took the MCC side to Australia in 1950-51. At evening drinks, after a hard day in the field, he would often ask the twelfth-man to bring him a whisky, not just because he doubted Australians' ability to create a gin and tonic. He had a successful tour on the field and in the last Test led England to their first victory over Australia for thirteen years. It is strange now, in cricket's reduced circumstances, to understand what an emotional event that was. Legend has it the Sydney market advertised lettuces with hearts as big as Freddie

Brown's. You can question the aptness of the simile, but not the strength of its tribute.

He was inspirational on that tour - "So came the captain with the mighty heart" - a reflection in Brian's mind of what he was achieving at Northampton and probably the reason he was there. As so often with FR, there is something of Tennyson's sublime simplicity about his very appointment as MCC's captain. He knew that Norman Yardley and George Mann had been approached ahead of him, but had rejected the invitation. At the end of July 1950, at Lord's on the first day, he hammered 122 for the Gentlemen in 110 minutes, finishing off with a six into the pavilion. That kind of bravura partly explains Brian's enthusing about his "leading from the front". On the second evening of that game he was invited into the Lord's committee room and offered the captaincy to Australia. As Mike Brearley once said in a Cambridge lecture on captaincy: "In some contexts action needs to be headstrong."

That innings for the Gents against the Players typified his approach throughout his career. Robertson-Glasgow had written in a portrait of him in 'The Observer' before the Second World War that he was a notable hitter "who shattered logical arrangement" and "magnified the power of correctness" by daring to drive into the areas behind the bowler and short of the deep fielders. In his time at Northamptonshire, contemporary reporters frequently applaud innings that are "bright", "lively", and "forceful", with particular reference to his "powerful", "aggressive", "bold" driving. Different eras, but the same response. Aggression, of most kinds, was central to his credo. In 1953, he stated that a captain should instruct his batsmen to dictate the policy of play, and expect his side to make between 300 and 400 in five hours play, declare, or be all out and bowl at the tired opposition for the last hour. Ah, the sublime simplicity of it all.

He was also a fine attacking bowler. At the age of forty, he took eighteen Test wickets in Australia, not with leg spin, which he had practised for most of his career, but at medium pace. He took 391 wickets for Northamptonshire, at a cost of 23.23, and scored 4,331 runs at 30.93. The way "he could bowl a long time with a lovely, rolling rhythmic action" is one of Brian's clear memories. Colin Cowdrey's description of his bowling in the nets in Australia in 1954 echoes that. He also remarks on the slow rhythm with the classical shoulder action. Brian judges his all-round talents as the more remarkable because they were still to the fore in his forties, after playing little or no cricket for about ten years. That absence included three years in prisoner of war camps, during which he lost four and a half stone.

Heroic indeed. It is easy to understand why, at the time, many should be in awe of the man and his achievements, not least a young recruit to the groundstaff making his way in the first team under Brown's leadership. "He had this imposing presence. He was a tall, strong figure, but surprisingly mobile. Larger than life in everything he did." Like several amateur captains - Jardine, ERT Holmes, Yardley among them - he wore a raffish 'kerchief, knotted at the neck. A kind of dandyish badge of office, rather as "swank clubs" (Brian's phrase) have colours seemingly designed by Dali.

As it happens, FR bore an astonishing physical resemblance to my kind uncle William, so I was not overawed, even aged fourteen, when asked to bowl before the great man in the County Ground nets. After a while he summoned me to the presence and said: "The wrist is important." My school's motto was 'Manners maketh man', so I thanked him for the advice.

Perhaps he was demonstrating his renowned 'bluffness'.[1] Critics saw him as brusque, too ready with the captain's choleric word in 'Measure for Measure.' There was no shortage of them, often directed at Vince and, in particular, his fielding at third man in front of 'millionaires' row' at the County Ground. As befits someone categorised by 'Playfair' as "stylish" or "elegant", female admirers lobbed sweets at Brod, as yesterday's groupies threw underwear at Tom Jones. Less welcome were the showers of sarcasm from the choleric Brown. On which, it is rumoured, James Robertson Justice based his performance in the 'Doctor' series.

Accounts of Northamptonshire games contained the statutory references to "Brown's reputation as a disciplinarian being clearly seen in the field" or "under Brown's firm leadership the ground fielding was consistently good". However the means are interpreted, Brian is certain that, "he made other people play better than their potential." When asked to name which people, he replied, "All of us", adding after a Pinteresque pause, "you dare not do otherwise." Prior to 1949 it is likely that thinking of failure had seeped into Northants as a team, as it had individuals, and it was a key factor in Brown's successes as a leader that he overcame that. "We played purposeful cricket. The skipper had a confident air and he seemed to enjoy playing." A view also expressed when he was with Surrey: "He never suffered from boredom or satiety." Contrast that with some of today's players lamenting cricket's 'treadmill'.

The Richie Benaud philosophy is that captains should have the regard and respect of their players. It's a bonus if they are liked by them, although that isn't essential if they are winners. For Brian, his first skipper fulfilled each of those requirements. He also saw a good deal of him on the golf course. Brown was a useful golfer, good enough to represent his school, the Leys in the Halford Hewitt Trophy, the annual competition for public school old boys. "His own brand of humour came through on the golf course, just as it did on the cricket field. Much of it was directed at the golfing limitations of the rest of us." The tables were occasionally turned, in one instance at the Ashridge Golf Club where the County Cricketers Golf society had been playing under the captaincy of FR, several years after his retirement from cricket. Brian and Laurie Johnson were the last to leave the clubhouse after what's known as a 'convivial evening'. Outside it was pitch black as Brown, with increasing fury, was attempting to retrieve the society's flag from the flagpole, unaware it had already been removed. "Looks like you could be

---

1 To add to Brian Slough's personal recollection of FR, there are many examples of 'bluffness' in Brown's 1954 autobiography. There, one learns that Bob Clarke (477 wickets for Northants) "has not got a very acute cricket brain". Indeed "there are times when his concentration wavers and he does not appear to be playing in the same match as his colleagues. He wanders haphazardly about, and very often I have felt impelled to scratch a mark on the ground with the spikes of my boots to indicate just where I wanted him to stand". Nevertheless Clarke was "a generous and great-hearted cricketer".

The boy Reynolds got a mention - many others didn't - though it was as a footnote to Brown's favoured 'keeper, "a player with a really big heart" Ken Fiddling. "Well as Brian Reynolds deputised, there is no doubt that we missed Fiddling, especially on wickets where the ball turned". Of Brian's batting, "I am very hopeful that the role of No.1 or 2 will eventually be the lot of Reynolds; he has improved considerably as a batsman."

some time getting that flag down skip," said Johnson, as he drove away with Reynolds and the flag in his car.

It's no secret, and no surprise, that FR Brown was not universally liked at Wantage Road and beyond. And in Benaud's view, not even necessary. An aristocratic mother of an Oxford student of the fifties described Brown as, "a splendid cricketer who nevertheless epitomised the worst traits of someone from a minor public school." Maybe that remark throws some light on several well-documented dust-ups in his cricketing life, three of which involved Yorkies: Close, Laker and Trueman. Strong-willed, even abrasive, individuals, like Freddie Brown you might say. In Close's case, hostility started on the 1950-51 Australian tour, when he was only nineteen. After rows with Brown, he "felt like a leper." Laker, who had little time for a certain kind of amateur, talked of Brown's "uncomfortable jurisdiction", while the explosive potential of Laker and Trueman's touring under his management in 1958 is chronicled in Don Mosey's biographies of both. One confrontation involved Brown, Trueman and Trevor Bailey, in which Fred's anger was fermented when addressed by his surname. Surprisingly, perhaps, Brown viewed Bill Edrich with "extreme disfavour", regarding him as a "problem".

Jeremy Newton, Chief Executive of the National Endowment for Science, Technology, and the Arts, interviewed in 'The Guardian', was asked which management guru he believed in. His answer was William Shakespeare. Brown's style of management was Antony. His advocates, like Brian, talk fondly of his being a captain 'of the old school'. What that partly implies is that old-time captains like Percy Fender, 'Gubby' Allen and Freddie Brown found it easier, and were accustomed, to be autocrats. That was the natural order of things. The skipper was no believer in captaincy by committee, nor in anything by committee..

Frederick Richard Brown was born on December 16th, 1910 in the Peruvian capital of Lima, where his father was in business.

A Cambridge blue and Surrey amateur, his Test debut was against New Zealand at the Oval in 1931. He played another twenty-one Tests, fifteen of them as captain. His final Test was against Australia at Lord's in 1953 - the famous game in which Trevor Bailey and Willie Watson batted through most of the last day to secure a draw. Brown's major contribution was four second innings wickets, though his 28 (caught off Richie Benaud in the last over) after Watson had been dismissed ensured that the good work was not wasted. Brown was, at the time, the Chairman of Selectors.

A Wisden Cricketer of the Year in 1933 and MCC President for 1971-72, his last Championship appearance was in 1953, though his final first-class game was in 1961 when he captained Free Foresters against a Cambridge University side whose third wicket partnership involved Mike Brearley and Northamptonshire's John Minney.

FR Brown CBE died on July 24th, 1991.

Freddie Brown as he appeared in 'Cricket Musketeer', in the days when it was politically correct to wear gloves when smoking.

```
┌─────────────────────────────────────────┐
│                                           │
│  P Roy c Reynolds b Tyson 0               │
│                       Northampton, 1952   │
│                                           │
└─────────────────────────────────────────┘
```

1952 - 1953

"Still ending and beginning still"

William Cowper,
'The Task'

```
┌─────────────────────────────────────────┐
│                                           │
│          Not the first century            │
│                                           │
│           Keeping wicket                  │
│                                           │
│             On the buses                  │
│                                           │
│        First time at Lord's               │
│                                           │
└─────────────────────────────────────────┘
```

"Fred slipped in another short one. 'Just testing', he grinned."

1951 provided little cricket for the serviceman - just a handful of Second Eleven matches - and little progress towards the goal of a first team place. 1952, though, provided an opportunity to make the breakthrough as well as a three-year contract.

Northamptonshire County Cricket Club

T. E. MANNING, Esq., President

SECRETARY:
Lt.-Col. A. St. G. COLDWELL

———

HON. TREASURER :
H. C. DEVITTE, Esq.
Westminster Bank, Northampton

County Cricket Ground

Northampton

Pavilion Phone 697

PHONE : 4 9 1 7

May 29th. 1952

Dear Reynolds,

I am to offer you a three-year contract from the 1st. April 1953 to 31st. March 1956.

The terms offered are £200 per annum, plus £5 for each First-class match played, plus current rate of expense allowance when playing away for First-class matches, plus match money.

The match money is £3 per player for each First-class match won, and £1 per player for each match won on 1st.

The terms would be subject to review according to *ability* shown at the end of the first season, i.e. end of August 1953.

If you would like to come and discuss things with me you know where to find me.

Yours sincerely,

asacoldwell

Secretary.

Pte. B. Reynolds,
Quebec Barracks.

The bowling 'prodigy' of Stamford Road School had not materialised, despite the time spent bowling to members in the nets. "I used to bowl leg-spin and googlies, but only dropped them anywhere near about once a week." In 1952, with Brian completing his National Service in Northampton, an opportunity arose. "When you get a chance, you take it. I'd kept wicket a few times for the Town, particularly in Knock-out matches. Ken Fiddling was unwell, Jock Livingston didn't want to keep on a regular basis, having been hit in the teeth. Nor did Percy, who couldn't read George Tribe's bowling. So I had a go," is Brian's summary of the club's stumper situation. Percy 'Sparrow' Davis's wicket-keeping lapses made him the frequent target of FR Brown's Swiftian satire. "Buddy, you move to your left a bit, Nutts you move a yard to your right, Sparrow, you stand in the middle and, if it comes your way, let it hit you." That's the clean version.

Brian's first-team debut as wicket-keeper was against Essex at Northampton in the middle of July. It was a high scoring match which featured three double centuries and a new fifth wicket record partnership for Northants. 'Sonny' Avery led the way for Essex with 224, putting on 294 for the second wicket with Paul Gibb (132). Northamptonshire went a long way past Essex's 428 as Dennis Brookes made 204 not out and Des Barrick recorded 211. Brian watched their partnership of 347 which greatly exceeded the previous Northamptonshire record, 236. That had been made by George Thompson and Bob Haywood at Dewsbury in 1911, a pairing that in the same season (Northamptonshire's seventh as a first-class county) set a seventh wicket record with 222 against Gloucestershire. The 347 of Brookes and Barrick was not overhauled until 1998 when Mal Loye (322*) and David Ripley (209) battered the defending Champions, Glamorgan, at Northampton.

In its brief review of the game, Wisden highlighted another individual. "Reynolds, a 20-year-old soldier in the Northamptonshire Regiment, allowed only six byes and altogether gave a praiseworthy display." Brian didn't bat (FR declared when he was sixth out) but took his first catch, Dick Horsfall, and late in the game made his first stumping, Bill Greensmith (off Tribe).

Brian played six consecutive matches as wicket-keeper, five of them at Northampton. The only away game was at Glastonbury which Harold Gimblett chose for his benefit; it was the first time anybody had chosen Northants for his benefit match. There were few batting opportunities; nine was the usual position and in half the games he did not make it to the crease.

He did bat against the Indian tourists, being not out on 12 when the declaration came. Ten minutes later he was standing (a long way) back for Frank Tyson's debut over. "Frank sprayed it about a bit for three balls. Off the fourth there was an inside edge. I dived to leg and caught him." 'Him' was Pankaj Roy who made forty-three Test appearances for India, though he had an appalling tour in 1952: five ducks in his seven Test innings.

After one more game, a rain-affected draw with Leicestershire, Brian's season came to an abrupt end. "I was about to set off from Wootton to Kettering on my motor bike but it suddenly became very dark and I decided to go back into the barracks to get some more water-proof gear. There were no lights on and as I turned a corner I was aware of someone coming the other way. I instinctively put my hand in front of my face and immediately felt a tingling sensation. The chap coming the other way had just come out of ablutions and was carrying an open razor. I was cut on my right index finger, palm and forearm. There was plenty of blood, so it was off to the General for quite a few stitches. That was the end of cricket for that year."

Brian's first match in 1953 was against the Royal Air Force. Although a three-day game, some committee in the depths of Lord's decided the game should not have first-class status, despite the presence in the visitors of many players with first-class experience - included were Martin Horton, Roy Swetman, Alan Shirreff, Jim Pressdee, Roly Thompson and Mike Willett. Under Wisden's pseudonym of BC Reynolds and Playfair's BG Reynolds, he scored 121 in four hours which did not count as his maiden first-class hundred. The RAF's opening bowler was probably a bit miffed that his five wickets (for 77) did not count in his career record. He was AC2 FS Trueman.

Despite its lack of status the match received coverage in the national press, with generous praise for the way Reynolds and Tribe rescued the situation after

Northants were 90 for five (at that stage, Trueman four for 28). Livingston, Jakeman, Barrick and Broderick had "all been beaten by the England bowler's pace." However, "Reynolds batted beautifully, showing more confidence against Trueman than any earlier batsman and when the slow bowlers took over the partnership carried on until it added 138." Freddie Brown then clobbered 129 in 102 minutes, which probably contributed as much to Trueman's later antagonisms as 'kerchiefed Oxbridge hauteur.

The full scores did not appear in Wisden. The batting details of the Northamptonshire's first innings are:

D Brookes	c Fenner	b Thompson	9
VH Broderick		b Trueman	34
L Livingston	lbw	b Trueman	14
FS Jakeman		b Trueman	15
DW Barrick	c Pressdee	b Trueman	6
BL Reynolds	c Fenner	b Shirreff	121
GE Tribe		b Trueman	62
FR Brown	c Thompson	b Shirreff	129
A Lightfoot	not out		3
RW Clarke	did not bat		
M Tate	did not bat		
Extras			16
TOTAL		(8 wkts dec)	409

The fact that the RAF match was not recognised as first-class still rankles a little. "A month later, on my twenty-first birthday, I sat with my pads on all day dying to get in. Somehow Buddy and Brod had managed to go in first but we wouldn't have been all out if we were still playing today!" The birthday match - at Peterborough against Scotland - was deemed first-class. When Brod was out, Brookes declared, leaving nine 'did not bats'. Dismissed for 66, Scotland, following-on were 126 for four at the end of the second day. On the third it rained, non-stop.

Oldfield and Broderick's 361 appeared as the record first wicket partnership for Northants in every 'Playfair' until Richard Montgomerie and Malachy Loye made 372 against Yorkshire in the last match of 1996. No disrespect to Buddy and Brod, but quite a few at the County Ground were pleased to see a 'proper' first wicket record; those with Northamptonshire and Scotland allegiances were doubly delighted. "That partnership was in the record books for years. My hundred didn't count. And neither did Fred's wickets."

Brian batted thirty-eight times against Yorkshire, with a highest score of 77 (at Northampton in 1960). Yorkshire is one of the four counties against whom he failed to score a century. Trueman dismissed him on six occasions. Three of those were early in his innings, which had nothing to do with Fred's well known con-artistry. Brian confirms his habits of spending more time in opponents' dressing rooms than his own and wearing suits with padded shoulders, like a young Jack Palance. On the other hand, Northants reckoned it was possible to keep Fred sweet. An occasional "well bowled" when you knew you weren't playing at it, did no harm. "I liked Fred, and still do. We've met a few times since we stopped playing. He was certainly a tremendous bowler, who could be as fast as he wanted to be. Later in his career he could adapt his pace to suit the wicket. Fred moved the ball and was unpredictable; with Brian Statham at least you knew where it was coming from." Brian was hit on the head (before helmets, of course) by both of them. He once tried to hook Fred at Northampton, the ball flew off the edge and hit him on the cheekbone. Yorkshire encouraged him to leave the field. "They were always keen to remove you from the fray, whatever the means, but having reached the edge in front of the old pavilion, I returned. First up, Fred slipped in another short one. "Just testing, Renny," grinned Fred. He always called me 'Renny'."

Most on the county circuit called him 'Waddy' rather than 'Bronk' as he was known in Kettering. According to Frank Tyson, 'Waddy' stemmed from his being "an extremely competent trencherman who enjoyed a wad of sandwiches." David Steele thought that it referred to the wad of protective material Brian used on the bottom joint of the index finger of his bottom hand. "I think it was the sandwiches," admits Waddy.

Ken Fiddling played in only the first four Championship matches of the 1953 season. From May 23, Brian took over as wicket-keeper and was ever-present for the remainder of the season.

His encounter with Trueman was a useful introduction for during the season Brian confronted a host of international-standard 'quicks': Peter Loader, Trevor Bailey, John Warr, Alec Bedser, Tom Pritchard and Jack Flavell as well as Statham and Trueman. Northamptonshire had the quickest in Tyson. There was another, whom Brian and Fred rated as highly as any of them. Derbyshire's Herbert Leslie Jackson played in only two Test matches (and missed an entire decade - his first was in 1949 and his last in 1961), such was the strength of contending fast bowlers or the weakness of England's selectors. In August 1953, at Wellingborough School (where Derbyshire were the visitors three years in a row) the scorecard read: 'BL Reynolds c AC Revill b HL Jackson 0.' The fact that the card also read 'Jackson st Reynolds b Brown 15' was some consolation.

"Les Jackson was a mean bowler. For a start, he looked fearsome. He also had the habit of digging a pit, left foot about middle, which made it difficult for batsmen to stand at the crease in the second innings." Fred Jakeman, in a bid for the poet laureateship, put it this way: "If he's not hitting you in the rocks, he's tearing steaks off your arse." And they say Yorkshiremen don't have a way with words.

Brian had his problems with the Derbyshire Jacksons. Les (who retired in 1963) dismissed him seven times; the unrelated Brian (who started in 1963) five. Like all the best blue-eyed gunslingers, however, Bronk was set on revenge. On a benign wicket at Derby, in Les's final season, he dropped one short and was smacked over square-leg for six. "I've been waiting ten years for that." Les said nothing, but wouldn't die easily; the innings ended: 'Reynolds c Jackson b Smith 74.' Advantage Reynolds (just).

In that first full season Brian was dismissed more often by spin bowlers: Ray Smith, Jack Young, Jim Laker, Ray Illingworth, Doug Ring, Jack Walsh, Cec ('Sam') Cook, Jim McConnon, and Doug Wright (and Louis Devereux) among them. Not a bad batch for starters, at whatever stage of your career. The list is also significant in another way: it indicates the number, and range, of slow bowlers in the game at that time, not least the wrist spinners. Indeed, the first bowler to dismiss Brian in the first-class game was of that ilk: WE Hollies, known eternally as 'the hand that bowled Bradman'. How many of us would like that as our epitaph?[1]

That same year Brian was also lbw cheaply to Bedser, Statham and Wilf Wooller. No disgrace there and, anyway, fledglings rarely get the benefit of an umpire's doubt. That much hasn't changed. To be fair, would you turn down a Wooller appeal against a raw recruit at Neath? Doug Greasley also went 'lbw b Wooller 0' (there were three in a spell of six for 61). No ironic subtext intended; the umpire was the highly respected Syd Buller who umpired 33 Tests.

Bronk's first Championship match of '53, at home to Leicestershire, saw the boy start well; out for 59, caught by Maurice Hallam off Jeff Goodwin. A week later, on his first appearance at Lord's, he opened the batting (in the absence of Brookes) with Broderick, scoring 41 against the varied Middlesex attack of Alan Moss, John Warr, Don Bennett, Fred Titmus, Jack Young and Denis Compton. Northamptonshire had been sent in by Bill Edrich on a difficult wet wicket, another defunct species. Among his happy memories of Lord's is being warmly praised by 'Patsy' Hendren, then the Middlesex scorer, for the way he used his feet against the slower bowlers. EH Hendren scored 40,302 runs, average 49.81, for Middlesex and reached three figures 119 times in his thirty-one year career. Some compliments you never forget, just as he'd never forgotten that criticism of his art work at school.

To cap a satisfying HQ debut, he caught Compton (Denis, not Leslie who was also in the team) off Bob Clarke for 52. "Denis was one of those great players, with an original talent that is a gift from God. Colin Milburn was another. No one could coach that ability into players. Denis would dance down the wicket and then late cut. Mind you, he couldn't run between the wickets. I think it was John Warr's famous one-liner that 'a call from Denis was merely the start of negotiations.' Don Bennett reckoned he never seemed to own a bat, but it didn't matter as he'd score hundreds with a plank." The last day of that Middlesex game was Coronation Day. There was no cricketing celebration at Lord's, where persistent showers prevented any play.

A month later, at a very different venue, but special to Brian, he recorded an unbeaten 48 against Essex. It set up an engrossing finish. Local pride is reflected in the evening paper's report: "As they came back to the pavilion the Kettering crowd cheered Reynolds and Freddie Brown. But, reaching the pavilion steps, the skipper smilingly stood back, and pushed Reynolds up the steps before him, clapping the youngster and indicating the applause should be for him." Essex, needing 300 to win, managed 232 for 9, Trevor Bailey batted for three and a quarter hours for his unbeaten 81 to save the game. Doug Insole became another of Brian's distinguished victims, when he was stumped off Tribe for 47.

---

1 It was Warwickshire's Eric Hollies who bowled Don Bradman (for a duck) in Bradman's final Test innings at The Oval in 1948. Bradman needed to score four runs to aggregate 10,000 runs in Test cricket at an average of 100. Hollies' googly left him on 9,996 at 99.96.

LORD'S GROUND

(3ᴰ) **(3ᴰ)**

MIDDLESEX v. NORTHAMPTONSHIRE

SATURDAY, MONDAY & TUESDAY, MAY 30, JUNE 1, 2, 1953 (3-day Match)

NORTHAMPTONSHIRE		First Innings		Second Innings
1	Broderick, V.	c Bennett b Moss	20	
*2	Reynolds, B.	c Thompson b Young	41	
3	Livingston, L.	c Warr b D. Compton	34	
4	Barrick, D. W.	not out	117	
5	Davis, E.	st L Com'ton b D Com'ton	0	
†6	F. R. Brown	c Edrich b Young	39	
7	Tribe, G. E.	c L. Compton b Young	9	
8	Greasley, D. G.	b Moss	0	
9	Nutter, A. E.	c L. Compton b Moss	38	
10	Clarke, R. W.	c Young b Titmus	15	
11	Starkie, S.	not out	4	
		B 6, l-b , w , n-b ,	6	B , l-b , w , n-b ,

* Innings closed   Total ....*323   Total ....

FALL OF THE WICKETS

1....41   2....85   3....122   4....122   5....193   6....207   7....208   8....262   9....299   10......

1......   2......   3......   4......   5......   6......   7......   8......   9......   10......

ANALYSIS OF BOWLING		1st Innings					2nd Innings				
Name	O.	M.	R.	W.	Wd.	N-b	O.	M.	R.	W.	Wd.	N-b
Moss	29	3	99	3	...	...	...	...	...	...	...	...
Warr	16	2	49	0	...	...	...	...	...	...	...	...
Bennett	12	0	53	0	...	...	...	...	...	...	...	...
Titmus	20	8	36	1	...	...	...	...	...	...	...	...
Young	24	9	57	3	...	...	...	...	...	...	...	...
D. Compton	7	0	23	2	...	...	...	...	...	...	...	...
....	...	...	...	...	...	...	...	...	...	...	...	...

MIDDLESEX		First Innings		Second Innings
1	J. G. Dewes	l b w b Tribe	41	
2	Brown, S. M.	l b w b Nutter	16	
†3	W. J. Edrich	l b w b Brown	47	
4	Compton, D. C. S.	c Reynolds b Clarke	52	
5	Thompson, A.	c Livingston b Brown	55	
6	Bennett, D.	b Nutter	1	
7	Titmus, F.	run out	3	
*8	Compton, L. H.	b Tribe	8	
9	J. J. Warr	not out	5	
10	Young, J. A.	c sub b Brown	0	
11	Moss, A. E.	not out	4	
		B 7, l-b 5. w , n b ,	12	B , l-b , w , n-b ,

Total 244   Total ....

FALL OF THE WICKETS

1...34   2...90   3....130   4...184   5....187   6....190   7...219   8...240   9...240   10...

1......   2....   3...   4....   5......   6......   7......   8......   9......   10...

ANALYSIS OF BOWLING		1st Innings					2nd Innings				
Name	O.	M.	R.	W.	Wd.	N-b	O.	M.	R.	W.	Wd.	N-b
Nutter	35	6	78	2	...	...	...	...	...	...	...	...
Clarke	21	4	61	1	...	...	...	...	...	...	...	...
Brown	19	5	34	3	...	...	...	...	...	...	...	...
Tribe	22	3	59	2	...	...	...	...	...	...	...	...
....	...	...	...	...	...	...	...	...	...	...	...	...
....	...	...	...	...	...	...	...	...	...	...	...	...

Umpires—F. S. Lee & A. E. Boulton-Carter   Scorers—E. Hendren & L. Sherwin

† Captain   * Wicket keeper

Play begins 1st & 2nd days at 11.30, 3rd day at 2.30

Stumps drawn 1st & 2nd days at 7, 3rd day at 6.30

(Half-an-hour extra on the last day if necessary)

Spectators are requested not to enter or leave their seats during the progress of an over

This card does not necessarily include the fall of the last wicket

MIDDLESEX WON THE TOSS AND PUT NORTHAMPTONSHIRE IN

Extracted from the Northamptonshire Evening Telegraph's pre-Coronation edition, the lack of quality in the reproduction cannot conceal the identity of the opponents; Brian Reynolds is behind the stumps, Denis Compton is in front.

The Kettering ground was a few minutes walk to Brian's home in the Oval. Northampton required more effort. His routine for games at Wantage Road was to walk into the centre of Kettering and catch a United Counties bus shortly after eight o'clock. The journey, via Broughton, took the best part of an hour. He left the bus at St Matthew's Church and walked to the ground. At close of play came the identical, reverse journey, "though I admit to keeping a look out at the bus stop in the hope that someone would recognise me and give me a lift back to Kettering." This was a time when star footballers like Tom Finney travelled to a match on the same bus as spectators. Indeed, the last authenticated sighting of a Cobblers footballer waiting for the 256 to Kettering was winger Harry Walden. Harry played nineteen matches in 1965-66 when the Cobblers were in what would now be termed the Premiership. After evening matches he was always in the queue at St.Matthew's for the 9.30 pm from Derngate. Is it just home-spun philosophy that says there's a message in there somewhere?

Brian was also growing accustomed to other bus journeys. No sponsored cars, motorways, and Granada service stations. This was the age of Wesley's buses, B roads and fish and chip shops. The schedule could be demanding:

Tuesday June 16, day 3 at Northampton;
Wednesday June 17, day 1 at Neath;
Friday June 19, day 3 at Neath;
Saturday June 20, day 1 at Kettering;
Tuesday June 23, day 3 at Kettering;
Wednesday June 24, day 1 at Leeds;
Friday June 26, day 3 at Leeds;
Saturday June 27 day 1 at Bournemouth;
Tuesday June 30, day 3 at Bournemouth;
Wednesday July 1, day 1 at Chesterfield;
Friday July 3, day 3 at Chesterfield;
Saturday July 4, day 1 at Northampton v Australians

Brian is grateful that for much of the time they had a "superb" individual called Sid French as driver and 'twelfth man'. "He was actually much better than most twelfth-men," asserts Brian, perhaps recalling one or two who found it difficult to judge the ideal water temperature for the senior pro's bath.

After the war the Northamptonshire team sometimes travelled by train, but by the time Brian started, Wesley's had taken over. "I always preferred travelling by coach. It kept you together as a team. There was no hassle and you could put your feet up and have a kip."

Northamptonshire was probably the last county to abandon coach travel in favour of players' (then un-sponsored) cars. "There was always the memory of Freddie Bakewell and Reggie Northway. That's why the club was reluctant to use cars," Brian recalls. Returning from a match at Chesterfield (in which Bakewell hit 241*; it was the last of the 1936 season), Northway's car left the road south of Leicester and he was killed instantly. Bakewell, who had played in six Tests, was critically injured. "He wasn't expected to survive, so his broken arm wasn't set. So, when he did pull through, he wasn't able to play cricket again."

Three half-centuries in succession, 50* against Lancashire, 64 at Taunton and 60 at Leicester, towards the end of July represented Brian's best spell with the bat. In August there were disappointingly few runs but the young man had begun to make his mark in first-class cricket.

End of term plaudits in various cricket handbooks and annuals were directed at Tyson and Reynolds, more so for the young wicket-keeping batsman with his haul of 37 catches, 17 stumpings, and 816 runs. Wisden's final Northamptonshire sentence stated, "Reynolds, one of the younger players, showed promise as a batsman and wicket-keeper, and Tyson did enough to suggest that he might become a very fine fast bowler."

The Chronicle and Echo had agreed about Bronk's wicket-keeping in 1952. "Reynolds, whose batting has also earned him praise, has proved himself an efficient 'keeper who can take the ball cleanly and sometimes spectacularly on the leg side. His quickness behind the stumps has been noted and I think that Northamptonshire need not look any further for a deputy for Fiddling." However, after the RAF game, the May 15th 1953 edition had an article headlined, "An Opening Bat Discovered?" which questioned the best role for Brian.

"Now 20 years of age and free from Army duties he returned to the side to make a century, his first in county standard cricket. Back on the staff he can now concentrate on his cricketing career and it is also time for Northamptonshire to decide what they are going to do with him.

"In a very short time an opening batsman will be needed and Reynolds would appear to be a youngster worth trying there. If he 'came off' Northamptonshire would have a man for the position for about 20 years and that is the all important point, one which should outweigh any arguments between him and any 'stopgap' opener. Many people felt that after Saturday, if the selection committee share the idea of other counties who introduce young men, they will play him there for the rest of the season.. Yorkshire have put their young men in quickly and Australia are never afraid of trying out youth.

"Reynolds is one of the most level-headed young men in cricket and no one need fear that quick promotion would 'go to his head' and ruin him. On Saturday, let it be remembered, he comfortably weathered two spells of Trueman where established men fell, and throughout his innings there was not a trace of nerves. He timed some of Trueman's fastest deliveries perfectly and heavily punished the slower bowlers.

"I am not at all sure that keeping wicket is doing Reynolds any good. He was not picked out of the County trialists and offered terms on the staff with that idea. Because he has helped the club there in a difficulty is no reason for persisting with him in that position now. Why not concentrate on his batting?"

Events conspired to prevent the selection committee on this advice and Brian spent the season with gauntlets. Some other statistics indicate what a fine job he made of it. That season the leading wicket-keeper-batsman was Dick Spooner, who played in five Tests in India in 1951-52, averaged 31.50 as number four batsman for Warwickshire. Paul Gibb, another Test player, averaged 27.61 batting at three for Essex and Godfrey Evans 24.84 going in usually between three and five for Kent. Brian, generally at six, averaged 29.24 (FR Brown 27.12). Comparisons of catches and stumpings are difficult, "odorous" according to Dogberry, especially as the above played a different number of matches, but a reasonable conclusion puts them on a par. That is no mean achievement. It is proof of Brian's innate ability as a games player that, not only was he a high-class fielder in any position, but he kept wicket in the County Championship with little prior experience. He had no formal coaching, but readily acknowledges the help given by senior players, notably Jock Livingston.

In spite of the praise, what Arlott saw as a "modestly quiet man" is evident in Brian's self-critical assessment that he "probably had good hands but was really only a stopper." He relished the experience, which came his way largely by the default of others. Brian learnt many lessons from his skipper; one of them was to make the most of an opportunity. He is probably unfair to himself to suggest he was no more than a slip with gloves on. Like most keepers he derived his deepest satisfaction from keeping to spin bowlers: a test of intelligence, reflexes as well as concentration. He especially enjoyed the challenge of George Tribe, who bowled most slow left-arm varieties - chinamen, googlies etc. - but also what he called his 'squibber' (a quicker delivery that captured many lbws). Early on there were difficulties reading the googly, so hitched flannels became the signal. On the rare occasions where a batsman could pick it, George would adjust his field and give him a single, which is more difficult than it seems. Brian is amused that once he could pick George's assortment, the Australian avoided him in the nets. His overwhelming admiration for Tribe as a cricketer and a man is forthrightly expressed: "If I have one ambition left, it's to find another player like George Tribe. A super bloke as well, even though he's an Aussie."

Of his twenty stumpings, eight were off Tribe's bowling. In one innings against Gloucestershire at Rushden 'st Reynolds' appears in the scorebook thrice, but his most vivid memory is stumping the left-handed Brian Close down the leg-side off Des Barrick in 1952. Close, having scored just one, cursed succinctly and left. That kind of dismissal requires the skills Brian now looks for in assessing potential County keepers.

"There's little point in checking when they're standing back. It's speed of hand and eye standing up, the position of the head. Quickness of foot is important, but subsidiary. Top class batsmen leave their ground for such a short space of time that you're lucky to stump someone off a width ball."

In one game in 1953, against Cambridge University, Brian did not keep wicket. Young Keith Andrew was given the gloves and he caught two (one of them, Raman Subba Row, for 81) and stumped three. In 1954 he became first choice keeper and Brian rates him as highly as anyone he's ever seen.

The match against the Australians was a big occasion for every County in the pre-television era. The County Ground was packed on July 4th, 1953 for the visit of Lindsay Hassett's tourists. Drama came in the first over when Frank Tyson removed Colin McDonald and Graeme Hole, but the Aussies fought back (Neil Harvey 118) to win by an innings in two days. Brian took a rest from wicket-keeping duties and is here seen being presented to the Duke of Gloucester at the tea interval on the first day. Freddie Brown is making the introductions, Des Barrick and Bob Clarke have had their turn and next, on the right of the picture, is George Tribe.

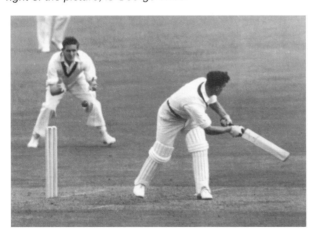

In the Northants' first innings of 141, Ron Archer took seven for 56. Brian rates him as one of the fastest he ever faced. Here, he turns him to leg, before departing c McDonald b Archer 21. The fielder is Archer's new ball partner, Alan Davidson.

1952 - 1957

"Champions fierce,
Strive here for mastery."

> 'Paradise Lost',
> Milton

With the Posh

On his bike

On Hold

Lawton's provider

"If he thought he could intimidate me, he was wrong."

Brian celebrated his imminent return to civilian life by making the first of twelve first-team appearances for Kettering Town during the 1952-53 season in the 2–1 home victory over Merthyr Tydfil on September 6th. Large crowds continued to support the Poppies and that fixture, against the side which had recently completed a hat-trick of Southern League titles, attracted a crowd of 5,020. The Poppies, whose success was founded on the strong defensive trio of Pascoe imports Peter Pickering, Bill Barron and Willie Waddell, ended the season in fourth place.

Interestingly, the Yeovil Town programme for the match against Kettering at The Huish on December 13th 1952, refers to the Poppies right winger as "the only local boy in the side". There is a tendency to assume that, at this rather humble level of the game, the town side would include a profusion of Kettering-bred players. In fact, during the fifties, in common with other post-war decades, Brian was one of the few locals to total over fifty appearances for the first team, sharing the distinction with Bobby Wyldes, Harry Johnson and Geoff Toseland.

In the summer of 1953, Brian was offered improved terms to join Peterborough United of the Midland League. The 'Posh', then one of the most ambitious non-league clubs in the country, were managed by Jack Fairbrother, the former Newcastle United goalkeeper. "Jack always used to say, 'Make them shoot from outside the area. There's no way they should beat me from there.' And of course with his great positional play and the heavy leather ball they rarely did."

During Brian's initial season at London Road, Peterborough enjoyed the first of the FA Cup runs which were to become such a regular feature during the rest of the decade. However, he took no part in the matches which ended in glorious defeat by First Division Cardiff City, featuring mainly in the club's reserve team - which played in the United Counties League - but made four Midland League appearances during the season. The first came just seven days after the epic battle at Ninian Park when he featured in a nine goal thriller against Corby Town, scoring two goals in the 5-4 victory. Team-mates that afternoon included Johnny Anderson, a member of

Spotlight

BRIAN REYNOLDS

When Brian signed for Peterborough United this close season, the club could feel well satisfied at adding to the staff a man who has such zest for sport. At the moment he is playing himself in, and from reports received from last Saturday's game, he certainly "went to town" at British Timken. Reports regarding his position suggest that he can play anywhere down the left side. What a player to have at your command. Noted in Kettering for his absolute whole heartedness, Brian also has a good knowledge of the game of soccer.

His cricket club think the world of him. He has just completed a very, very successful season in white flannels, and we at Peterborough hope that he continues his good form, and really enjoys his first season with the "POSH."

Manchester United's 1948 FA Cup winning side, Republic of Ireland international Paddy Sloan, long-serving centre-half Norman Rigby and geordie winger, George 'the electric' Hair, notable as one of the first footballers to play in contact lenses.

Jack Fairbrother made his final Peterborough appearance against Cardiff before taking the vacant managership at Coventry City. He was quickly succeeded by George Swindin, who had spent almost all his playing career with Arsenal in the First Division – one top-class goalkeeper giving way to another. Brian played just one game alongside the new player-manager, in the defeat at Scunthorpe and Lindsey United. It was to be his last Midland League appearance.

In 1954, the reserve side switched from the United Counties League to its eastern equivalent, the Eastern Counties League. The competition provided a good class of football as, in addition to trips to east coast resorts such as Lowestoft, Yarmouth and Clacton, opponents included the 'A' sides of Arsenal, Tottenham Hotspur and West Ham United. Among Brian's colleagues in the reserve side that season were inside-forward Denis Emery and winger Peter McNamee, players who would play significant parts in the sustained success which culminated in Peterborough's election to the Football League six years later. Such was the level of interest among supporters, that home gates for reserve matches were often in excess of 6,000.

George Swindin had retired from goalkeeping at the end of the previous campaign to concentrate on management. His long association with Arsenal shaped his expectations and he had high aspirations for his new club. There were major ground improvements at London Road, some players became full-time professionals and, as Brian recalls, all thirty members of the playing staff were expected to conform to the highest standard of behaviour both on and off the pitch. "I often used to spend Friday night at team-mate Colin Senior's house in Peterborough if we were leaving the ground early on Saturday morning for an away fixture. On one occasion, Colin, his wife and I went along to the local pub for a bit of relaxation. She had a couple of gin and tonics while Colin and I had orange juice. When I got to the ground the next Saturday, I was summoned to George Swindin's office and questioned about my drinking habits. When I told him what had happened, the manager seemed satisfied, explaining, 'You were seen in the pub by a supporter, who reported to me that you were boozing. I had to check it out.' It taught me a valuable lesson. After that I made sure that if I did any drinking I did it at home and not in public."

Brian was still relying upon his trusty motor-bike to transport him to and from Peterborough in all weathers. "On cold days I used to wrap layers of brown paper under my jacket and down my legs to keep warm. It was far from ideal preparation for a football match. Sometimes I'd get to the ground with little time to change, let alone defrost. There were no complicated 'warm-ups' in those days. You just went out five minutes before kick-off and fired shots at the goalkeeper. And as for 'cool-downs', the prospect of an hour's journey back to Kettering on my motor-bike was quite enough to chill me out."

At that time, the Eastern Counties League was populated by an interesting cross-section of players. The West Ham United 'A' side included wing-half John Smith, whose big money transfer to Tottenham Hotspur in 1958 would clear the way for Bobby Moore's entry into League football, centre-half Andy Nelson and

Tony Franklin (brother of Dennis, Brian's fellow Avondale Colt), who later played for Wellingborough Town. There were also hard-bitten veterans like March Town player-manager Oscar Hold. His programme notes for the game against Peterborough Reserves on Easter Monday 1955, in marked contrast to the rather bland prose which occupies most such publications today, ranged over esoteric matters like the right of footballers with strong religious beliefs not to play on Good Friday, the ownership of a gents mackintosh left in the grandstand and a less than flattering description of the playing surface at Stowmarket. "Our visit to Stowmarket brings the 'Curate's egg' immediately to mind. The officials proved delightful hosts, their appointments were excellent, the match was interesting, handled very efficiently by our old friend, referee Mr Everitt, the result was very gratifying but oh, oh, oh, what a blooming pitch!!!"

As Brian Reynolds recalls, however, Oscar's attitude on the field during the Bank Holiday clash was far from aesthetic. "He kicked me, deliberately and hard, in the first minute of the game, but if he thought he could intimidate me he was wrong. I waited until the ball had gone out of play and then confronted him face to face. 'There's nowhere for you to hide,' I said, 'and if you kick me again you'll be over the stand'."

Peterborough celebrated a double success in 1955-56, the first team crowned Champions of the Midland League for the first time and the reserves winning the Eastern Counties League. Additionally, Alf Ramsey's Ipswich Town, of the Third Division South, were beaten in the FA Cup before a crowd of 20,671, but despite these achievements the club received only eight votes in its quest for Football League membership. During the close season George Swindin demonstrated his determination to strengthen his squad by signing Henry Cockburn, thirteen times an England international. There were also departures from London Road, including Brian Reynolds who rejoined Kettering Town.

The club was now managed by Tommy Lawton, who had joined the club from Arsenal as player-manager in a blaze of publicity back in February 1956. Lawton had won the last of his twenty-three England caps in 1949 but was still such a big name that when he signed for Kettering Town he did so live on BBC TV's 'Sportsview' programme, under the watchful gaze of David Coleman.

Cricket duties over, Bronk made his first Southern League appearance of the season in the home match against Yeovil on September 29th 1956, but the occasion was overshadowed by grief. Both sides wore black armbands in memory of former Poppy and Leicestershire cricketer Maurice Tompkin, who had died the previous Thursday, aged just thirty-seven. Lawton's team left it late to secure victory. Only a minute of the match remained when football's most famous centre-parting leapt to head Reynolds' accurate left-footed corner past the visiting goalkeeper for the only goal of the game.

A fortnight later, in the game against Chelmsford City, Brian played a supporting role in a virtuoso Lawton performance. A crowd of 4,102 watched in admiration as the former England centre-forward produced a vintage display scoring four times, three with his head, in a thrilling 6–4 victory. During the first-half Brian had made a determined run down the right wing, only to discover on looking up to cross that he had outstripped all his team-mates and there was no red shirt in the penalty area. During the interval Lawton had words of advice. "Just aim your cross towards the penalty spot," he said, "I'll be there." Midway through the second half, Brian again found himself clear on the wing. He centred as instructed and there was the great man, having timed his run and jump to perfection, hovering several inches above the defenders before powering an unstoppable header past the hapless goalkeeper for his fourth goal of the game.

Although Lawton was an exceptional case, a significant number of 'big name' players continued to ply their trade in the Southern League during the fifties, including Jimmy Logie, Archie Macaulay, Charlie Vaughan, Ronnie Rooke and Billy Elliott. Most significantly, earnings were not subject to the constraints imposed by the rigid wage structure then operating in the Football League.

Brian played six times in all for the Championship winning side, scoring once, in the 4–2 success at Dartford, and never appeared in a losing team.

His position as a local sporting celebrity often led to invitations to officiate at functions in and around the town. One such occasion was an amateur talent competition held at Kettering's Savoy Theatre in Russell Street in October 1956. Tommy Lawton presented the prizes and Brian's fellow judges were goalkeeper, Jack Wheeler, wing-half Harry Johnson and winger, Maurice Robinson. While Jack played a mean ukelele and Harry's renditions on the piano were the stuff of legend around the town's pubs, Brian's presence probably owed more to the centuries scored against Worcestershire and Essex earlier that summer!

Tommy Lawton shakes hands with the talented winner who has a white sports coat but no pink carnation. Judge Reynolds tries to impress as Napoleon.

Changes at Rockingham Road during the close season saw Lawton make good his declared intention to accept the vacant managership at Notts County. He had originally joined the Meadow Lane club in 1947, his move from First Division Chelsea to the Third Division South side commanding Britain's first ever £20,000 transfer fee. Lawton's debut, at the County Ground, Northampton in November 1947, attracted a crowd of 18,272. He even won back his place in the international side, becoming the first player from the Third Division to be capped for England. Sadly, inevitably perhaps, the return would end in tears.

Keep it up, Kettering

Jack Wheeler
Goalkeeper

Ray Parker
Right-back

Harry McDonald
Left-back

Harry Johnson
Right-half

Norman Plummer
Centre-half

Amos Moss
Left-half

Brian Reynolds
Outside-right

Arthur Dixon
Inside-right

Tommy Lawton
Centre-forward

Bob Thomas
Inside-left

Maurice Robinson
Outside-left

Alf Mansfield
Trainer

The long defunct national newspaper, the 'News Chronicle' made much of Lawton's team early in the Championship season. In the accompanying text, Brian Reynolds is, "More widely known perhaps as a fine, forcing batsman for Northamptonshire. A great runner between wickets - and along touchlines".

B L Reynolds b Ralph 169

Westcliff-on-Sea, 1957

1954 - 1957

There is a tide in the affairs of men
Which, taken at the flood, leads on to fortune...
On such a full sea are we afloat.

'Julius Caesar',
Shakespeare

Last in, first out

The send-off

Winkles and whelks

No Gentlemen

"I always tried to give a hundred per cent, whatever the game or the circumstances. The old saying still holds good: 'If you don't give any away, you don't owe any'."

79

In his speech at the annual dinner of the Kettering Town Cricket League before the start of the 1954 season, Jock Livingston predicted that Brian would be the first Kettering cricketer to wear an England cap. "It's my honest opinion," he said, "that Brian Reynolds will be the best young opening batsman in the country in the next two or three years." Never mind the occasion, Jock never indulged in idle flattery. In any case, he was not alone in believing Brian had the right temperament, technique and toughness. Alec Bedser, more given to grimace than gush, had told him that Reynolds was "a good 'un."

WILL WEAR ENGLAND CAP?

BACK in 1946 his sports master described a 14-year-old Kettering cricketer as "a future county player." Last Friday "Jock" Livingston, Northamptonshire's opening batsman, speaking about the same player, predicted that in a few years he would be the first Kettering cricketer to wear the England cap.

Both were referring to Brian Reynolds who lives at 57 The Oval. The schoolmaster was right, for Brian began playing for his county in 1950, and this season was sixth in the county batting averages table with 29.24.

Only time will tell whether "Jock" Livingston's prediction about Brian will prove correct.

Ironically Brian, in his youth, was regarded as an "expert" bowler. But Livingston said he believed

Reynolds would become the best opening batsman in the country.

In the winter Brian, who is 21, plays football for Peterborough United. He was formerly with Kettering Town.

At around the same time, an Oxford cricketer, reputedly studying PPE (Politics, Philosophy, Economics), kept a guinea pig called Jeremy in his college rooms. Each morning, before setting off to play for the university, he removed the creature from his cage and confided in him: "We must all understand, Jeremy, some days are good days, others are not quite so good." He said his degree course had taught him little about politics and economics, but cricket had taught him some philosophy. It was a truth Brian Reynolds came to grips with between 1954 and 1957.

The 1954 season began with a new captain. Freddie Brown had departed with, unsurprisingly, just a hint of acrimony. The next captain, one might have assumed, had to be Dennis Brookes. In 1953 he had proved a more than capable deputy for the absent Brown, captaining Northants to victory over both Lancashire and Yorkshire. But Brookes was a professional.

There were other professional captains. Leicestershire's Leslie Berry had captained his county immediately after the war. In 1946, Wisden reported that Leicestershire had enjoyed their best season since 1935 and had recorded record gate receipts, much of this due to "the value as captain of Leslie Berry, senior professional, in the absence of any regular amateur player". In 1948 another midland county, Warwickshire, had introduced a professional captain, Tom Dollery, (albeit another minor public school product) in 1948. The world did not end, instead they won the Championship in 1951. Next, MCC appointed the ultimate professional, Len Hutton, as England captain, much to the chagrin of the game's reactionaries.

One such was the Northamptonshire committee member, Captain RHD Bolton. He was educated at a Lancashire public school, Rossall, the alma mater of a host of forthright and idiosyncratic characters, from the likes of Sir Thomas Beecham and Patrick Campbell to Peter Winterbottom and Liam Botham. Over the years its old boys have frequented cricket's hierarchy: England captain (Nigel Howard), manager, ECB management (Bob Bennett) and MCC president (Michael Melluish). Captain Bolton was not alone on the committee in wanting to appoint someone from a public school or Oxford and Cambridge to replace Brown. As Derek Birley observes in his 'Social History of English Cricket', these were still seen as the royal roads to cricketing success. "Leisure, coaching, good wickets, good fixture lists and easy access to the magic circle" were crucial elements. The Captain supported MCC's desire to keep amateurs in the game, "not, as popularly stated, for the sake of the 'old school tie', but with a sincere desire to regain and preserve the unfettered spirit of high adventure, which, since the Golden Age, had been the amateur's priceless contribution to cricket."

There was no shortage of RHD anecdotes. At Rossall he was remembered for driving along the tram track from Blackpool's north shore under the impression it was the road. Brian Reynolds' best memory of him is the time he played for the Captain's XI in a country house match in which RHD had opted to go in last. Throughout the innings Bolton sat in a deckchair wearing his Spy cartoon pads (with cane struts). Asked if he had no faith in his batting line-up, he replied, "I have to make the most of any opportunity to wear them these days." They were the pads he'd worn in his twelve innings for Hampshire between 1913 and 1922 (121 runs at 10.08 with a top score of 24).

While the supporters of shamateurism prevaricated, Brookes' appointment seemed the obvious solution to Brown's departure. "Whoever was appointed would be different to Freddie, but Dennis was a good choice," says Brian. "He was a shrewd captain, who knew the game and, equally important, his own players. His knowledge of opposing players' strengths and weaknesses was impressive. He had a super temperament and everyone liked and respected him". That's about as close to Benaud's job specification for captains as you can get. The chairman, GAT Vials, also commented on Brookes' "great knowledge and unswerving loyalty to the best spirit of the game."

Dennis, of course, had another priceless asset for the post: his serene batting could be inspirational. Tony Pawson saw him as the "classic stylist", a genre of player no longer in vogue. Brian shares the view of most of his contemporaries that Dennis was an outstanding player of slow bowling. "I'd also point to his ability to pace and build an innings, something which many modern players have lost. He was undoubtedly one of the very best. And, another thing, he never gave it away. If he hadn't had that injury in the West Indies, who knows?[1]"

In the first four games of 1954 Brian opened with Dennis Brookes, a role for which he seemed destined. After beating Sussex at Northampton, the next three games away were lost: Glamorgan and Surrey (both heavily) and Warwickshire, narrowly. The batting was shabby, with several pitifully low scores, some admittedly on rain-affected wickets: 89 and 105 against Glamorgan; 99 against

---

1 Brookes played only one Test, at Bridgetown in January 1948. He suffered a finger injury and returned to England early.

Surrey in an innings defeat. Amidst the general inadequacy, Brian had 31 against Sussex in the second innings (Bob Clarke top scored with 37), 26 in the 105 against Glamorgan, top score in the first innings against Warwickshire with the marathon 43, and the second highest score against Surrey with 20.

It's a brand new season and Brian Reynolds puts his front foot forward as he opens for the first time for the first team. It's the start of the professional era and for Bronk's opening partner, Dennis Brookes it's his first time as captain (as distinct from acting captain). On the extreme right of the picture is an enthusiastic second-year pupil at Kettering Grammar School. It may be Saturday morning but Bruce Thompson has, as one did in those days, turned up at Wantage Road in full KGS uniform.

At the Oval, Oldfield had scored 106 out of 180. Brian describes it as "a brilliant knock, one of the most memorable I've ever seen. He mastered the lot of them, Bedser, Laker and Lock. Norman was forty-three then. Soon[2] afterwards he became an umpire. He played the spinners off the pitch, which takes some doing. Even at the start of the season his Gunn and Moore had that sweet sound. A terrific cutter and hooker. The war meant that we probably never saw the best of him"

There was another hundred in that Surrey game, 169 from Peter May. "A great player and a gentleman." No one disputes that he was a glorious batsman, but contrary to the general opinion that he was over-sensitive and introverted, Brian found him invariably pleasant and approachable. "I remember once at the Oval

---

2 Very soon. In fact less than a month after his final innings for Northamptonshire, he was standing as an umpire in a Championship match.

when a wicket had fallen and I was taking a look at his bat. It was a beauty. Peter said it weighed 2lbs 7oz, but it picked up better than my 2lbs 3oz. When I said so, he smiled and said 'If we can't get a good bat from Stuart Surridge, who can?' It was flattering that when he was in charge of England selection, he used to contact me about prospective players." Raman Subba Row also notched more runs against Northamptonshire, with an unbeaten 66. Just coincidence, or was predestination dropping hints.

For the fifth match, at Old Trafford, Oldfield opened. It was his last first-class appearance; he finished with 57, a signing-off chit to both his county employers. Brian batted at five, which was his aggregate for the match. It was his last for a month. Doug Greasley took advantage of a Trueman-less RAF attack, recording 103 and 62 and when the scorecard for the visit of Nottinghamshire on May 29th was printed, it revealed that Oldfield and Reynolds had been replaced by Greasley and Eddie Davis.

Brian's next Championship appearance was against Glamorgan at Peterborough in July. Buddy Oldfield umpired, Brian got 5 and 0, done twice by AJ Watkins, whom someone once described as a pugnacious batsman. built like an armchair, but never static. He had later links with Northamptonshire as coach at Oundle School. Brian batted at seven against Yorkshire, falling to Johnny Wardle and Bob Appleyard on a rain-affected pitch: the County 90 all out in two hours. Wardle he depicts as "cantankerous, even on the golf course." But then, aren't we all?

Left out again, he was recalled as Champions Surrey graced Kettering, to the background noise of the annual fair and steam trains packed with holiday makers. The game was a merry-go-round for Laker and Lock. Brian now batted at six as the side managed 125 and 133 (Laker six for 58, five for 36 Lock three for 31, three for 62). Brian was twice among Laker's victims as Surrey won by one wicket (Laker 33*). To make matters worse, before the match when some Surrey players joined in an impromptu game of rounders with some Kettering lads, Lock hit my new tennis ball onto the railway embankment. It still rankles[3].

"Locky threw his quicker one, mind you, he's not the only spinner to do that. Jim was probably the best off-spinner the game has seen. It can't be proved, but I reckon he got more wickets caught behind, or at slip, than in his leg-trap. You'd play for the turn and it wasn't there. His control was excellent. To be honest, though, he wasn't one of my favourite people."

After scoring 88 not out against Yorkshire seconds at Rothwell (batting at four) he reappeared for the final match of the season. It was at fondly-remembered Trent Bridge. His second innings score of 34, the highest in an abject 93 as Northants collapsed against Bruce Dooland (five for 19) and Gamini Goonesena (four for 44) at least ended the season on an optimistic note.

A season that had begun with so much promise had produced little. With Keith Andrew firmly established as number one wicket-keeper, Brian had needed to make his mark purely as a batsman. His Championship average plummeted from 29.24 in '53 to 10.53 in '54. He wasn't the first youngster to find that success the second time is more elusive than the initial dose.

---

3 A claim that the tennis ball belonged to Dave Allbury, rather than Brian Slough, was published in 'West Stand Story', c.1995.

The Seconds at Rothwell against Yorkshire II, August 11 & 12, 1954.
Back row (l to r): Malcolm White, John Wild, Myles Arkell, Stan Leadbetter, Mick Duck,
Doug Greasley.
Front row (l to r): Mick Allen, Brian Reynolds, 'Dick' Wells (capt), Eddie Davis, Percy Davis.

In the 1955 Northamptonshire Year Book, Brookes wrote, in his first Captain's Report: "B Reynolds was tried as my opening partner at the start of the season. Lack of form and consequent omission from the team was disappointing because of the loss of his top-class fielding."

If it looks from a distance like 'last in, first out', that isn't Brian's loyal response. "The skipper thought someone else should be given a go, that's fair enough." Did he ever feel pressure or disappointment? "Pressure isn't a word I remember being used in those days. And we certainly didn't know what a learning curve was! You were always disappointed when you didn't do well but we were young men serving an apprenticeship. To qualify as a craftsman requires a lot of time and a lot of hard work."

It was the chairman's view that "Reynolds was given fewer opportunities in 1955 than his skill probably warranted." He only played eleven times in the Championship (ten in 1954), finishing with an average of 25.53. The high spot was his significant part in the win against Glamorgan, at Cardiff in July, when Northamptonshire raced to 204 in 135 minutes. Brookes acknowledged that Brian made a vital contribution to the victory, scoring 64 in the first innings after leaving his sick bed against medical advice. He had developed a severe bout of tonsillitis, with a soaring temperature. His resulting weight loss is evident in the photographs of his brother's wedding, which occurred soon afterwards.

Brian might have had more opportunities, had it not been for a new signing: Raman Subba Row arrived from Surrey. Subba Row, a twenty-three old Cambridge blue, had presumably arrived because Northamptonshire wanted an amateur captain. "I suppose," says Brian, "they thought Brookie might not last much longer." In one of his less charitable moments Brian lets slip, "he probably came because he was offered more money." Whatever the behind-the-scenes machinations and whatever the seemingly deferential pros really thought about amateurs, the harsh fact was that Subba Row's arrival increased the competition for batting places. "Players come and players go," shrugs Reynolds reverting to his ability to imply far more than he has actually expressed.

In '55 there were several praiseworthy performances from Brian, often when the side was struggling, as in 1954. Wisden mentioned his "fine batting" against Middlesex at Rushden in his first game. At the start of June, he was second top scorer with 38 (lbw Shackleton) as an opener in two low totals against Hampshire at Peterborough. "Derek wasn't a particularly friendly individual, unlike Butch White, with his big in-swingers and smile to match. Shack wasn't really my type, but he could pitch it on a threepenny bit for two hours before lunch and not break sweat. He was quick enough, with a bit of nip off the wicket." He remembers one innings against him, when he resumed after the lunch break. Brian pointed out to Mick Norman the spot where Shack was pitching the ball; the patch on the wicket was clear to see. "It'll land there, so I'll charge him first ball." An intriguing tribute to Shackleton's accuracy, Reynolds' footwork, and Brown's influence?

After the 38 against Hampshire, Brian opened in the next game against Warwickshire and was then omitted. Brookes had batted at five for four matches, but returned to open with Peter Arnold against Sussex. In his re-emergence (at four) against Gloucestershire, at Kettering, Brian made a fighting 50 (Tribe top scored with 51) in a second innings total of 153. He then disappeared until his 64 at Cardiff, the illness making him unavailable for a while.

In August he contributed an unbeaten century for the seconds against Yorkshire (yet again), before completing the season with 47 (run out) and 30 (c Fagg b Wright) against Kent. The press described Wright as "spinning the ball sharply". At least Fred Jakeman was not there to be haunted by him. Brian corroborates another of the County Ground's favourite tales, that Fred was once so agitated at the prospect of facing Doug Wright, that he went to the wicket without a bat. Fred, who joined the staff in 1949, had left after a mediocre year in 1954. An aggressive lefthander, it seems odd to picture him smoking nervously while waiting to bat. 1951 was his golden year: 1,989 runs (average 56.82) and a highest score of 258 not out. His son, Stuart, played three times for Northamptonshire in 1962 and 1963. Both Jakemans (Jakemen?) were born in Holmfirth.

In 1955 another Yorkshireman played his final games in the Championship for Northamptonshire: the last of another species in cricket's vanishing world. Jack Webster was one of several public school masters who surfaced in county cricket at the start of their summer holidays. They would have nets coaching pupils, but no other cricket apart from an occasional game for the likes of the Free Foresters or the MCC. This tradition (and its disappearance) raises questions about relative standards of the first-class game, the role of amateurs, and past perceptions of them. Not least, the feelings of professionals who made way for them. Social historians agree that the older ones were reared to be deferential and biddable. Indeed, many professionals who felt for the game's traditions mourned the amateurs' removal.

Brian liked Jack and was never aware of any animosity at his arrival. He had also done a useful job in his last season, as Brookes reported: "With lack of young material of sufficient potentiality the selectors wisely relied on J Webster to augment the seam attack. His ability to bowl a length and dispose of early batsmen proved an asset in our run of six consecutive victories." Jack, who died in 1997, the year Brian retired, played sixty times for Northamptonshire between 1946 and 1955, and was captain for nine games in 1946. In 1948 he had six for 118 against Nottinghamshire at Trent Bridge and a fortnight later five for 32 against Lancashire at Wellingborough School.

Northamptonshire triviaphiles tell you of his many county connections. Opposing captain in the 1939 university match was Oxford's EJH Dixon, who also played for the County. John Dudley, Headmaster of Kettering Grammar School in the fifties, was his contemporary at Bradford Grammar School and Percy Davis was appointed coach at Harrow during Jack's time as master in charge of cricket.

There were many accolades for Brian's fielding during the 1955 season. He had now moved from the slips to the covers, where Brookes spoke of his being "a joy to watch and an inspiration to everyone." He was fit, mobile, skilful and could concentrate. He also had another Reynolds asset. "I always tried to give a hundred per cent, whatever the game or the circumstances. The old saying still holds good: 'If you don't give any away, you don't owe any'."

At the end of 1955, chairman Vials had forecast Northamptonshire could well see further progress by Arnold and "a big advance by Reynolds - a very good player needing a send-off which seems bound to come." As it turned out, Arnold moved from 1,523 runs (average 30.46) in 1955 to 1,155 (average 24.06) in 1956. Reynolds from 383 (25.53) to 1,046 (30.76).

Whatever Vials meant by the ambiguous "send-off", 1956 saw a major advance in the fortunes of Brian and Northamptonshire, who finished fourth in the Championship, then the highest in their history. Subba Row was called up for National Service. He became, not a Private at Wootton Barracks with the Northamptonshire Regiment, but a Pilot Officer with the RAF. He was only available for two matches. Players come and players go. As in 1953 during Fiddling's absence, Brian took advantage of the opportunity and played in all twenty-eight Championship matches.

If "determined" and "resolute" were adjectives often applied to Brian during his career (they're still valid) the prospect of a regular place and position in the batting order were factors in Tubby Vials' "send-off". For Brian, that kind of certainty is crucial to any player's confidence, an obvious truth often ignored.

Three men who had "send-offs" in 1956. On the left is left-arm spinner Michael Henry John Allen who made his debut in 1956 and topped the County's bowling averages. On the other side of Brian is Sydney Starkie. An off-spinner and another Lancastrian signed from League cricket, 1956 was the last of his six seasons on the Northamptonshire staff. He was a direct replacement for Gordon Garlick who was, yes, a Lancastrian.

On May 22 at Leicester, batting at five, he scored a personal best, 71 not out as he batted, mainly with Tribe, to save the game. The following day, he scored his maiden first-class hundred (precisely) against Worcestershire at Northampton. Some felt it was his second maiden first-class hundred. The innings lasted two hours thirty-five minutes and contained fourteen boundaries. Sometimes a cliche is forgivable: "I felt on top of the world." The bowling line-up is worth a mention: Jack Flavell, Len Coldwell, Bob Berry, Roly Jenkins and Martin Horton. Genuine balance from five Test bowlers, including Horton, who had taken some stick during Brian's hundred against the RAF.

One of 'Test Match Special's' favourite cliches is "the game's a great leveller", or as Jeremy could tell you, "Some days are good days, others are not quite so good." After Worcestershire, it was Reynolds c&b Dooland 0. "Bruce was a fine bowler. You had to avoid playing back. He got loads of lbws." Dooland, who also dismissed Brian twice at Trent Bridge in 1954, played a couple of times for Australia against England in 1946; George Tribe's three Tests were in the same series. From 1953 to 1957 Dooland took 770 wickets at 18.86; Tribe 1,021 at 20.25 from 1951 to 1959. Magnificent figures, in a different game. Just as Nottinghamshire played leg-spinners Dooland and Goonesena in the same side, so Northamptonshire included three left-arm spinners in Tribe, Jack Manning and Mick Allen. Another, Vince Broderick was still on the staff. Mind you, in the nineties they occasionally fielded three off-spinners: Rob Bailey, Graeme Swann and Jason Brown.

After the Dooland dismissal, the good days soon returned. Four days later, in fact, against Essex in a drawn game at Brentwood. Tribe scored his third century for Northamptonshire, but by general consent "the best innings of the match came from Reynolds". Brian had had to wait a long time for his first century; for the second the wait was ten days. Over twelve days he had improved his personal highest score three times. At Brentwood he batted a tad under three hours, hitting eleven fours, his fifth wicket partnership with Tribe adding 208. One tangible by-product of this double century stand was receiving a commemorative, inscribed tankard from William Younger & Co Ltd (plus twenty four 'Double Century' ales). It now stands proudly, and invariably highly polished, among his other trophies in the sitting room.

Cricket's quirks of fate ensured the presentation of the Double Century tankard, during the Warwickshire match, by Eric Hollies, the first to dismiss Brian six years earlier. Warwickshire supporters always boasted that Hollies was so good that he took more wickets (2,201) than he scored runs (1,544). At Edgbaston the Rea Bank was renamed "The Eric Hollies Stand". That's the noisy part.

Brian had a taste for the Essex bowling. In July, at Peterborough, another rapid partnership of 82 with Tribe set up the victory by 202 runs. Brian enjoyed batting with George. It was one of those successful duos which the game fosters, based on complementary talents and personalities. They repeated the act in the same month, when Kent were beaten for the second time in less than a fortnight. In a stand worth 99, achieved in an hour, Brian hit five successive fours in an unbeaten fifty. The bowler was the ubiquitous Dave Halfyard, who took 769 wickets in his career, but not much stick.

Several other scores of fifty plus were valuable in the team's successes. Surrey, the champions, were beaten twice. In May, Brian had two red inks against Bedser, Loader, Laker and Lock; his 54 assisted the seven wicket win. Northamptonshire took only eighty minutes for the 136 and only the second victory in the Club's history at the Oval. Just as Alec Bedser had made complimentary remarks to Livingston about the young Reynolds, so Brian holds Bedser in high regard. "As with most of the Surrey players, Alec enjoyed a moan, but I liked him a lot and he was a terrific bowler. Modern bowlers could learn a lot from his practice methods in search of accuracy. He also did a great job as an England selector."

There were good times against Yorkshire and Lancashire. His 61 out of 257, top score against a white rose attack boasting Trueman, Appleyard, Wardle and Ray Illingworth, received high praise. The following extracts from press reports capture the style of Brian's batting and the mental approach that informed it. First, JM Kilburn: "Reynolds contributed a determined spirit and many handsome shots. He stayed for half an hour without scoring, but the delay was not of his choice, and when opportunity presented itself he square cut and drove through the covers with attractive rhythm and the confidence that considers the ball and not the bowler's name." HLV Day was equally impressed: "Having got under way he batted with power and fine judgment. Particularly pleasing was his readiness, even eagerness, to use his feet to the spin bowling of Appleyard, Wardle and Illingworth. He realises, as so many batsmen either are unable or refuse to do, that a half volley or long hop is meant to be hit, no matter by whom it is served up. He caused a readjustment and dispersal of the fielders by his cheerfully vigorous attack." At Blackpool, in Ken Grieves' benefit game (it rained) his 51 not out secured first innings points.

So to Kettering's 'feast week', when he fell in both innings to Wilf Wooller, for 23 and 25. It was a low scoring game, won by Glamorgan by 67 runs. It was Wilf's match. He top scored with 99 (c Reynolds b Clarke) and took 8 for 63 in the game, ending it with three wickets in five balls. Like Freddie Brown, he spent time in a prisoner-of-war camp, in Wooller's case a Japanese camp. The novelist Leslie Thomas says that when Wooller played his first match after repatriation he was like a big yellow skeleton. It took more than the enemy to daunt Wooller, who organised a game of cricket at the notorious Changi prison camp in Singapore on Christmas Day, right in front of the bewildered guards. Lieutenant LW (Dick) Curtis, then of the Royal Norfolk Regiment and Captain Ben Barnett of the Australian Imperial Forces, went one better. They organised an 'Ashes' game in Changi. Dick, who played for the Kettering club with Brian (and had been "very unlucky to miss his half-century" in the 1949 Knock-out Cup final), would certainly have watched Wooller's outstanding all-round performance with mixed emotions, pride amongst them. They don't make them like that any more.

There were many other good days in 1956. Two, in particular, different in kind, but of lasting significance. The first was being awarded his cap, a proud occasion for a Northamptonshire-born man. It was a vote of confidence in his ability as a professional cricketer: he had arrived. It also meant a pay rise.

The second award was the MCC Advanced Coaching Certificate. A considerable achievement for a relatively young professional and commendably forward looking. There was a foretaste of Brian's future career in this statement from the County handbook: "It is our desire to make increasing use of these coaches in improving the standard of cricket throughout the county."

Brian again played in all twenty-eight Championship games in 1957, increasing his run tally to 1,157. There were three distinct highlights. In May, Gloucestershire were beaten by seven wickets at Northampton. The win owed most to Brian's brilliant unbeaten 157, with twenty five boundaries, in four hours. While he was at the crease, his seven partners between them scored only forty-two. The most successful was Harry Kelleher, with whom he added eighty-four for the last wicket.

At the beginning of June, Middlesex were beaten by 47 runs at Lord's. Brian opened and once more played a key role in the win. A vibrant stand with Livingston (both scored 93) of 174, in as many minutes, effectively won the game. This had become a sign of his progress in 1956 and 1957: the capacity to control a game's outcome by his own performance.

He also opened against Essex at Westcliff-on-Sea later in the month, when Northamptonshire followed on 178 behind. His 169 (twenty-three fours) lasted six hours, with only one sharp chance. This innings, the highest score of his career, not only saved the game but gave Northants a chance of victory. Fifty of Brian's 169, including eight fours, were from Trevor Bailey's bowling. But Bailey had the last word (if not laugh). Set 244 to win, Essex were happy to reach the close on 152 for 7. Their saviour, with 79, has already been mentioned. Brian's Aunt Jessica was delighted with her nephew's success. She knew the reason for it, revealed in the congratulatory telegram.

K   16   GTG 2-56   SHIRLY BM 17

GREETINGS   = BRIAN REYNOLDS NORTHANTS
CRICKET   TEAM WESTCLIFFONSEA-ESSEX

= THATS WHAT WINKLES AND WHELKS DO FOR YOU

= AUNT JESSICA   ++

Message to today's stars: Forget the carbos and isotonic drinks and get stuck into a plate of whelks.

Northamptonshire's season ended with them in second place. It was the second time Northants had been runners-up. In 1912 rain, some argue, deprived them of the title; in 1957 it was Surrey, winning the sixth of their seven consecutive Championships. Surrey were 94 points in front of Northamptonshire; 14 points was the maximum that could be acquired in one match. When Wisden wrote, "eventually Northamptonshire became Surrey's closest rivals without ever threatening to overhaul them", it was an incontrovertible fact.

"They were dominant, they just seemed so far in front of everybody," recalls Brian. "Yet we always seemed to play well against them. I'm not saying we always won, but we usually gave a good account of ourselves."

'We' certainly gave a good account of 'ourselves' at the Oval at the end of May, though Brian's contribution was one to be glossed over. A second innings century from Dennis Brookes and Frank Tyson's eight for 60 and five for 52 were the major contributions to a 72 run success. At Northampton a week later, ten wicket revenge was extracted. Northants went for 111 in the second innings, Reynolds c Stewart b A Bedser 26, the second highest. Mickey Stewart caught six others in that innings. It's still in the record books, though now it's a joint record: in 1966, Gloucestershire's Tony Brown also caught seven in an innings.

Not, unfortunately, in the record breaking innings in 1957, but here is Mickey Stewart fielding at Northampton with Brian batting. This is in 1965, when Northamptonshire were again runners-up. Stewart, by now the Surrey captain, is at second slip, Stewart Storey is at first and Arnold Long is the wicket-keeper.

Brian's season ended with his selection for the Players against the Gentlemen. Among exalted company, in front of 12,000 spectators at Scarborough, he and Frank Tyson produced a century partnership for the seventh wicket (Reynolds 75, Tyson 63). RA Roberts of 'The Daily Telegraph' described Brian as "hitting the ball with the finest of intentions off either foot". The Amateurs' bowling was far from amateurish, with John Warr, Trevor Bailey, Ted Dexter and Goonesena, but Reynolds fell to deadly Doug Insole. This wasn't a new experience. It was Insole who had earlier ended his 102 at Brentwood.

Suggestions that Brian was 'Doug's bunny' are not well received. "I expect I fancied some free hits and didn't concentrate. You should never do that."

The Players team at Scarborough in 1957. From left to right, Dick Richardson (Worcestershire), Brian Taylor (Essex), Bob Gale (Middlesex), Brian Close (Yorkshire), Tom Graveney (Gloucestershire), Godfrey Evans (Kent), Johnny Wardle (Yorkshire), Freddie Trueman (Yorkshire), Frank Tyson (Northamptonshire), Brian Reynolds (Northamptonshire), Don Shepherd (Glamorgan).

Wisden chronicled, "Aggressive stroke-play by Reynolds and his Northamptonshire colleague Tyson, who shared in a stand of 114, turned the tide," The Northamptonshire duo return to the pavilion at tea on the second day.

Scarborough Cricket Festival

President : T. L. Taylor, Esq.

GENTLEMEN v. PLAYERS

Played on the Scarborough Cricket Ground September 4th, 5th & 6th, 1957

GENTLEMEN

		First Innings		Second Innings	
1	P. E. Richardson ... (Worcs)	c GALE B SHEPHERD	54	LBW B TRUEMAN	2
2	W. H. H. Sutcliffe...(Yorks)	B TYSON	1	NOT OUT	0
3	M. J. K. Smith ...(Warwick)	B TYSON	1	c CLOSE B WARDLE	50
4	W. J. Edrich ... (Middlesex)	c REYNOLDS B SHEPHERD	29	B GRAVENEY	34
5	D. J. Insole (Capt.) .....(Essex)	B WARDLE	35		
6	A. C. Walton ... (Oxford)	c GRAVENEY B WARDLE	28	c SHEPHERD B GRAVENEY	30
7	T. E. Bailey .... (Essex)	NOT OUT	31		
8	E. R. Dexter ... (Cambridge)	c EVANS B CLOSE	6	c TAYLOR B TRUEMAN	88
9	G. Goonesena .... (Notts)	NOT OUT	22	...	
10	J. J. Warr ...... (Middlesex)			...	
11	M. E. L. Melluish (w.k.) (Mid'x)				
		b... lb 3 w... nb 4	7	b 4 lb 5 w... nb 5	14
		Total......	219 -7d.	Total......	226 -5d

Fall of the Wickets

1	2	3	4	5	6	7	8	9	10	1	2	3	4	5	6	7	8	9	10
9	20	74	106	121	127	173	...	...	...	2	93	163	209	226	...	...	...	...	...

Analysis of Bowling

	First Innings				Second Innings			
	Overs	Mdns.	Runs	Wkts.	Overs	Mdns.	Runs	Wkts.
TRUEMAN	14	1	44	0	8	1	23	2
TYSON	13	4	22	2	7	1	26	0
CLOSE	11	7	18	1	2	0	21	0
SHEPHERD	24	7	70	2	12	0	47	0
WARDLE	23	5	53	2	10	1	60	1
GRAVENEY	...	...	...	...	6.2	0	35	2

PLAYERS

		First Innings		Second Innings	
1	D. B. Close ....(Yorks)	B WARR	4	RUN OUT	79
2	R. Gale .... (Middlesex)	LBW B BAILEY	4	ST MELLUISH B GOONESENA	83
3	T. W. Graveney ......(Glos)	B BAILEY	13	B WARR	6
4	D. W. Richardson...(Worcs)	B BAILEY	0	NOT OUT	54
5	B. Taylor .... (Essex)	LBW B BAILEY	6	c INSOLE B WARR	2
6	B. L. Reynolds ... (Northants)	c EDRICH B INSOLE	75		
7	T. G. Evans (Capt. & w.k.) (Kent)	LBW B DEXTER	13	NOT OUT	4
8	F. H. Tyson ...... (Northants)	c EDRICH B INSOLE	63		
9	J. H. Wardle ......(Yorks)	c BAILEY B GOONESENA	1		
10	F. S. Trueman ....(Yorks)	RUN OUT	7		
11	D. J. Shepherd (Glamorgan)	NOT OUT	10		
		b 4 lb... w 5 nb 1	10	b 4 lb 3 w... nb...	7
		Total......	206	Total......	235 -4

Fall of the Wickets

1	2	3	4	5	6	7	8	9	10	1	2	3	4	5	6	7	8	9	10
4	8	8	24	35	52	173	174	188	206	133	200	219	226	...	...	...	...	...	...

Analysis of Bowling

	First Innings				Second Innings			
	Overs	Mdns.	Runs	Wkts.	Overs	Mdns.	Runs	Wkts.
WARR	17	1	52	1	12.4	2	72	2
BAILEY	20	6	38	4	17	2	62	0
DEXTER	8	0	32	1	4	0	24	0
GOONESENA	11	0	55	1	4	0	31	1
INSOLE	4.1	0	16	2	4	0	39	0
	...	...	...	...	...	...	...	...

Umpires : H. G. Baldwin, A. R. Coleman. Scorer : C. Turner.

Wickets pitched 11–30 a.m. Lunch 1–30 p.m. Tea 4–15 p.m. Stumps drawn 6 p.m.

A New Ball may be taken, at the option of the fielding captain, after 200 runs or 75 overs.

PLAYERS WON BY SIX WICKETS

93

In Brian's first year as a professional 175 of the 450 county players were amateur. By 1961 the number had fallen to 72 out of 370. In November 1962 the Advisory County Cricket Committee recommended that the distinction between amateur and professional should be abandoned and that thenceforward all who played the game should be known simply as cricketers. In its wake, another of the game's traditions, the Gentlemen v Players fixtures, went the way of Accrington Stanley. That said, it had now become a creative exercise of Daliesque proportions to pick a Gents XI worthy of the name. As Humpty Dumpty said, "When I use a word, it means just what I choose it to mean."

In 'Sport and Society', PC McIntosh is quite clear that the distinction between amateurs and professionals at the same club had become solely hierarchical. Historian Richard Holt believes that the ending of what was little short of class distinction had less to do with the democratic drive of professionals than with the amateurs' decline.

Even Oxbridge men had less time and money to spare. Added to which, entrance requirements were more stringent. As Oxford and Cambridge tightened its academic criteria for entry, the quality of its cricket dropped. That process is now complete. The start of the new millennium marks the end of a sporting epoch. After 137 years, Oxford University's first-class status has finally gone. Matches against the counties in 2000 were played by a combined Oxford universities side using players from the ancient university and the new Brookes university. The end was nigh after Lord McLaurin's plans for reshaping English cricket, in 'Raising the Standard', recommended the setting up of six university 'centres of excellence'. Yet again, a change in the structure of cricket was influenced by money.

In Wisden 2000, Ralph Dellor wrote, "six university centres of excellence have been established, each of which will play three fixtures against first-class counties in 2001, although it has yet to be determined whether they will be consecrated as first-class."

And when the appropriate committee is looking at this matter is there any chance of certain matches being looked at retrospectively? Can Fred have a few more wickets? Can Brian have a century consecrated? And Stanley did return; a reformed club revived the name in 1968 and keep the flag flying at a new ground in Accrington.

Clacton Town 5   Kettering Town 0

March 1959

1957 - 1959

"O that a man might know
The end of this day's business ere it come!"
Brutus in 'Julius Caesar'.

Against the Posh

Day Trip to Clacton

Golf

Or refereeing?

"When I got back to the dressing room I was too tired to unlace my boots."

Kettering replaced Tommy Lawton with Harold Mather. Like Lawton, Mather had played for Burnley. There the similarity ends. Although Mather had played in the FA Cup final in 1947, he was no substitute for his exalted predecessor and the euphoria of the previous season soon evaporated with a string of poor results.

When Brian Reynolds reported for training, barely a week after batting for the Players against the Gentlemen at Scarborough he found a club in crisis. Several of Lawton's championship winning side had moved on, injury and illness weakened the squad still further and Brian found himself pressed into first-team action more rapidly than he'd expected.

"Harold Mather took me on one side and said he wanted me to play at Yeovil that Saturday. He was desperate. 'You must be fit,' he said, 'playing all that county cricket.' I explained that there was a world of difference between being cricket-fit and football-fit, but he wouldn't hear of it. I played at left-half and could hardly drag my legs around the field. We were a goal down in five minutes, Bill Draper equalised and then little Hughie Morrow somehow put us in front. We were under constant pressure for most of the game but Jack Patterson performed miracles in goal and we managed to hold on to win 2–1. When I got back to the dressing room I was too tired to unlace my boots, let alone climb in the bath for a soak."

The victory proved a false dawn. The situation worsened with an ignominious defeat at Corby in the second qualifying round of the FA Cup at the beginning of October. Losing four of the next five League games increased the disquiet at Rockingham Road.

Ignominy indeed. The Occupation Road terraces were healthily populated for Kettering's FA Cup exit. An attendance of 6,121 watched the home team win 3-1. Here Brian is thwarted by home 'keeper Pat Egglestone. The Corby defender is Barry Parsons and Kettering's number eight is Geoff Toseland, ex Avondale Colts and Sunderland.

Towards the end of November the board acted and signed the former England star, Jack Froggatt as player-coach. The move signalled the end for Mather. Although for a time they worked in tandem, by February 1958 Froggatt had taken over as player-manager.

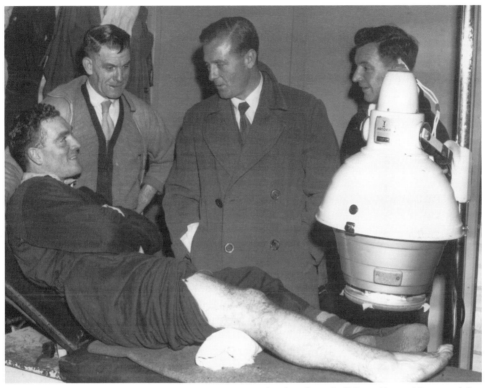

On Froggatt's first day as player-coach, he found Brian Reynolds receiving treatment for an injured ankle. Trainer Alf Mansfield is on the left and player-manager Mather is on the right, far from centre stage.

Brian played in nine first-team games during the season, at left back, left half or left wing. He scored one goal, the second in a 2-3 home defeat to Gravesend & Northfleet. His last appearance of the season, on March 24th, was a 2–0 victory at Rexville Stadium, Newport, the home of Welsh works side, (and makers of Toffee Rex), Lovells Athletic, before a crowd of 100. How different his next appearance would be.

On Saturday November 15th 1958, the Poppies had travelled to Peterborough in the first round proper of the FA Cup. The game, attended by a crowd of 17,800, ended in a draw and the replay, held the following Thursday afternoon, generated immense interest in the area. Kettering's town centre bore a strong resemblance to Goldsmith's 'Deserted Village' as shops and factories closed, hundreds of schoolboys shunned lessons and all thoroughfares led to Rockingham Road. Jack Froggatt made something of a surprise choice to replace former Cobblers defender, Maurice Marston, who was taking accountancy examinations and unable to play. While many, including the local press, had expected the vacancy to be filled by club stalwart, Bobby Wyldes, the player-manager selected Brian Reynolds, who hadn't played a first team game all season but was the regular reserve right-back.

Back in November 1947 a similar tie between a Kettering team, including both Maurices, Dunkley and Tompkin, and Peterborough United had attracted Rockingham Road's biggest ever attendance, 11,526. The huge crowd witnessed a thrilling contest, the Posh scraping home by the odd goal in seven when, as survivors have no difficulty in remembering, the Poppies' captain, Rex Smith, missed a penalty with the last kick of the game. Yet it's surprising how few of the 11,400 supporters present on that fateful afternoon eleven years later can recall the game's dramatic sequence of events with similarly unerring accuracy. Kettering took the lead after just forty-five seconds when centre-forward Bill Draper headed home a cross from his former Cobblers colleague, Hughie Morrow. Seventeen minutes later it was 2–0, Draper converting a centre from local boy Alan Dadswell. However midway through the first half, when injury forced the Poppies' vastly experienced centre-half, Norman Plummer, to the rôle of a passenger on the wing, the tide slowly began to turn. Denis Emery reduced the arrears after seventy-one minutes and Peterborough relentlessly piled on the attack.

In the words of the Daily Mail reporter, "Posh maintained a siege which would have shaken Mafeking." The infamous own goal was not a last minute winner, as so many seem to think, but the Peterborough equaliser, which levelled the scores at 2–2 and took the game into extra-time. From a distance of forty-two years, Brian recalls the incident with remarkable clarity. "'We'd been under tremendous pressure for most of the second half. Peterborough were a great attacking side, they threw everything at us and our backs were really against the wall. A cross came over and I tried to head it out for a corner but it flew off my forehead into the corner of the net. No-one felt worse than I did. But what people often forget is the dreadful goal that originally brought Peterborough back into the game. Goalkeeper Peter Roberts had been a hero in the first match at London Road but Denis Emery's scuffed shot from the edge of the penalty area went right under his body and into the net."

A Billy Hails goal won the game in extra-time. Posh went on to beat Headington United in the next round eventually falling to Fulham in a Third Round replay, after holding the First Division giants to a draw at Craven Cottage. Such was the quality of that Peterborough side.

Publicly, player-manager Jack Froggatt was phlegmatic about the outcome, describing events as "typical of the twists and turns that make football such an entertaining game." It was more difficult for Brian Reynolds to appear philosophical. Unlike most of the Poppies team he actually lived in the town. He faced the situation with typical fortitude; the following evening he joined fellow guests at Kettering Town Cricket Club's annual dinner and on Saturday afternoon resumed his place in the Poppies' reserve side at King's Lynn.

Even today, there are still people quick to remind him, good naturedly of course, of that moment of indiscretion. A popular, but no doubt apocryphal, story tells of the day in 1963 when Brian scored 124 not out against Nottinghamshire at Northampton. On the way home he stopped for fish and chips in Burton Latimer and, as he entered the shop, was recognised by several people in the queue. After a minute or so, someone plucked up the nerve to address the newcomer. There was no mention of the century. "You're the one who scored that own goal in the Poppies cup match," he said. Brian is convinced that the local paper has already written his obituary, its opening line referring, not to his twenty years as a county cricketer, but to that injudicious moment at the 'Tin Hat' end in 1958.

There were three more first team appearances that season before the game which brought his footballing days to a premature end at the age of twenty-six. Once again Jack Froggatt selected Brian Reynolds in preference to Bobby Wyldes for his side's almost meaningless fixture at Clacton on March 18th 1959. "Almost meaningless" is an understatement.

The Southern Football League had operated with only one division since 1946. It was a very strong competition and there was no shortage of ambitious clubs wanting to join. The decision was therefore taken to expand, the additional division commencing in the 1958-59 season. Instead of the existing clubs forming the first division and the new clubs constituting the second division, the clubs were split into two geographical divisions, the North Western Zone and the South Eastern Zone. For 1959-60, the top eleven clubs in each zone would form the top division, to be known, radically, as the Premier Division. The others would form the second division, to be known, radically, as Division One.

There should have been forty in membership for the 1958-59 season. However the Kent FA refused to allow Bexleyheath & Welling, Dover, Folkestone and Tunbridge Wells to join the Southern League as they had not given sufficient notice of their intention to withdraw from the Kent League. Their entry to the Southern League was delayed a year. A fifth club, Llanelly (as it was then spelt), were prevented by the Welsh FA from re-joining. This left the Southern League with only thirty-five clubs for the 58-59 season.

As late as August 9th, 1958, a meeting of the Southern League decided to organise an Inter Zone competition divided into seven geographical groups. Early in March 1959 the Management Committee decided that, in order to prevent fixture congestion, and as the competition had achieved its object of filling vacant Saturdays, it would end when all clubs had played their eight group games.

The final table for Kettering's group was:

	P	W	D	L	F	A	Pts
Cambridge United	8	5	0	3	25	17	10
Bedford Town	8	3	4	1	22	17	10
Chelmsford City	8	3	4	1	16	14	10
Kettering Town	8	2	2	4	13	21	6
Clacton Town	8	1	2	5	13	20	4

The game at Clacton was Kettering's last game in the competition. Neither side could win the group; the winners received a 'small trophy'. The official attendance at Clacton was 311. Perhaps as the home fans celebrated their only victory, they found some meaning in the game.

Meaningless it may have been, but just as when Bronk was selected for the Peterborough replay, a dramatic consequence ensued. Proof indeed that Thomas Hardy had no prerogative over coincidence. With Kettering losing 0–5, and only ten minutes of the match remaining, Brian could have been excused the challenge that ended his career. As he prepared to shoot, he was involved in a sickening collision with the opposing centre-half, who made what might euphemistically be called a blocking tackle. There was no doubting it was a serious injury, the crack on impact resounding around the ground. The Poppies outside-left was stretchered from the field and rushed to hospital, his tibia and fibula shattered.

Coach driver Bert Orsborn drove the rest of the team home that evening before breaking the news to his son, another Brian, and a cricketing colleague from the young Reynolds' Headlands days. "I can picture him now. He was in tears. I don't think he'd seen an injury like it in all his years of travelling with the Poppies. Words couldn't express his feelings. We all knew what it meant for Bronk's cricket. The new season was only a few weeks away."

The staff at Clacton Hospital plastered the leg from thigh to toe and he spent an agonising, sleep-free night, rendered even more excruciating by a mysterious stabbing pain in his heel. Inspection the following morning revealed that when the cast had been applied, plaster had trickled down the back before setting to form a razor sharp sliver which penetrated the flesh, forming a huge hole.

At Kettering General, the Poppies' doctor, Fred Harlow, consultant Frank Radcliffe and the saintly Sister Parry, took good care of the patient, replacing the heavy cast with a light walking plaster. The injury, just weeks before the start of the new cricket season, could hardly have come at a worse time. However early in April, and within days of leaving Kettering's convalescent hospital in Rockingham Road, his burning aim to get back into flannels before the end of the summer was reported in the local press, in the article accompanying this photograph. "I think I can do it. In fact I've set myself a target for the end of June."

As his recovery continued, the plaster was in regular need of attention. When Sister Parry expressed surprise at its poor condition, suggesting misuse, Brian reassured her that he was only walking on it. The fact that he was carrying a set of golf clubs at the same time was sensibly omitted.

Despite his determination to regain fitness, June proved a shade too optimistic for a return to County Cricket. Fortunately, after spending a winter at the club's indoor school, Brian was back to full fitness at the beginning of the 1960 season. Unwilling to jeopardise his cricketing livelihood, Brian announced his retirement from football. Still only twenty-seven, he could look back on his career with considerable satis-faction. Instead, he took up an interest which some might consider even more hazardous than playing – namely, refereeing.

His progress through the ranks was spectacular and within three years he was officiating in the Metropolitan League as a Class One referee. He might well have made the Football League, had he been willing to compromise his own high standards. While considering his position after suffering unwarranted abuse from the Bury Town manager, two incidents occurred which confirmed his intention to resign from the County list. After training hard all day for the impending cricket season, Brian hurried to Corby for an evening match. When he arrived at the ground off Cottingham Road shortly before the appointed kick-off time, no goalnets had been put up and there was no sign of the opposition. It was a very murky evening and the possibility of playing a full game was already in doubt. By the time the visitors turned up in penny numbers, and still awaiting the arrival of their kit, Brian's mind was made up. He broke the news that he'd called the game off and went home to write his report for the County FA. It wasn't well received.

The die was finally cast a week or so later, following a cup-tie at Thrapston. "One of the players cast serious doubts about my parentage and I sent him off. To my surprise he then maintained, very vociferously, that he wasn't talking to me but one of his team-mates. So I decided to call it a day and concentrate on golf. The ball doesn't always go where I want it to, but at least it doesn't answer me back!"

Today, Brian rarely watches football other than the occasional game on television. An exception was during a recent holiday trip to Madeira where he took advantage of the generosity of a friendly waiter who had a spare ticket for the Portuguese League game against Vitoria Setubal. "The match kicked off at four in the afternoon, it was scorching hot and there was no cover. The football was diabolical. The referee blew his whistle about four hundred times, there were seven bookings, the game couldn't flow, the players were all pushing and pulling each other and the only goal came when a penalty was awarded to the home side for a most innocuous challenge. At least I spotted a familiar face grimacing in the crowd opposite. It was Brian Munton from Barton Seagrave. Another footballing, cricketing, referee!"

Although alleging indifference to the current state of the game, Brian retains an enduring affection for football. Like many of his generation he fears that, at the two extremes, the recent huge influx of foreign players in the Premiership and the absence of youngsters playing impromptu games in the park, augur badly for the future. Whatever that holds, we are unlikely to see many more Dunkleys, Tompkins, Barrons or Reynolds. Men for both seasons.

HON. REFEREE'S SECRETARY
HARRY W. SYKES
PHONE NORTHAMPTON 36629

111 RUSKIN ROAD
KINGSTHORPE
NORTHAMPTON

6th., June., 1966.

Mr. Brian Reynolds.,
202, St. Peters Avenue,
KETTERING.

Dear Brian.,

    I have to acknowledge with **regret**
your letter of the 5th., June.,'66.,
notifying me of your resignation as
an active Referee with this County F.A.
which terminates a standard of refereeing
during the six seasons of service which
both I, and the Referees Committee have
been highly appreciative.
    Whilst I was expecting this confirmation
of your verbal decision to retire from
the ranks of our Senior Referees, I am
never-the-less deeply sorry to lose your
services.
    However, the decision is yours and
this County F.A., is the loser.
    Please accept the sincere thanks of
myself and the Referees Committee **for**
your most **valued** services with the Whistle
during your period of service with us.
        With kind regards and best **Wishes,**
            Yours sincerely

            Hon. Referees' Secretary.

```
╔══════════════════════════════════════════════╗
║                                                ║
║   B L Reynolds  not out  102                   ║
║   Northants won by four wickets; Dover, 1961   ║
║                                                ║
╚══════════════════════════════════════════════╝
```

1958 - 1961

Sed ut acerbum est, pro bene factis cum mali messim metas.
(How bitter it is, when you have sown benefits, to reap injuries.)
                                                Plautus, 'Epidicus'

```
┌──────────────────────────────────────────────┐
│                                                │
│                   Subba Row                    │
│                                                │
│              A walking guide                   │
│                                                │
│                Elgar or Elvis                  │
│                                                │
│              Brighter cricket                  │
│                                                │
└──────────────────────────────────────────────┘
```

"I didn't feel anything, but there was a lot of blood."

Jack Hobbs, 'The Master', was one of many professionals who voiced regrets at the amateurs' demise, believing their independent position allowed greater freedom in the way they played. This view ignored the reality that, by the end of the 1950s, most amateurs were no longer independent. For example, County clubs had often found them administrative employment; 'assistant secretary' was one convenient euphemism. In 1961, Alec Bedser said he doubted if there were any players in first-class cricket who were amateurs "in the old-fashioned sense." He also saw no reason why professionals shouldn't make successful captains.

In 1958, another Surrey man and an amateur of the right stock (Whitgift and Cambridge) took over the captaincy of Northamptonshire. Raman Subba Row had been promised the captaincy at least eighteen months earlier. Now, his National Service ended, he took charge, an officer and a gentleman. Whether 'The Master' would have approved, we don't know.

The County's own master, Dennis Brookes, had returned to the ranks. He might have been forty-two years of age, but he was still one of only three Northants batsmen to reach 1000 runs in the wettest season in memory. Many groundsmen say that every year; in 1958 it was justified. Northamptonshire had only eleven complete days of cricket in their first twenty-one.

There were compensations. The game against Yorkshire at Bradford could not start on the Saturday, so Arnold and Reynolds beat Close and Illingworth 4 and 3 on the Beckfoot golf course. On the Monday, the same pair put on 128 for the second wicket, at a run a minute, in bright sunshine, before Brian was out on 61 - caught Close bowled Illingworth. Cricket's like that. Arnold was unbeaten on 85, before the wretched weather beat everyone. "Peter had a very effective method, very much his own style, with little backlift and punchy shots from a weighty bat. It's not how, but how many."

After second place in 1957, whispered expectations were of the first ever top spot. The doubters (there are one or two at Northampton) referred to the loss of Bob Clarke and Jock Livingston, both ranked highly in Brian's estimation. "Jock was exceptional all round the wicket. Quick on his feet, he could dominate the spinners. I remember batting with him against Bill Greensmith, the Essex leg-spinner. At the end of one over he said, 'I'll just plant him in the bowling green, but not so often they'll take him off.' There's good players, and good players who are lucky. Jock didn't need the luck, but he seemed to have it. Against Worcester once he hit the biggest ever dolly to mid off and Reg Perks shelled it. Jock took full advantage. He loved talking, especially about cricket. That's something else young players could learn from him."

Brian speaks with special warmth of his fellow local-born cricketer. "Bob Clarke was a genuine, wholehearted character. Everything about him said that. I used to call him, Eddie (Davis), Jakie, and Des, the 'four musketeers.' Everyone liked him. He once had a standing ovation at the Oval after scoring fifty. He visited the ground shortly before he died, but I was coaching and now regret that I only had time for a brief word. Bob was a lovely man."

By the end of July, after six successive victories, Northamptonshire were again in second place. August was disastrous, however, and they finally finished fourth. Once upon a time that would have brought celebrations from Brackley to

Barnack, but Brown and Brookes had changed all that. For the west stand, known as the moaning capital (and capitol) of the British Empire, fourth was nowhere.

In the Championship Brian scored 915 runs and, according to a rather curmudgeonly phrase in Wisden, played a number of "sound innings". He certainly had a "sound" technique (you don't last twenty years at the top level without one), but the press were now more often applauding his attacking prowess. One such example was a 'Daily Telegraph' account of his 97 against Gloucestershire, when he and Subba Row put on 163 in 150 minutes, retrieving a poor start of 69 for three, in "a rousing piece of batting." Michael Melford wrote of "Reynolds playing an attractive innings, full of fine strokes. Some aggressive batting which, combined with the admirable running between wickets, made a splendid day's cricket." His powerful driving was a delight: "He always banged it cheerfully back past the bowler when he had a chance." Witness the ten fours in his first 60.

The Reynolds-Subba Row stand was appropriate fare for the opening of another stand. The indoor cricket school was open to spectators for the first time. It offered protection for 585 spectators, though it's doubtful if 585 were in the ground on a cold, gusty day of spitting rain. Not untypical of the County Ground, according to Vic Marks.

The faithful were also entertained by a 'What happened next?' incident, now deemed politically incorrect. One of Brian's boundaries was acquired from a ball which slipped from Sam Cook's hand and trickled towards square leg. Slip and keeper raced in front of Brian to protect the long leg area, while he set off after the ball and dispatched it for four through long stop's territory. Further evidence of the Reynolds philosophy: never waste an opportunity, whether it's a leftover bun or a free hit.

At the opening of the indoor school are (from left), Arnold Payne (club chairman), Dennis Brookes, GAT Vials (club president), Eric Harrison (chairman, Supporters Association, the main benefactors) and Brian Reynolds. During the summer the long hall was used as a buffet and bar. It still is, but now it's a smoke-free zone.

This 97, alongside his 53 against Essex in low totals at Leyton, continued the good times against these two counties. His final tally was 1271 (average 37.38) against Gloucester and 1300 against Essex (average 34.21). Not that statistics appeal much to Brian. He'd be more satisfied with the team's early season wins and his contribution to them. Batting at three against Glamorgan, he had a 79 and 42, while his 62 against Middlesex secured first innings points.

He was again selected for the Players at Scarborough and was again in fine form scoring 58 in the second innings (st Petrie b Dexter) as the professionals won by 55 runs. This was one of three stumpings in the innings by EC Petrie, who had toured in 1958 with the New Zealanders. In the fast fading anachronism of 'gentlemen and players', Dexter was the last amateur to be registered with Sussex. There's something fitting about that. Corinthian Lord Ted was never one to go gently into that particular good night; he was too fond of his pale blue Jaguar.

Northamptonshire's batting highlight in 1958 was undoubtedly the partnership of 376 between Subba Row (300) and Albert Lightfoot (119, his maiden century) at the Oval, after sinking to 95 for five. It involved all kinds of records, until along came David Ripley and Malachy Loye in 1998. "I had a lot of time for Albert," says Brian, "he was a smashing man and a good all-round cricketer. It's often forgotten that he played nearly three hundred times for Northamptonshire. Raman's record shows what a fine player he was, capable of big hundreds. He was especially talented on the leg side, with neat deflections, and he could run well between the wickets."

Brian was a popular guest at many cricket functions, especially in his own part of the county. Local players had the chance to talk to the local hero and he would always tell them what they wanted to hear. "It is from enthusiastic villages like this that the players of the future will come", was said at Great Oakley and elsewhere. In 1958 he was able to include the indoor school in his speech, "the biggest asset Northamptonshire cricket has ever had", he told Burton Latimer, adding the obligatory, "we need local boys".

As well as club dinners (or 'suppers' as some less pretentious clubs termed them), there was a variety of other engagements in an age not yet TV-dominated. At the Kettering & District Schools Cricket Association presentations at the Technical College, the Evening Telegraph photograph shows him surrounded by "eager young autograph hunters". A Sports Forum organised by the Rockingham Road Men's Brotherhood at the Baptist Church Rooms received extensive coverage.

Four local sports personalities answered questions posed, on the audience's behalf, by Mr KS Tingle of Kettering Swimming Club. The most controversial was, "Who are the fittest of sportsmen?"

Mr C Mandeville, a Kettering Harriers official for many years plumped, not for a track and field man, though he conceded, "a marathon runner would be a close second", but for a boxer. "A professional boxer is faced with roughly an hour's physical exertion, during which he would have to sustain a great deal of punishment."

Brian Reynolds was less adamant. "Different sports require different sets of muscles. A sportsman trains to be 100% fit for his particular sport."

Another question led Jimmy Potts, a Kettering councillor, Poppies winger and Oxford double blue (cricket and soccer) to admit that an amateur footballer sometimes did not get a fair share of the ball when playing for a professional team. "I myself have come across a few isolated instances of this but in the main it is exaggerated. There can be faults on both sides when it happens."

The fourth member of the panel, Dennis Wildman, a soccer referee was more forthright. He was in favour of retaining the maximum wage in football. Why? "Otherwise you might get a player concentrating on being an individual, rather than a member of a team."

The panel at the Baptist Church Rooms (left to right): HJ Potts, D Wildman, KS Tingle, BL Reynolds, C Mandeville.

In 1959 there was a broken leg, recorded in some publications, for several years, as a broken hip. It's axiomatic that a professional sportsperson's greatest fear is serious illness or injury. Even Brian admits, "I did wonder, but I was lucky. From the outset they assured me the recovery would be a hundred per cent, with no damaging after effects." The cricket club treated him well, but made it clear they couldn't countenance another football injury. "I realised my longer term future was with cricket, so that was the end of football." As a Warwickshire supporter put it:

"The injuries that they themselves procure
Must be their schoolmasters."

At the start of the 1959 season Brian believed he would play before it ended. "Bravado really. I did turn out for the seconds at Horton, but it was a mistake. I drove the ball towards long-on and called for three. I had a job to run one. Still, I was lucky with injuries. I didn't pull a muscle until I was nearly forty." Perhaps that has less to do with luck than a disciplined regard for fitness. As early as 1961 Bedser was lamenting that "there are far more pulled muscles nowadays". He put it down to insufficient net practice and the motor car: "strong limbs cannot be developed by sitting in a car." In Alec's youth you walked or rode a bike to get from A to B. Today, you pay exorbitant fees to a health club, to walk or ride a bike on machines that keep you in the same place. And some people accuse Alec of being an old cynic.

Brian was hit on the head by Trueman and Statham (if it's inevitable, pick the best) and he remembers being "furrowed" (his word) by Terry Spencer at Grace Road. "I didn't feel anything, but there was a lot of blood." In June 1960, he was again felled against Leicestershire (CT Spencer again). Having scored 50 in a century opening partnership, he had to retire after being struck twice by balls that kicked. That was one of his ten fifties in a Championship run total of 1,400, his highest to-date and testimony to his consistency. Brian, and his opening partner Mick Norman - Desperate Dan and Fred Astaire in David Steele's eyes - were the County's heaviest scorers by some distance. Both played in each of the twenty-eight championship games, whereas Raman Subba Row appeared in ten, because of England calls and a broken bone in his thumb, sustained in the fourth Test. His selection as one of Wisden's five cricketers of the year was a possible consolation.

Fred Astaire gives Ossie Wheatley some tap. Desperate Dan is the non-striker.

"It's not the quantity but the quality," a universal truth all cricketers should remember. It certainly applied to another (possibly the best) of Brian's fifties in 1960. In May, against Somerset, Alley took five for 46 on a spiteful, rain-ruined wicket, as Northamptonshire were shot out for 138. The weather cut eight hours from the game; twenty wickets fell in the match, of which seventeen were catches and Jim Lomax retired with a broken wrist. Local umpire, Ron Lay, was kept busy.

A sentence from one report sums up the County's collapse and Brian's strengths, of technique and temperament: "Reynolds alone shaped confidently in face of a lifting ball."

Brian has no clear recollection of that game, but a vivid one of Bill Alley that reflects well on the Australian and the cricketing morality of yesteryear. He caught Bill, while fielding at forward short-leg, taking the ball near the ground. Brian gestured it was a clean catch. "If you say so Brian, then that's good enough for me," said Bill and left the crease immediately.

Cricket needs that kind of integrity. If it loses its honesty, it has nothing left to lose, and "hark what chaos follows." In 'The Guardian' on April 15, 2000, Mike Selvey wrote: "Cricket has become a game for cheats and charlatans. No-one trusts anyone else on the field of play these days anyway and now, thanks to Cronje, the same will apply off it, even within the same team."

In these cynical times, it has become fashionable to dismiss cricket's past as full of defunct, sentimental idealists, or even hypocrites, mocking the time with fairest show. The so-called 'realism' of today's players is yet another convenient cop-out that seeks to rationalise an acceptance of the morally unacceptable. One such argument is that standards are always in decline. As far back as the sixth century BC, full-time professional athletes incurred the contempt of Aristotle and Euripides, not for the stigma of performing for profit, but from neglecting the ideals of the good and wise, the temperate and just.

Neglect of ideals, of course, doesn't make them invalid. At the start of Brian's career the majority of batsmen 'walked'; the con-artists were soon rumbled. The tradition lingered, certainly until May 1985, when Graeme Fowler said this: "on the county circuit, where it is a tight-knit community and you are playing against the same people year in and year out, walking is right, because otherwise it creates so much bad feeling, and most people do walk. Besides, I think it is the right thing to do." Fifty-two years earlier, FGJ Ford (Cambridge, Middlesex and England) in a letter to 'The Times' had used the phrase "the moral value of the very word cricket." Was that a different cricket from the game that started the twenty-first century awash with allegations of match rigging?

There is good news. At key stages of the game's 'pyramid' the will still exists to assert its rightful values. Two contemporary publications illustrate the point. In schools the national curriculum encourages young people to: "observe the conventions of fair play, honest competition and good sporting behaviour; understand and cope with a variety of outcomes, including both success and failure; and be aware of the effects and consequences of their actions on others." In the Northamptonshire County Cricket League's Handbook for 2000 the editor has published the MCC's definition of 'the spirit of cricket' which, among other recommendations, urges players not "to indulge in cheating or any sharp practice."

Cricket once stood for the presentation of parts of life of lasting quality. That is one reason why many people loved playing and watching it, for all its foibles. It can never be played in a world outside of time, sealed off from the surrounding ugliness, but it should still offer a glimpse of the real thing, or it will soon be nothing special.

Late May 1960 was special for Northamptonshire, as South Africa suffered the first defeat of their tour. In the game's last over (bowled by former Northamptonshire all-rounder, Jon 'Pom-Pom' Fellows-Smith), the County scrambled the required three runs to secure their first victory over a touring team for twenty-seven years. It owed much to an opening stand between Reynolds and Norman of 64 in an hour, Brian starting the victory charge with sixes off Hugh Tayfield, one scorched the bell tower in the old pavilion. David Steele reckons that, in the right mood, Brian "could hit the ball as far as anyone." He had also made 44 in the first innings. Brian believes that, when South Africa batted a second time, Tayfield saw it was turning and fancied his chances. "He was heard to say they'd got enough," before adding with the born competitor's edge, "but they hadn't."

DJ McGlew c Reynolds b PD Watts 52; South Africa 92-1, Northampton, May 25, 1960.

Reynolds and Norman were a purposeful double act, excelling in their running between the wickets. They were quick, confident and enjoyed it. As local men, it might have been the Weetabix. Brian sees Mick as "a highly effective worker and nudger, skilful at manoeuvring the ball and always looking for runs others wouldn't contemplate. He was also a high-class fielder."

Urgency, in the field and between wickets, contributes to so-called 'brighter cricket', a hot topic at that time, heated by concern about falling attendances. Locally, Des Barrick joined the debate while speaking at a dinner organised by the Wellingborough branch of the County Supporters Club. He urged his colleagues: "Play attractive cricket . . . in these modern times youngsters would rather rock 'n' roll than watch a match, and so it's up to the players to get them to the boundary." Throughout 1960 Brian, preferring Elgar to Elvis, did his best to oblige. A 'Daily Express' banner headline gives the flavour: "Reynolds slogs 35 off 16 balls on a tricky pitch." With a nice sense of context, the venue was Wellingborough, the acting captain, Barrick. True to his earlier plea, he ordered his side to "Go out and play your shots hard." Brian - "we love a captain to obey" - did just that. Pat Marshall depicted him as "the executioner with the bludgeoning bat". A later paragraph endorsed Patsy Hendren's delight at his footwork. "Reynolds' bold batting had paid off by showing that any terrors in the wicket could be overcome by moving to the pitch of the slower, more flighted Sussex spin - then driving." One of the suffering spinners was Robin Marlar (Harrow and Cambridge) strongly touted as Northamptonshire's captain before the appointment of Brookes. His six overs brought one for 54.

On several other occasions Brian's readiness to attack found approval in the press and points for the side. A seven wicket win over Lancashire and a 72 run success against Gloucestershire both included a Reynolds 83 (four sixes against Gloucestershire). His 51 and 36 against the same opponents earlier in the season had also benefited from sixes, when others had struggled. Yorkshire were sorted out by six wickets (Reynolds 77 and 34), likewise Somerset (Reynolds top scored with 49). In trouncing Derbyshire by ten wickets Donald Ramsamooj had 123 and Brian 47; others very few. It was the 28 year old Trinidadian's first Championship appearance, having waited three years while qualifying. Strangely, after such a sparkling start, he added just three more hundreds. In a six wicket defeat by Worcestershire Brian was again top man, with a fifty that contained nineteen scoring strokes. Remember Jeremy? In July, in a nine wicket hammering by Glamorgan (with an all-Welsh side) he bagged a 'pair'.

There was no time to dwell on it. Both teams left Cardiff on Friday evening, heading for Northampton where they resumed the battle on the Saturday morning. It was Des Barrick's benefit match and the beneficiary was also the captain: Subba Row was at Old Trafford, breaking his thumb for England. Also injured was reserve wicket-keeper Laurie Johnson who had deputised for the injured Keith Andrew at Cardiff. Andrew was still unfit, so Des's benefit keeper was BL Reynolds (42 and 6 - as suits used to be - and one catch).

In an article at the end of that season, Alec Bedser wrote that "Cricket on the whole had become slower," to the game's detriment. "Attractive batting and stroke-play have declined." The consensus view agreed with Des Barrick's at the dinner in Wellingborough, that this was the main reason for the slump in attendances. In 1947, total attendances - exclusive of members - had been 2,300,910. In 1960, the figures fell to 1,046,104, a decrease of 323,569 compared with 1959. Daily attendances for county matches in 1960 fell on every day of the week compared with 1959. Significantly, Saturday showed the largest decrease; work alone could not explain the decline. Brian says the players were obviously conscious of the diminishing support, "but in a busy season you just got on with playing. That was your job."

At the end of 1960 Northamptonshire were ninth in the Championship, two places higher than 1959. Brookes and Tribe had retired in 1959, now it was Barrick and Tyson. In three years, the side had lost six players of genuine class. Brian remembers Des as a "naturally gifted cricketer, an incessant bat twirler, and a joker (still is). He had the cheek to claim we were relatives, having married a Reynolds. I learnt a lesson through Des. Keeping wicket in rubber soled boots, I slipped running in and was struck behind the ear by one of his rapid returns, much to everyone's amusement Mind you, Jack Jennings sorted him out once on the massage table, with 'chilli paste' on his backside." Brian still enjoys a curry.

Frank Tyson took 525 wickets in 170 matches for Northamptonshire at 20.95. David Larter, who started in 1960, had 511 wickets in 134 matches at

18.19. Pity they only overlapped for one season. "It is generally agreed that Frank was one of the fastest bowlers of all time," says Brian, before chuckling at the memory of the committee man who, during the lunch interval at the Oval, asked the sweat-soaked Tyson if he was 'turning it'. "It was sheer pace with Frank, who was immensely strong. I was once at slip when Frank kept having serious chats with Keith Andrew. Keith said Frank was delighted with how much he was swinging the ball away from the bat, but he wouldn't disillusion him. 'If he thinks that, he'll bowl better.'" Even the greats can sometimes need cosseting.

Brian speaks admiringly of the respect fierce competitors could have for each other in County cricket, by referring to a game at Lord's in July 1954. Bill Edrich (who never needed cosseting) was hit in the face by a Tyson bouncer. He spent the night in hospital and returned to bat next day. "Bill resembled a casualty from the Boer War". Frank treated him to another bouncer first ball and Edrich went for the hook. Edrich, said Tyson, "was the man who displayed to him the indomitability of the human spirit". Alan Hill's biography of the Middlesex man recounts the story that years later, when asked to nominate favoured rivals, Frank Tyson and Ray Lindwall headed Bill's list. Fred Trueman, who was present, was not impressed.

For much of 1961 Northamptonshire were bottom of the table and, in the end, only Nottinghamshire were below them. Representative calls restricted Raman Subba Row to fifteen matches. Norman (1,563 runs) and Reynolds (1,342) again headed the County's run gatherers.

Brian had three centuries in the Championship and another against a Cambridge University side containing two future England captains in Tony Lewis and Mike Brearley. His 155 included four sixes and twenty-two fours. His outstanding achievement was in the win against Kent. Requiring 192, Northamptonshire owed everything to Brian, who batted with supreme confidence for an unbeaten 102, when everyone else missed out.

"We seemed to play at Dover quite often. I never played at Canterbury; I don't think we were ever on the list to be considered for a game there. Still, I liked Dover. It was an impressive location, cut into the hillside below the football ground. We'd finished at Swansea late on the Friday - we won with about ten minutes to spare. It was a long haul, no motorways, no Severn bridge. It took hours and we arrived at Dover early in the morning. We managed some sleep on the bus but we weren't best pleased when KV lost the toss. However, Crump and Scott bowled them out just after lunch and we went on to win."

Earlier, 107 against Leicestershire, in three and a half hours, saved the game at Grace Road and, in August, the third hundred (109, two sixes, fourteen fours) against Sussex secured first innings points. That match was most memorable, however, for Mike 'Tex' Dilley's second hat-trick of the summer, involving a useful trio of Les Lenham, Ken Suttle, and Ted Dexter. The earlier one, against Notts (Cyril Poole, Mervyn Winfield, 'Bomber' Wells), occurred during his first appearance for two seasons. He took thirty-eight wickets in thirteen appearances in 1961, with several distinguished scalps among them. 'Tex', another local man, played thirty three times for his home county, "and should have played longer and more often," says Brian. He left the staff in 1963 and bestrode the County League world like a colossus.

KENT v NORTHAMPTONSHIRE at Dover on August 26, 28, 29, 1961

KENT

Batsman	First innings			Second innings		
PE Richardson	c Norman	b Crump	25	c Scott	b Crump	132
JM Prodger	c Crump	b Scott	16		b Crump	3
RC Wilson	c Crump	b Scott	25		b Crump	4
*AH Phebey	run out		0	c Reynolds	b Scott	75
DJ Constant	c Lightfoot	b Scott	1	c Lightfoot	b Scott	0
PH Jones	c Andrew	b Wild	31	not out		87
AL Dixon		b Crump	1		b Crump	7
+DG Ufton		b Crump	43	c Reynolds	b Crump	11
DJ Halfyard	c Ramsamooj	b Scott	0		b Crump	0
A Brown	c Larter	b Wild	15		b Crump	4
DW Baker	not out		1		b Larter	4
	b1, l4, w1		6	l6, w5		11
			164			**338**

	1	2	3	4	5	6	7	8	9	10
	43	45	45	58	81	88	105	108	137	164
	47	53	197	212	223	251	299	311	311	338

	O	M	R	W	O	M	R	W
Larter	4	0	19	0	6.3	0	9	1
Dilley	4	0	15	0	3	2	11	0
Crump	13.5	2	53	3	48	19	129	7
Scott	19	7	46	4	27	7	86	2
Wild	9	4	25	2	24	5	85	0
Lightfoot					2	0	7	0

NORTHAMPTONSHIRE

Batsman	First innings			Second innings		
BL Reynolds	c Richardson	b Halfyard	21	not out		102
MEJC Norman	c Prodger	b Brown	77	c Prodger	b Baker	24
A Lightfoot	c Richardson	b Dixon	90		b Dixon	9
D Ramsamooj	lbw	b Dixon	4		b Halfyard	5
C Milburn	st Ufton	b Baker	28		b Halfyard	19
*+KV Andrew		b Halfyard	35	not out		0
BS Crump	c Richardson	b Jones	1	c Brown	b Dixon	18
ME Scott		b Halfyard	13			
J Wild	c Brown	b Halfyard	25			
MR Dilley		b Halfyard	0		b Halfyard	0
JDF Larter	not out		0			
	b14, l3		17	b2, l15		17
			299	(six wkts)		**194**

	1	2	3	4	5	6	7	8	9	10
	37	186	195	204	243	244	277	278	292	299
	48	85	108	140	140	169				

	O	M	R	W	O	M	R	W
Brown	16	6	42	1				
Halfyard	17.4	4	55	5	24	3	61	3
Dixon	31	10	80	2	17	4	48	2
Jones	21	8	46	1	15	7	38	0
Baker	23	5	71	1	8.3	1	30	1

Umpires: JS Buller, CS Elliott

NORTHAMPTONSHIRE won by four wickets

Two of his thirty-eight victims were Norman O'Neill and Alan Davidson in the tourist match, when Brian and Mick Norman put on 128, the highest first wicket stand for Northamptonshire against Australia. Before a crowd of 4,500 (takings £585) Brian made 60 before falling to Davidson, who opened the bowling with Ron Gaunt, 'Garth' McKenzie appearing as third change.

Other highlights included a quickfire 94 against Somerset and a top score of 86 in the win against Glamorgan, in difficult batting conditions, in the match before the Dover triumph.

In July, against the Combined Services, Brian became the first player born in Northamptonshire to captain the side since Jack Timms at Kettering in 1946. Opening the batting for the Services was RT Virgin (c Lightfoot b Dilley 4), who played 103 times for the County and was chairman of the cricket committee at the time of Brian's retirement. Meantime, the 1961 committee had to find another captain after a less expected retirement, that of Subba Row.

This card does not necessarily include the fall of the last wicket   Match Drawn   PRICE 3d.

JULY 12th, 13th and 14th   NORTHAMPTONSHIRE v. COMBINED SERVICES   Services won toss and put Northants. in

THE PUBLIC ARE REQUESTED TO KEEP OFF THE PLAYING AREA DURING INTERVALS

Northamptonshire	1st Innings		2nd Innings	
1 †Reynolds B	c Fenner b Stead	41	c Stead b Pratt	50
2 Milburn C	c Newsom b Stead	56	b Buss	0
3 Watts J	c Virgin b Buss	39	not out	108
4 Lightfoot A	c Hatch b Buss	18	not out	71
5 J Minney	c Virgin b Buss	2		
6 Scott M	b Buss	6		
7 Watts P	not out	86		
8 Williamson G	c Buss b Stead	19		
9 Dilley M	c Fenner b Buss	13		
10 ‡Johnson L	c McIntyre b Pratt	6		
11 Wild J	c Virgin b Buss	0		
	Extras	8	Extras	2

†Captain ‡Wicketkeeper   294   Declared for 2 wkts 231

(Rate of runs per over   )

1st Ins. 1-83   2-112   3-139   4-145   5-163   6-176   7-245   8-280   9-293   10-294

2nd Ins. 1-0   2-94   3-   4-   5-   6-   7-   8-   9-   10-

Bowling Analysis	O	M	R	Wk	N	W	O	M	R	Wk	N	W
Stead	24	6	69	3	....	....	9	1	45	0	....	....
Buss	31.3	1	131	6	....	....	25	3	66	1	....	....
Earnshaw	19	4	68	0	....	....	7	0	35	0	....	....
Pratt	9	2	18	1	....	....	24	2	83	1	....	....

Umpires—F Jakeman and J Langridge
Hours of play—1st Day, 11.30 - 7   2nd Day, 11.30 - 7   3rd Day, 11.30 - 5 or 5 30

A NEW BALL may be taken after 85 overs

NEXT HOME MATCH—
JULY 19th, 20th and 21st—NORTHANTS. v. AUSTRALIANS (at Northampton)

Combined Services	1st Innings		2nd Innings
1 P G Hatch	c Johnson b Williamson	0	
2 R T Virgin	c Lightfoot b Dilley	4	
3 D J Newsom	c Lightfoot b Dilley	23	
4 N Durden-Smith	b Dilley	0	
5 †M D Fenner	b Watts (J)	46	
6 A Buss	b Williamson	36	
7 K Robinson	c Wild b Scott	18	
8 D Pratt	lbw b Scott	12	
9 ‡T F McIntyre	c Johnson b Watts (J)	18	
10 B Stead	c Reynolds b Scott	14	
11 R O Earnshaw	not out	2	
	Extras	2	Extras

†Captain ‡Wicketkeeper   175

(Rate of runs per over   )

1st Ins. 1-4   2-4   3-4   4-30   5-79   6-96   7-139   8-155   9-169   10-175

2nd Ins. 1-   2-   3-   4-   5-   6-   7-   8-   9-   10-

Bowling Analysis	O	M	R	Wk	N	W	O	M	R	Wk	N	W
Dilley	15	3	51	3	....	....						
Williamson	17	9	25	2	....	....						
Lightfoot	5	1	19	0	....	....						
Watts (J)	8	1	32	2	....	....						
Scott	7.3	1	34	3	....	....						
Watts (P)	15	9	12	0	....	....						

Scorers—R Smith and J M Mason
Lunch 1.30-2.10   Tea at 4.30

Cushions from under Press Box and New Pavilion—6d. per day

B L Reynolds lbw b Statham 141

1962 - 1964

"Matches are made in Heaven."
Robert Burton.

Andrew

Senior pro

Pie and Beans

It's a Knock Out

"Everyone has to field well, there's no hiding."

Among those bucked by the appointment of Keith Andrew as Northamptonshire's captain for 1962 were advocates of the cyclical theory of history. The sequence rolled on: Cambridge, northern nous, Cambridge, northern nous. Brown, Brookes, Subba Row, Andrew. It also heralded five successful years, including the runners-up spot in 1965. Brian was a sure supporter of his new boss: "Keith was an astute captain. Quiet and unassuming, but ruthless enough when necessary. He mastered the difficult art of being captain and wicket-keeper at the same time. His philosophy was, 'Just give them enough rope'." Alan Curling, then sports editor of 'The Northamptonshire Evening Telegraph', welcomed Keith's appointment as "a man who always thinks before he speaks or does anything." You have the same impression with Mike Brearley, even when he's arguing otherwise.

For Brian, also, the five seasons from 1962 to 1966 were the peak years of his career. For starters, he played in 139 of the 140 Championship games, a proud record of reliability. One year, however, was undeniably special. In 1962 he married Angela, became the Club's senior professional, and was at his most prolific as a batsman with 1,714 Championship runs at an average of 34.28). To cap it all, Ijaz Butt of Pakistan lost the will to live (allegedly) after his dismissal in the tourist match: Butt c Allen b Reynolds 17.

Brian had ended the 1961 season with a century against Kent; he began 1962 with another (110, seventeen fours) against the same opposition. Michael Melford, a confessed Reynolds admirer, had this to say: "It is never hardship watching as willing a driver as Reynolds, but today he hooked and cut as fluently as he drove, his timing impeccable from the start. His batting had a midsummer bloom, while that of others was palpably in early May." Brian and the Watts brothers were paramount in the County's innings and the lively pace of their run gathering, followed by comparable flourishes from Cowdrey, set up an intriguing finish, ruined alas by you know what. It should be said that Melford, who died in 1999, was one of the most respected sports writers of his day. In 1961, he became 'The Sunday Telegraph's' first cricket correspondent, and in 1965 succeeded EW Swanton as 'The Daily Telegraph's' chief cricket writer, with flair and style. A glimpse of those qualities is evident in his writing about Brian Reynolds. His tributes, like those of Bedser, Hendren, Livingston et al, are worth having.

Brian's dynamic start set the tone for 1962, which continued through the next two years, bringing his three highest aggregates. To begin the season with a hundred was also an ideal introduction to his time as senior professional. "It was my job to back up the captain and look after the needs of the team. If I thought it relevant, I'd offer my views." It also meant that the twelfth-man had to run his bath, not always a blessing, especially later when David Steele was, briefly, given the responsibility. Steele's judgement of water temperature lacked the certainty of his close catching. The wrath of Lillee and Thomson was nothing set against a scalded Reynolds. The role of senior professional was important yesteryear and Brian was suited to it. Talk to his fellow players (including David) and they tell you of his exemplary professionalism. "Brian was dedicated, disciplined, and clean living - everything about him was right," said one.

William Watson, the poet not the batsman, described May as a month of "prosperity" and "confident prime". It was certainly so for Brian in 1962. Immediately after the Kent game, he had 99 and 90 against Somerset, for whom Bill Alley (b Dilley) also succumbed in the nineties. Roger Prideaux's 140 was his first century for Northamptonshire. The local paper wrote of Brian's "spirit, concentration and heart"; maybe you can concentrate too intensely in the nineties? The reporter also forecast (rightly) that this would be his best season. In the same month, in the win against Glamorgan with six minutes to spare, Brian contributed 67 and 115 (run out). His partnership with Norman, of 198 in 150 minutes, was crucial to the result and some entertainment. Otherwise, it was grim going; Northamptonshire's first innings run rate was 1.98, Glamorgan's 2.05.

Ron Yeoman's' gently ironic poem, 'County Cricket' contains the lines:

But don't forget
In county cricket,
That a ball well off the wicket
Never should be hit for four;
So the batsman carefully plays it
Slowly back
Along the floor.

With the football stand behind, Brian is on his way to 115 against the Welsh county. John Evans is the bowler, Jim Pressdee is the fielder.

At Kettering, in the next game, against Gloucestershire, the cricket was equally tedious. Kinder critics resorted to the old standby that it "lacked purpose". The locals called it a "bloody disgrace", claiming there was more entertainment in the Town League on the adjacent recreational ground. It was the kind of cricket that was driving the Advisory County Cricket Committee to even more gin and tonics. Their pleas were for "brighter cricket" and a determination to entertain the general public. The home side were so lethargic on the last day that all the visiting team, except Arthur Milton and wicket-keeper Barrie Meyer, bowled in an attempt to raise the tempo. In one over Harold Jarman bowled three balls with his right arm and three with his left. Brian, meantime, was not guilty, having long since departed (lbw b Brown 0). It was a rare failure, likewise for Wisden, who probably caught the general malaise in recording his first innings dismissal as "caught Mortimore bowled Hilton" (presumably on loan from Lancs). Arthur Milton (it was he) didn't bowl during the second innings circus, but had figures of 9-4-11-1 in the first. Arthur, like Willie Watson, a double international at cricket and football, played County cricket from 1948 to 1974. He took five more wickets in 1962, three Cambridge students and Ray Julian and Jack van Geloven at Ashby de la Zouch.

Peter Roebuck tells a lovely story that illustrates Arthur's gentle nature. At slip once, he took a low chance, and held up the ball to show it was a clean catch. "I caught it, Peter," he said to the batsman, Sainsbury of Hampshire. "I'm not so sure about that," came the reply. "Oh well, stay in if you like," said Arthur.

Milton's six wickets that season put him five ahead of BL Reynolds, in spite of Bronk's 0.4-0-0-1 against Pakistan. The tourists had failed to accept the declaration challenge of making 175 in just under two hours not, as one participant (Reynolds) suggests, from the lurking threat of his 'off-breaks'. However, he had been one of the few batsmen to show much initiative, with a 79 and 50.

Also in June, at the Oval, the drawn game against Surrey was belittled as "doing nothing to foster interesting cricket." There was plenty from Brian that did. For example, in that same month, he and Lightfoot whacked 77 in 38 minutes in a run chase against Middlesex (Brian 69). In July, opposing Glamorgan at Swansea, forceful batting from Brian (83) and Jim Watts (72) almost brought an unlikely win following a stiff declaration. A month later, rain prevented a victory over Sussex, after Brian's unbeaten 104, with two sixes and thirteen fours, had established his side's ascendancy.

Michael Turner, secretary of Leicestershire, also did much to "foster interesting cricket" in 1962 by instigating the Midlands Knock-out Competition, involving Derbyshire, Leicestershire, Nottinghamshire and Northamptonshire. It was the first limited-overs competition at this level, with 65 for each side.

It began with the two semi-finals on the first Saturday in May. Leicestershire beat Derbyshire, Wisden opined, "an excellent match showed that one-day cricket could be most interesting." At Trent Bridge, Northamptonshire stormed to 168 for nine off 65 overs, a dozen of which were maidens. Notts were bowled out in 54.2 overs for 137; spinner Malcolm Scott took five for 23 in his 15 overs.

Brian didn't play in that game but he was selected for the final the following Saturday, taking the place of Colin Milburn. "Scoring was slower," reported Wisden, "than in the semi-finals mainly because this time there was no limit on the number of overs allowed a bowler". Gus Williamson was in his 19th over when he bowled last man Brian Boshier to finish with five for 58. Northamptonshire won by five wickets after Reynolds and Norman put on 98 for the first wicket. Bronk's 55 was one run off the highest score of the match; he was a strong contender for 'Man of the Match' but that idea was still in the future. He didn't come away empty-handed; GAT Vials presented each player with an inscribed ashtray, similar in weight, if not appearance, to an Exocet missile. Perhaps 'Tubby' foresaw the arrival of the John Player League in 1969, or the popularity of Heavy Metal.

Turner's midlands tournament was the experimental forerunner of the national knock-out competition, which arrived on the first-class scene in 1963, almost a century after it was first suggested. Driven by dire necessity, some said.

Midlands Knock-out Competition Final

LEICESTERSHIRE v NORTHAMPTONSHIRE

Grace Road, Leicester, May 9, 1962

LEICESTERSHIRE

MR Hallam	c Scott	b Larter	4	Larter	16	2	52	3
J Birkenshaw		b Larter	2	Dilley	14	3	68	0
A Wharton		lbw b Williamson	53	Williamson	18.2	2	58	5
S Jayasinghe	c Crump	b Williamson	14	Watts	3	0	9	2
*D Kirby		b Larter	21	Scott	6	1	22	0
LR Gardner		lbw b Watts	56					
J van Geloven		b Williamson	42					
+R Julian		b Williamson	9					
CT Spencer	not out		9					
RJ Barratt		b Watts	2					
BS Boshier		b Williamson	1					
Extras		(b2, l6, w1)	9					
TOTAL			**218**					

NORTHAMPTONSHIRE

MEJC Norman	c Birkenshaw	b van Geloven	46	Spencer	11	2	55	0
BL Reynolds		b Kirby	55	Boshier	13.2	4	36	1
RM Prideaux		b Kirby	4	van Geloven	18	2	55	1
A Lightfoot	c Julian	b Kirby	6	Barratt	5	1	28	0
PJ Watts		b Boshier	47	Kirby	12	3	42	3
BS Crump	not out		52					
JG Williamson	not out		6					
*+KV Andrew								
ME Scott								
MR Dilley								
JDF Larter								
Extras		(l3)	3					
TOTAL		(five wkts)	**219**					

Umpires: CS Elliott, FC Gardner

NORTHAMPTONSHIRE won by five wickets

    In the introductory year of the national competition, matches were 65 overs per side, subsequently reduced to 60. It was sponsored by Gillette, who gave £6,500 to be divided equally among the counties, a trophy, and Man of the Match awards. The purpose was to stem the decline in attendances by providing the more "enterprising" cricket which administrators had called for in the Championship, with limited reward. There was the prospect of a result in the day, weather permitting, and excitement during it.

    In the initial first round Brian scored 34 in a six wicket win against Warwickshire. Needing a comfortable 141, he and Prideaux adopted the sensible approach of batting cautiously to make sure they got there. If not exciting, it was "enterprising" - the paradoxically pragmatic kind: Building Society passbook rather than dotcom share dealing. The next round saw an equally easy win against Middlesex, again by six wickets.

Northamptonshire lost in the semi-finals, however, to Sussex, the competition's first winners. "Sussex won the cup before the other counties had woken up to what was required," according to Lord Ted. Brian had reservations about the aloof Dexter, but he had sorted out the one-day tactics. Moreover, his 115 was largely responsible for setting a testing target, soon to become formidable as Reynolds and Milburn went cheaply. Brian was run out for two, in pursuit of a theoretical run as a ball from Ian Thomson went through to the keeper. His theory was that a run existed if the ball went down the leg side. "Unfortunately," he admits, "this one didn't go far enough."

"One of the Wad's two crap theories," according to a team-mate. The other, a decision to lap Kent's Derek Underwood, which cost him his wicket and torn flannels. Brian acknowledges only the first. "I did lap left-arm spinners in certain situations, I remember doing so against Norman Gifford, but not with Derek. He had phenomenal accuracy. On a turner, you had no chance. He was too quick through the air to get down the wicket to him."

Cricketers love a theory and the Gillette spawned a host of them, as it became an established feature of the first-class fixture list, even though it was never regarded as first-class. 1963 started a new era; the immediacy of the shortened version boosted the game's appeal, not to mention its coffers, through the gate and sponsorship. It was possibly the most dramatic change that first-class cricket has experienced. Of the game's elder statesmen, Richie Benaud is not alone in having no truck for those cricketing bigots who believe the only way to save the game is for those who care about it to combine forces in depriving others of the opportunity to enjoy the abbreviated version. Birley believes the original objections were another manifestation of the "elitist smokescreen" that has often stopped cricket responding to change. "There was some anti-feeling to start with," says Brian, "even a light-hearted approach on occasions, though maybe that was more true of the Sunday League when that started." He remembered that in 1963 the players "could see drawbacks, but it was fun to play." One such drawback was that "batters and bowlers could develop bad habits which would spill over into the longer game."

Brian agrees with some of the oft-repeated views that limited-overs cricket "denatures" the game. "It's mainly about containing, though bowling the other team out is still the best way of doing just that. It does encourage negative bowling and nagging medium-pacers, while further reducing some varieties of spin." Indeed, in his speech at the annual dinner of the Kettering Town Cricket Club in 1963, he had foreseen some of the potential negatives, proposing that there should be laws to prevent fast bowlers from monopolising the attack. He had also argued that the 65 overs should be reduced. Shortly after his speech, Ted Dexter expressed similar fears about "stereotyped, defensive bowling, mostly of the medium-pace variety," and the corresponding decline in the spinners' art.

Brian is also quick to stress the positives. "Everyone has to field well, there's no hiding, so the general standard of fielding has improved. Similarly in running between the wickets." The over-limit intensifies the conflict between bat and ball, rather like the conflicts in a short story compared with the novel, or an episodic 'soap' against a five act play. The balance sheets show that the uncommitted watcher likes it, prefers it; this is an age of instant gratification.

Brian makes another observation about the shortened version, which spectators might not appreciate, unless they've played the game. "It's a hectic business, there's no let-up. You need to be very fit." In his award-winning 'A Lot of Hard Yakka' Simon Hughes puts it this way: "To lose one of these breathless tip-and-run skirmishes is to feel as exhausted and demoralised as the defeated crew in the boat race." He reckons that the eight over spell and the fielding is as debilitating as a day and a half's normal cricket.

Northamptonshire rose one place in 1963 to finish seventh in the Championship. At the end of July they had been third, a mere thirteen points behind the leaders. Thereafter, their batting was too variable, especially against the spinners. David Larter and Brian Crump both took a hundred wickets, the first time two seamers had achieved this in the County's history. "Crumpy was a very good performer, but he benefited from bowling with David, who got lots of bounce. You sometimes felt they were happy to get away from David, but Brian was much better than they bargained for. He's still playing. I wonder if he's still visiting Dr Barker - I think that was his name - in the Potteries. He must have been a miracle worker, the way he used to sort out Crumpy's aches and pains."

Northamptonshire could also claim the most consistent opening batsmen on the circuit. Desperate Dan and Fred Astaire accounted for over one third of the total runs in the County's Championship games. In 1962 Brian had 1,714, Mick 1,719; in 1963 it was 1,550 and 1,740 respectively. That wasn't all: both were superb fielders, morally upright, and ever present. Some of us boasted of their local origins. One of Brian's memories of MEJC concerns a game at Cardiff. "Mick used to like to go to morning mass. I had no objection as long as he didn't wake me up. Sometimes he was a bit late for breakfast but on this day we'd all finished and there was no sign of him. We decided we'd better get down to the ground and hope he'd turn up. As we walked out of the hotel, Mick was walking down the steps of the hotel next door. He'd enjoyed his breakfast even though he'd wondered where the rest of us were!"

On several occasions they topped the bill as a double act. In May, on a soft Romford wicket against Essex, they provided a promising opening of 55. Doesn't sound many, but the rest of the side were 'Lakered' (after his move from Surrey), all out for 132. In June, their rapid 73 secured the win over Leicestershire with three minutes to spare. In Keith Andrew's benefit match in July, Northamptonshire won by an innings against Derbyshire, helped by a Norman-Reynolds stand of 125 (Brian 89). A month on, the County collapsed against Glamorgan's Don Shepherd and Jim Pressdee, who took eighteen wickets between them on a "doubtful" wicket. Brian and Mick alone stood firm, (Brian 51, Mick 69) the only ones to show any "dogged" resistance. Shepherd's career span (1950-72) was similar to Brian's; he took 2,174 wickets for Glamorgan, at 20.95. Fifteen of those were a certain BL Reynolds; including unwilling participation in Shep's career best, nine for 47 at the Arms Park in 1954.

Brian's most obvious triumphs were centuries against Nottinghamshire, Gloucestershire, Kent, Warwickshire and Oxford University. His 115 against Kent at Kettering (Prideaux was the only other contributor with 42) looked important to a result, before rain swelled the nearby brook. There was plenty of Bronko biff in his not out 124 to beat Notts (three sixes and sixteen fours) and his not out 135 (three sixes and twenty five fours) against Oxford. University matches were still taken seriously, Wisden recording, "Reynolds getting a splendid hundred". His aggressive 74 and Milburn's 74, both cracked four sixes, brought the win at Derby, after being set 198 in two hours.

In that match Brian and Colin were both caught off Edwin Smith: Brian by Les Jackson, who had him lbw in the first innings. Between times Brian had caught Les. Quite like old times. Edwin Smith played for his county for twenty years, overlapping with Brian for nineteen of them. Reynolds (74) and Milburn (65) had also struck thirteen boundaries each against Middlesex at Peterborough, before Alan Moss and John Price's lifting deliveries, from wet turf, proved virtually unplayable, at least with the bat.

In their second innings of this match, as Northamptonshire slumped to 47 for seven, there were eight interruptions, as the rain repeatedly freshened an already impossible wicket. This kind of scenario is but one reason why statistical comparisons between eras, pre and post covered wickets, are of limited value. Today's batsmen rarely confront wickets made treacherous by the elements; it could be their techniques are consequently the poorer. For example, photographs and contemporary reports confirm Brian's impressive footwork, in attack and defence, where he went right forward or right back. You learnt the necessity for that by playing on uncovered wickets.

Sir Learie Constantine once said he would discard averages and all the game's tables, believing them pernicious, the bane of cricket. One of his reasons was their encouragement of "plodding, dogged, poisonous stickability at the crease." There's nothing like hyperbole to stir the pot, as Mr Boycott is well aware. Brian provided "stickability" on many occasions, if only to deny the opposition and benefit his team, not his average. It was never "poisonous". In early July 1963, against Glamorgan at Cardiff, painstaking batting was required to retrieve the loss of quick wickets; Brian (50) and Prideaux (124 not out) did the necessary. Against Hampshire at Wellingborough School, the opening pair grafted, because the rain-affected conditions again demanded it. "Norman and Reynolds gave the game a dull start, but the 122 scored by them proved of inestimable value." The other thirty-nine wickets were to fall for 288 runs. Derek Shackleton took eleven for 104 but Larter, Crump and Jim Watts bowled Northamptonshire to victory by 108 runs - not that different a number to Fred and Dan's stand.

The finest example of Brian's "stickability", when the situation demanded, occurred at Edgbaston at the end of August, when he denied Warwickshire their hopes of sharing the Championship with Yorkshire. MJK was not best pleased. Northamptonshire had been forced to follow on and began the last day still needing 46 to make the opposition bat again. In the morning, Alex Bannister of 'The Daily Mail' had confidently predicted a Warwickshire victory. It foundered, however, on Brian's obdurate 113 in four and a half hours. JM Solan of 'The Birmingham Post' wrote of his innings: "As an exercise in dedicated obstructionism it was a model of its kind." He had remained on 99 for half an hour, after appealing against the darkness for the second time when two short of his century. This gritty denouement was a sharp contrast to the previous day, when 'The Guardian' had enjoyed his "powerful driving and hooking" and effective lapping of Bob Barber's leg-spin. He and Prideaux had moved swiftly to 110 in as many minutes. This was a game which again encapsulated Brian's ability to bat in various modes appropriate to fluctuating contexts, including the absence of light. His last day defiance an example to those players who, at the end of the nineties, appeared unwilling or unable to battle for a draw.

1963 saw in the new - the Gillette - but for Brian it ended with a reminder of the old. He accepted his invitation to appear at the Hastings Festival with relish, opening for Arthur Gilligan's XI against the West Indians. "It was a lovely way to finish the season. The West Indians were a very sociable bunch, and although in the latter stages the game was not too serious, I can assure you that on the first morning when I opened, Wes Hall wasn't holding anything back."

In the 1964 Wisden, photographs of Reynolds and Crump headed the County's annual review. Both Brians featured in the game against Lancashire at Old Trafford in May that year, when Brian Reynolds played, what many pundits consider, his best innings. Lancashire had gained a first innings lead, after Ramadhin (48-17-82-5) had exercised his mysterious control; most of the Northamptonshire batsmen agreed with Clive Lloyd, it was "baffling and unreadable spin." Brian had been lbw Ramadhin for 16. Steele had top scored with 72.

In the second knock Brian was again out lbw, (the umpires were Fred Jakeman and Ron Lay) but this time to Statham, and not before he had reached a blistering 141. He mastered an attack with Statham and Higgs for starters and Ramadhin the main course. One journalist spoke of "his driving being a delight to the eye," and he was particularly severe on the West Indian spinner (15-0-74-1). He had swept and driven him for two fours in an over to complete his fifty and then smashed a huge six on the leg side. The little man's "intricacies" (Cowdrey's word) no longer bemused. "To be fair, he was coming to the end of his career, but it was still difficult to pick which way it was going. So I aimed to get there before it dropped." His 141 included a century before lunch, and you don't get many of them to the pound.

There are many stories about pre-match rituals. Some involve food, such as Mike Gatting's cheese and pickle sandwiches. There are conflicting accounts of events prior to this Old Trafford game, but a pie is central. It seems Brian agreed to travel to Manchester with the Staffordshire cousins, Messrs Crump and Steele, having heard of the invitation to have lunch with the Crump parents en route. "You will not taste a finer steak and kidney pie anywhere in the British Empire", Steele had assured Kettering's ace trencherman. He was right and Reynolds duly tucked in, as he did later to Ramadhin. He was still going strong, when Crump junior ("the wretched Crump" as MJK Smith christened him) flaked out mid-course. BLR ignored the hosts' stricken son, aware of his hypochondria, finished his own pie and then the wretched Crump's, not wishing it to go to waste. That's the, uncorroborated, Steele version.

There's a mutual respect between Reynolds and Steele, both dedicated professionals who always gave their all in the cause of the team. But as so often happens with professional sportsmen, the respect is frequently hidden within pointed anecdotes. Brian, who continues to grow high quality beans, can remember the time they went missing. "Angela and I were away for a few days one year, just about the time the beans should have been at their best. We suggested

The coach at work. Watched by Brian Crump, Tony Durose and (right) Bert Lightfoot, Brian demonstrates to an earnest young Steele how to bowl both the stock delivery (above) and the wrong 'un (below).

to my father-in-law that he should help himself. When we got back, I saw they were gone and asked him if he'd enjoyed them. He said he'd come round to pick them and there were none there. At the time the Steeles lived close to us and it turned out he'd been round. 'I knew you were on holiday and I didn't want them to go to waste', he told me." Again, uncorroborated.

Tales of opportunism and waste. There were no wasted opportunities from Reynolds and Steele in 1964. David began to emerge as "a more than useful all-rounder", while Brian cemented his reputation as one of the best openers in the country. He scored 1,467 runs in the Championship. David maintains that Brian would surely have been 'capped' for England, had he been playing in recent years. Perhaps the closest he came was his selection as twelfth-man for the final three days of the first Test against Australia, at Trent Bridge in June. Coincidentally, the venue of his first youthful visit to a Test. He spent some time on the field after Boycott injured his hand. The other original opener, John Edrich, was pronounced unfit just an hour before play was due to start and Fred Titmus filled the breach.

His obdurate 113 against Warwickshire in 1963 was followed by 112 against them in 1964, dismissed, on both occasions, by Rudi Webster, the Barbadian who represented Scotland whilst studying medicine and later became an important member of the West Indian administration. This time, however, Northamptonshire won by 64 runs. Milburn and Reynolds set them on course with an opening stand of 176 in just over two and a half hours. The same pair led the way in a ten wicket win over Middlesex, hitting 188 in 150 minutes of exhilarating stroke-play (Reynolds 81, Milburn 104). Brian also played a key role in wins over Leicestershire (56 not out), Gloucestershire (65 and 52), Somerset (47 and 62) and Leicestershire again (80).

In the tourist match he was twice dismissed by McKenzie (29 and 38), one of Wisden's five cricketers of that year. The Australians 436 included 84 from Bob Cowper, who fed pleasurably on the phantom off spin of BL Reynolds. His remorse at falling lbw remains to this day. He should have heeded the warning of the poet William Cowper, written not that far from Wantage Road, of "Remorse, the fatal egg by pleasure laid." The wicket (his fourth and last) gave Brian almost as much pleasure as one of Angela's beef curries. Three of the four were in tourist matches and were Test players. His only Championship wicket had come a year earlier, Somerset's Peter Wight caught by Larter ("nobody else would have reached it") in front of the old scoreboard at Northampton. Wight, from what was then British Guiana, served Somerset for thirteen seasons and was a first-class umpire for thirty years. He never played a Test match, those others of that ilk did, which was unfortunate not just for the man himself, but also for Brian. It meant that in his bowling career, only 75% of the victims were Test players.

Brian's two centuries and nine fifties played their part in helping Northamptonshire rise to third place in the table. During the winter he was out and about spreading the message. It was "a great team effort" was what the members of Overstone Park, themselves winners of the Third Section of the Northampton League, heard at their annual dinner. "We think we have a good enough side to bring the Championship to Northamptonshire." The fare wasn't entirely bland. "Poor fielding probably cost Northamptonshire the title," was the message to Billing. "In all my years in top-class cricket I have never seen so many poor pitches. They were a disgrace to county cricket," he continued. "People like to see the ball struck and they want to see the batsmen score runs." Ever the diplomat he commented on the things that had impressed him about the Billing club, "the team spirit, the abundance of young players, and the 'livewire' secretary, Mr John Malfait.

It wasn't all dinners. Fashionable then as means of fund-raising for charity was the pile of pennies (and the knocking down of). The photograph extracted from the Evening Telegraph shows the deed being done at a Kettering pub.

Knocking down a pile of pennies at The Piper, Windmill Avenue, Kettering, on Wednesday is Northamptonshire county cricketer Brian Reynolds. With him is the landlord, Mr. F. Lewis. The pennies are in aid of Kettering's old people.

A similar event, at the Rose and Crown in Rushden, merited a preview ("Mr HW Catlin, Headmaster of Rushden Secondary School for Boys, has been asked to be present") as well as the report and picture of the event. The Chronicle and Echo also gave extensive coverage. The Telegraph recorded: "Brian Reynolds, Northamptonshire opening batsman, knocked down a pile of pennies for the spastics, worth £14 6s 6d, at the Rose and Crown, High Street, Rushden, last night. It took about half an hour for four people to count the pennies, which went all over the floor and not in a blanket provided." Bert Catlin's opinion was not reported, though Mrs Catlin, like Mrs Reynolds, was presented with a bouquet.

It was all good practice for 1965, the benefit season.

B L Reynolds b Marner 5

Benefit match, Kettering, 1965

1965 - 1966

"When you confer a benefit on a worthy man, you oblige all men."
Publilius Syrus

Second best

The Beneficiary

A mug's game

On Sunday

"A tribute to one of Northamptonshire's sons who has brought nothing but credit to his town and county, both on and off the sporting arenas." KV Andrew

127

One title stands out above all others among the cricket books on my shelves, maybe on account of its white dust jacket: Jack Fingleton's 'Cricket in Crisis'. Its presence is a reminder of Gerald Smith, to whom it belonged before his untimely death. Alongside his devoted wife Elsie, Gerald was a loyal supporter of Northamptonshire cricket and an admirer of Brian Reynolds. Like Brian, he enjoyed his classical music, stood for integrity on and off the field, and was himself a gentleman. In EW Swanton's phrase, "a sort of a cricket person".

Fingleton's book is also a reminder that cricket always seems in crisis, as a glance at the titles in a catalogue of cricket books quickly confirms. The 1960s were no exception. In 1965, aged 35, Brian Statham took 137 wickets, at 12.53, but said the principal reason for his success had been "the atrocious pitches." That same year Norman Preston wrote that the game was being "tarnished by squabbles and petty tactics." There were controversies over throwing, intimidatory 'bumpers', and cheap practices. Attendances at Championship games continued their decline to 659,560 in 1965, influenced, according to some commentators, by the prevalence of medium-pace bowling on sub-standard wickets against static batsmen. And in Northamptonshire, ladies were still advised to use the lavatory before they came to the County Ground.

A cricket crisis, however, is no more conclusive than Sherlock Holmes's plunge over the Reichenbach Falls. Indeed, for Northamptonshire and its senior professional, 1965 was "as happy as the grass was green" Well, almost. The Club was second in the Championship, with the run-in to the title as tense as it gets. Worcestershire finally triumphed, by a mere four points, after beating Hampshire and Sussex while Northamptonshire waited and wondered, their season having ended on August 24.

Among the season's oddities, which included controversial declarations involving Northamptonshire and, at the death, Worcestershire, was the absence of any consistent, gilt-edged individual performances. True, Brian Crump had one of his best seasons, with 784 runs and 112 wickets, otherwise it was a combined effort suggesting that cricket is a team game after all. Four players reached just over a thousand runs (Jim Watts 1,166, Reynolds 1,146, Steele 1,145 and Prideaux 1,098) and there were only four centuries (Reynolds, Steele, Milburn, Norman). Crump alone took a hundred wickets, though other bowlers produced magic spells.

Wisden's summary of Northamptonshire's season stresses one of the game's frequent truths - it's a team game. "Strangely," reports the 103rd edition of the almanack, "this summer which so nearly brought the title to Northamptonshire was to a large degree one of mediocre performances individually, which perhaps stressed that it was a team effort controlled admirably by the captain, Andrew."

Justification for the charge of mediocrity is that "only four centuries were hit". That's four - three more than Warwickshire, two more than Derby, Hants and Notts, one more than Essex. Leicestershire scored ten and finished fourteenth. If "Crump alone took 100 wickets" is intended to be an indictment of the bowling, perhaps it should be pointed out that no county had more than two hundred-wickets men (one of these was Nottinghamshire, who finished last) and six had none at all.

Brian Reynolds contributed significantly in a number of games, including his side's top score of 59 in a dismal May encounter against Middlesex. Any watching administrators, already despairing of cricket's future, must have crept back to the Lord's committee rooms. The scoring rate did not quite reach two and a quarter per over, even though the over-rate was over twenty an hour. And why not now? Fred Titmus's match figures were 58-34-65-7. That's partly why not. Brian knew Fred well, having also played golf with him on many occasions. "He was a class bowler, with terrific control and the ability to drift it away. No off-spinner will succeed unless they can do that." Like Brian, he came into the game, and stayed in it, because he loved it, playing from 1949 to 1980.

Brian was the game's top scorer in Northamptonshire's first win of 1965, against Warwickshire at Peterborough in June. His 75 on another unsavoury wicket was the foundation of victory. 59 in the next match against Sussex was followed by 62 against Essex, when David Steele notched his first century for the Club, "praiseworthy more for lack of error than quality of stroke," according to one churlish reporter. Error-free performers, especially in defence, make for successful sides. Ask Bill Shankly. Ask Brian about David and he'll tell you of "the complete pro, who loved the game. He had the ideal temperament. Nothing bothered him. If the ball went by his eyebrows, he pulled his cap down and got on with it. I wish we had a few more like him." He was also, recalls Brian, a bit of a home handyman at one time. "He used to keep coming round to borrow my drill. Then I didn't see him for a while. When I did eventually see him again, I asked him if he'd finished all the work. 'No', he replied, 'but I've found someone with a better drill'!"

Also in June, Somerset were beaten by 113 runs, Brian hitting 117, with eighteen fours. Bill Alley replied with 110, but everyone else struggled on the seemingly inevitable frisky pitch. In July, Brian (58), Milburn and Steele built a total sufficient to hammer Nottinghamshire by an innings at Trent Bridge. The game against New Zealand was drawn; Brian top-scored in the second dig with 48. He repeated the feat in a low scoring Gillette Cup victory against Gloucestershire, before the team's shame-faced exit (all out 97) against Surrey in the next round.

The Gillette was soon forgotten, the Championship was everything. At the end of May though, it seemed as if the Gillette was the only hope. Northants were bottom and winless, but on June 1st, they won their first match, trouncing Warwickshire at Peterborough. The Crawthorne Road ground was not renowned for the high quality of its pitches - "it lived up to its reputation for helping the faster men" - but by the time Brian was out for his 75, caught by Warwickshire's later Chief Executive, Dennis Amiss, off Michael Mence (not one of the faster men), the visitors' 131 had been left well behind.

There was a setback against Sussex and a rain-affected draw against Essex despite a second innings 59 in the former and a first innings 62 in the latter from Brian. Mediocre? Next, at Edgbaston, a pair of 31s contributed to the team's second eight wicket victory over Warwickshire. The charge was on.

"We knew we weren't a bad team, certainly nothing like a bottom of the table side. Somehow we found it difficult to get going. We started at Derby - there was rain - and found it slow at Lord's. At Gravesend there was a heatwave but once we got a victory under our belts we all felt better."

Wisden's accusation of mediocrity looks more difficult to refute when one searches for outstanding batting performances. But in low scoring games it was the bowlers who won the points. Consider the early August fixture against title contenders Glamorgan at the Arms Park. Northants won by 18 runs; no innings reached 200. Northants had a half-century in each innings (David Steele and Jim Watts); Glamorgan had just one (Peter Walker). Twenties and thirties were valuable; it was a bowlers game. Don Shepherd aggregated 65-35-83-11 and was the outstanding bowler but Brian Crump who bowled unchanged for three and a half hours in the second innings (which lasted three and a half hours) took an aggregate eight (for a total of 142 in 76.3 overs), Jim Watts four for 43 in the first innings and Albert Lightfoot, "almost unplayable" three for 24 in 20 second innings overs.

"We knew when we won that game that we would never have a better chance of winning the title" is the straightforward Reynolds assessment following a game which Andrew described in print as, "I am sure, the greatest match ever played by Northamptonshire." The Glamorgan match had been preceded by a visit to Clacton, a much happier one from Bronk than his 1959. His contribution was not outstanding but useful - 22 and two catches - in a match notable for Trevor Bailey's controversial declaration after Essex had saved the follow-on. Northants second innings lasted one ball (nobody had thought of the now obvious idea of forfeiting an innings) and Essex, set 146 in two and a half hours, collapsed to Crump and Malcolm Scott for 88.

Returning from Cardiff to Wellingborough, Notts were polished off by ten wickets (Brian 49, 27*), Kent went under at Wantage Road and Lancashire succumbed at Old Trafford inside two days. Northamptonshire stood at the top of the table with 138 points and two games left. Glamorgan were second with 110 points and five matches left, third were Worcestershire on 104 with four matches to play. The maximum points per match was ten - for a win. There were no other complications except for the two points awarded for first innings lead in matches drawn or lost. Northamptonshire's penultimate fixture was at Worcester. A win for Northamptonshire would leave Worcestershire too far behind. This was the crunch, the big one, the decider. Northants lost.

Post-match wisdom, and Wisden, thought that "Northamptonshire must have regretted omitting their off-break bowler, Haydn Sully, in favour of Larter, for not only did the pace man break down with a recurrence of muscle trouble after four overs on the first day, but the pitch favoured spin." Brian does not concur.

"There was no way you could leave 'Fred' out. He was a matchwinner. And it was a lively pitch, dangerous even. It certainly had Don Kenyon worried. It was flying all over the place. Even after Larter's injury, KV kept bowling him. He was still faster than anyone else."

The scorecard certainly confirms Kenyon's distaste for the pitch, c Reynolds b Larter 0. Worcestershire gained a first innings lead (217 against 211) and then dismissed Northants for 130. Jim Watts was the star, adding 55 to his first innings 67. Second best was Brian, who ground out 25 before falling to Doug Slade, who finished with five for 16. "It wasn't the first time he'd done well against us. But it wasn't so much a spinner's wicket as a bowler's wicket. They had to get 125 and we thought we were in with a chance, especially when Don went for a pair."

However, without Larter, Worcester reached the target in the 56th over. Three Test batsmen got them there, Ron Headley 34, Tom Graveney 45* and Basil d'Oliveira 33*. Worcester's slow left armers had taken eight for 72 in the second innings, the Northants pair took one for 62. Victory kept Worcestershire's hopes alive but a win over Gloucestershire at Wantage Road, Northants' last match, would have brought the title to Northampton.

It rained. It rained until nearly five o'clock on the first day. Andrew won the toss and Milburn opened. He batted into the second day; he batted for a total of three and a half hours and was 152 not out when Andrew declared at 227 for five. But Arthur Milton with "just as valuable, if more sedate batting" was Gloucester's backbone. There were two more declarations and the visitors were possibly favourites at 87 for one when the rain cut short their chase for 181 and Northants' quest for the ten points that would have finished off Worcestershire. The early finish allowed the groundstaff a little longer to prepare the County Ground for the following evening's Division One opener against Arsenal. The news from Worcester was not encouraging; Surrey were beaten by an innings.

Now the destination of title was in the hands of Worcestershire or the weather. Northamptonshire could only sit and wait - or play golf. Worcester made an ominously good start at Bournemouth, Headley and Graveney both registered centuries and Len Coldwell had Roy Marshall out before the close of play. More than half the second day was lost to rain; as the barometer fell, Northamptonshire hopes rose.

"I played golf at Kettering with KV on the Friday morning. We were sure it would be a draw. After we'd finished, he came home with me. We turned the wireless on and waited for the lunchtime scoreboard." As soon as Hampshire had saved the follow-on, their captain, Colin Ingleby-Mackenzie, declared. "I shall always remember Keith's reaction. 'I can't believe he's declared!' I suppose, though, it wasn't all that surprising. Ingleby-Mackenzie had a reputation for being a gambler - though perhaps that's not the word to use these days!"

Kenyon declared at 0-0 and set Hampshire 147 in 160 minutes. They lasted 99 balls, Coldwell took five for 22, Jack Flavell five for 9 and were all out 31.

Worcestershire travelled east along the south coast to Hove. Northamptonshire's hopes went west. Flavell's first innings seven for 26 gave Worcester the upper hand and despite John Snow's best efforts, Worcester inched their way towards their target of 132 in 260 minutes. It took over 70 overs - and they had been 70 for five - but a four wicket victory appeared in print. Two years previously neither Northamptonshire nor Worcestershire had won the Championship, now it was 2-0 to Worcester.

In 1965, the Championship was decided with poor pitches and allegations of collusion. In 1999, Derbyshire lost to Hampshire in such a way that both gained places in the new Division One. Warwickshire were squeezed into Division Two and complained about the collusion. Warwickshire had won their last match in two days, the losers, Sussex, were thus consigned to Division Two. Their captain, Chris Adams, took a dim view of the Edgbaston pitch; the phrase "blatant cheating" appears in Wisden. The world keeps turning.

1965, in case it has been forgotten, was Brian's benefit year. He had been on the staff for fifteen years and a 'capped' player for nine of them. The benefit has remained vital to the county cricketer and with diligent organisation, innovative thinking and sheer hard work, the sums raised have swollen. The comparison has been drawn between two off spinners: Jim Laker, probably the best ever, and Jack Simmons, county stalwart but Test standard only as a trencherman in the Reynolds mould. Jack could eat fish and chips for England. It is believed that over thirteen years Laker made a total of around £26,000, from Test match fees, his county salaries, and a benefit of £11,000 in 1956. (Dennis Brookes received £3,280 in 1958). In 1980, however, Simmons made £120,000 from his benefit alone.

Another Lancastrian, Cyril Washbrook, had set records in 1948 with a £14,000 benefit, achieved through well organised activities, merchandising, and circa £4,000 from his county's game against Australia. In contrast, one year earlier, Northamptonshire's Reg Partridge had received £1,476 and, a year later, Jack Timms £1,650. In those days it mattered which county you played for.

Long before Washbrook, Laker and Simmons, Syrus said "to hope for a benefit was to sell one's freedom" and counties knew this ensured player loyalty, in the meanest sense. At one time, benefits were a hazardous business. Players had to find match expenses, whatever the weather. Insurance against loss was possible, but premiums were expensive. The old joke about the player who, when asked if he wished for another benefit, said "Thanks all the same, but I can't afford it," sadly carries some truth. AW Shipman of Leicestershire lost £60 on his benefit.

Harold Gimblett had a similar experience. Whereas Lancashire had granted Washbrook his request to have the Australian match, Somerset refused Harold's for the Gloucester game. His benefit came in 1952, after completing 20,000 runs and reaching 2,000 in a season for the second time. Instead of Gloucestershire he was offered - you've guessed it - Northamptonshire. Brian played in the fixture at Glastonbury, when Harold made a glorious 104 after Freddie Brown had taken seven for 33 in Somerset's first innings. Unfortunately, his monetary achievements were less spectacular: "there was an excellent raffle which brought in nearly £500 and thank goodness it did. In those days the beneficiary had to defray all the expenses. We played for three full days but my net profit from the match itself was between £7 and £8."

Harold Gimblett was an outstanding talent, who deserved reward for loyal service. A benefit, after all, is a kind of deferred payment, which lures many players to stay in the game. That was especially so after the House of Lords' judgment in Seymour v Reed in 1927, which made them tax exempt.

Brian was luckier than Harold in being allowed the local 'derby', against Leicestershire. Better still, it was on his home town ground in June. Northamptonshire won by 142 runs in a game of three low totals; Jim Watts had the only fifty on either side and brother Peter's leg breaks brought him five for 46. Brian was lbw to John Cotton, a pace bowler recently moved from Nottinghamshire, who finished the season with 76 wickets at 21.42 and did the hat-trick at the Oval. Peter Marner, another import, did him in the first innings for 5 - "one glorious boundary stroke after the traditional single afforded to batsmen in their benefit game", chronicled Alan Ford in the Green 'Un. It was "a push past point" that got Brian off the mark and then, "square-cutting with a powerful punch from shoulders and wrist, Reynolds took a boundary off Marner's first ball."

Brian tossed up with Maurice Hallam. Later coach at Uppingham School, he sent the likes of Jonathan Agnew and James Whitaker to his old County. They agreed to toss up several times for the benefit of the photographers. Maurice called "heads" correctly each time. "The next one's for real," said Brian. Maurice stuck with heads, this time incorrectly. Some days, Maurice, are good days, others. . .

The pair had remarkably similar careers. Both made their first-class debuts in 1950, both finished in 1970, both became coaches. Both played only for the County of their birth.

Hallam lost both the toss and the match, Northants successful by 142 runs.

Early in the match, as the beneficiary stretches forward, the members' area on the brook side of the Kettering ground was far less well populated than the benches beneath the poplars at the bottom of the railway embankment. The second spectator from the left is 'Nip' Collier, Brian's schooldays contemporary from The Oval. Cec Pepper, once targeted by Northants, observes.

The big cities still have their Saturday night sports papers. Northampton's 'Green Un' and Kettering's 'Pink Un' both disappeared long ago. Reproduced from its original green page, is this illuminating view of Bronk's Benefit Saturday.

In 1965 the benefit match was not the only source of revenue, although there was no 'benefit committee' working on Brian's behalf, as is the current practice. The brochure was not an elaborate production; the fourth, and last, page listed the events.

FUNCTIONS AND MATCHES ARRANGED IN THE BENEFIT SEASON

APRIL 9   **DANCE at EARLS BARTON**

MAY 30   **EARLS BARTON C.C.,** Earls Barton
2.0 p.m. to 7.0 p.m.

JUNE 6   **ROSS GROUP C.C.,** Grimsby
2.30 p.m. to 7.0 p.m.
or 7.30 p.m.

JULY 4   **PETERBOROUGH UNITED F.C.,** Peterboro'
2.0 p.m. to 7.0 p.m.

JULY 9   **BARBEQUE AT WELDON**

JULY II   **WELDON C.C.,** Weldon   2.0 p.m. to 7.0 p.m.

AUG. 8   **SYMINGTONS C.C.,** Market Harborough
2.0 p.m. to 7.0 p.m.

AUG. 22   **LEIGHTON BUZZARD C.C.,** Leighton Buzzard
2.0 p.m. to 7.0 p.m.

Benefit Ties

Thirteen shillings and sixpence.

Autographed Tankards

Five shillings

The mugs caused Brian a little consternation. He ordered five gross (for the benefit of those without access to the back of a Silvine exercise book, 720), but instead, for a reason never explained, 1,620 were delivered (that's eleven and a quarter gross).

Wags in the national press enjoyed the predicament ("bit of a mug, eh?", 'Daily Mirror'), but the publicity helped shift them. Those who wanted one, the local press helpfully stated, "should contact Brian at the County Ground, where he coaches boys in the indoor cricket school, every day between 4.30 pm and 6 pm."

It was also a hectic time socially and in fund raising for others. He continued to speak at dinners, present awards and receive them, help with charitable functions, and demolish piles of pennies on pub bars. The benefit is recorded as raising £3,886 (annual membership of NCCC was £2 10s). Keith Andrew said it "paid tribute to one of Northamptonshire's sons who has brought nothing but credit to his town and county, both on and off the sporting arenas". Amen to that.

After the heady heights of third and second in the two previous years, fifth place in the Championship in 1966 seemed more than a stumble. It was Keith Andrew's last season and a tribute to his reign was that the expectation of honours was feasible. Hindsight support for this was the double defeat of Yorkshire, the eventual Champions. In the first, at Headingley in July, Brian was Northamptonshire's leading scorer with a notable 72 in a game of feeble totals. There was also a useful contribution to the four wicket victory over a powerful West Indies side, the second such - the first had been in 1933. In the second innings he was caught by Charlie Griffith off Lance Gibbs, "a really top notch bowler". Griffith, who bowled Brian in the first, had been called by Arthur Fagg in May for throwing. Umpire and bowler both suffered criticism, not least from former Test players. Brian is more charitable: "He probably threw his bouncer, but so do some other fast bowlers."

Brian had had another encounter with CC Griffith during the previous tour by the West Indies, while batting with Mick Norman. Charlie had been rumbling along, bowling within himself, when one stood up. Norman nicked it, Gibbs, at slip, tipped it over the bar and it flew to the old pavilion for four. Charlie was riled, slipped into top gear and let rip. At the end of the over Mick, having turned even paler than usual, said to Brian, "I can't understand it, he seems five yards quicker." Brian agreed, before adding, "You've stirred him up, so you can stay at that end." MEJC Norman b Griffith 18.

Brian played a central part in several other victories in 1966. In May, Lancashire were beaten on an awkward wicket, under-prepared during April's showers. Reynolds (56 not out) and Mushtaq Mohammad ensured a seven wicket win via a rapid stand of 109. In June, he made 60 and 67 as Nottinghamshire sank by 245 runs. Prideaux made a century in both innings, the first Northamptonshire batsman to do so since Brookes in 1946. Brian's hard-hitting 57 was the side's top score as they beat Leicestershire by 80 runs (Lock 23-13-33-5). In Leicestershire's first innings, Mick Norman recorded 102 for his new county: only to be expected really. To emphasise the point, it was August, but the first century of the season on the Northampton ground.

Brian also performed creditably against Kent (65 and 89) in a 77 run success and at Worcester (74 not out), but was rock 'n' rolled over against Oxford University, bowled by Richard Elviss (Leeds Grammar, not Gracelands) for 11. 'All shook up' by the swing presumably.

There were experiments in 1966; two met at Northampton when Somerset were the visitors on June 11, 12 and 13. In twelve Championship matches, the first innings were restricted to 65 overs; June 12th was a Sunday. There were still problems with the law which didn't allow admission to be charged on Sundays. Some clubs admitted by programme (or scorecard) only, some members only (instant day membership available) and some complied with the law by having a gate through which the public could walk free of charge (but it wasn't necessarily easy to find). The tide was moving rapidly against the Lord's Day Observance Society. In 1966 there was play on three Sundays at Wantage Road, in 1967 all home Saturday Championship games continued on Sunday.

On May 21st of 1966, taking advantage of a rare free Saturday, Brian won the Kettering Golf Club Championship. Rounds of 74 and 77 secured the title. At his best, his handicap was three; twice more, in the seventies, he won the Kettering Club's Championship.

Ask him a hypothetical question about whether he would, in this day and age, have become a professional cricketer and golfer and he says little. Yet the implications for cricket in the twenty-first century are obviously exercising his mind.

Brian was finally third in the County's run stealers, ahead of Steele and Mushtaq, but behind Prideaux and Milburn. Aged 34, he was probably still the fittest on the staff and had played in every game; Crump, the alleged hypochondriac, was the only other ever-present. He'd scored a total of 1,323 first-class runs and held another 22 catches. Brian had now played in 354 first-class matches in seventeen seasons. He was to play another 75 in the remaining four, and deserved more.

B L Reynolds run out 11

Grace Road, August 16 1970

1967 - 1970

"Farewell happy fields,
Where joy for ever dwells."
John Milton,
'Paradise Lost'

Prideaux

Longevity

Through an umpire's eyes

Some mistake, surely

"You play better when you feel you're wanted."

Brian played under five Northamptonshire captains and, rather like the five act 'well-made play', some say there was a foreseeable inevitability about the conclusion. Of course, as Thomas Nashe said, "Everything hath an end, and a pudding hath two", but it wasn't just that. His benefit year had gone; Prideaux and Milburn were now the regular openers and Brian had no fixed home in the batting order; he was 34 years old; and Keith Andrew's retirement brought down the curtain on Act four. Whether the final curtain needed to fall in 1970, however, was another question altogether.

If the end of Brian's playing career was inevitable, so was the appointment, in 1967, of Roger Prideaux as Andrew's successor. The captaincy sequence demanded a Cambridge man and fate had lined him up since his runs for the University against the County. He was also, in Brian's words, "A very fine player. A big man, he could play all round the wicket." An attack of shingles in mid-season was the only reason he missed 2,000 runs in 1967. There were mixed views about his captaincy, though in his first year of office, he could hardly be blamed for the team's drop from fifth to ninth position in the Championship. Larter retired; Malcolm Scott had an unfortunate season through injury and suspicions about his bowling action; Mushtaq and Milburn had Test calls; and the foul weather hit Northamptonshire harder than most. It really was, allegedly, the wettest May since 1733. The counties even talked of beginning the season a fortnight later and extending it into September. In the year 2000, the season began on April 7 and ended on September 17, though this was more to do with the resurrected Benson and Hedges Cup than global warming.

Disciples of Lord McLaurin were probably taken aback by the B&H rising from the ashes (you might say). Most of them claiming to see sense in his advocacy of the 'pyramid' structure for cricket, would find interest in MCC Secretary, SC Griffith's, 1967 speech to the county secretaries. In it, he urged the counties to interest themselves more in club cricket and the club cricketer. "I would like to see club cricketers given their chance alongside the Cowdreys, the Graveneys, the Titmuses, and so on." Northamptonshire did exactly that at the end of July, probably from necessity, when Brian captained the side as they defeated Middlesex by 79 runs. Playing against "the Titmuses and, so on" was John Minney (Oundle and Cambridge) born in Finedon and a gifted club cricketer. He was Northamptonshire's highest scorer in the match with a swift 58, as Titmus held sway with seven for 78 in 47 overs. Two other locally-born players also contributed effectively in a game of low scores. Roy Wills, who opened with Brian, made 37 and Peter Lee (14-4-30-2). The fourth, the skipper, was run out for 0. Roy, who has been associated with the county club for close on forty years, had obeyed his captain's call. In 737 first-class innings, Brian was run out twenty-six times. What conclusions can be drawn from that are best left to the actuary and Ladbroke's.

It is worth noting that SC Griffith made other observations that were echoed by McLaurin and his gurus some thirty years later. He argued that County Clubs were carrying staffs that were too large and saw this, not only as a financial burden (top performers could then be paid more) but as an opportunity to play club cricketers, if there were fewer professionals. It was around this time, incidentally, that the Editor of Wisden commented on another idea that was being mooted yet again: "I can imagine nothing more dreary than a four-day county match," (as opposed to three).

It is arguable that four-day captaincy requires less decision making than three-day. Brian has no criticism of Prideaux's captaincy, but found him sometimes "a bit dour". He recalled an incident against Sussex, centred on Laurie Johnson, who had succeeded Andrew as keeper with considerable aplomb. The ball had been skied to a surprising height, followed by Laurie's bellowed "Mine". Fielders duly scattered, as Laurie stood first in splendid isolation and then began to rotate, eyes on the swirling ball. He finally collapsed on his back, an outstretched glove at least a foot from where the ball eventually landed. Farce has universal appeal and everyone present fell about with laughter except 'Prid', whose curt, "I can't see anything to laugh at," only provoked further hilarity.

Brian missed just one Championship game in 1967, finishing with 1166 runs at an average of just under 30. Again, it was fewer than Prideaux and Milburn, but more than Mushtaq and Steele. His highest score was a century against Somerset at Northampton (when everyone else missed out) in three hours forty minutes, hitting two sixes and fourteen fours. It saved the game for Northamptonshire. A captain's innings, at the time he was deputising for the injured Prideaux.

He had nine scores of fifty or more, and others in the forties that were significant. For exámple, in May, after Kent amassed a large total, Northamptonshire collapsed on a spiteful wicket against Derek Underwood (38.1-17-72-6). Only Steele (39) and Reynolds (43), and the rain, prevented an innings defeat. No such luck with his 48 ("a courageous effort", wrote Michael Booth in 'The Daily Telegraph') in a hammering from Yorkshire, built around an undefeated 220 from Geoff Boycott. Brian's sentiments reflect those of many others: "You have to admire what he achieved as a player, whatever you think about him otherwise." Milburn was the only other successful batsman in that match. Is there any other game that can host such contrasting personnel as Milburn and Boycott?

In 1967, Brian's personal performances influenced - directly and positively - the course of over half Northamptonshire's games. A case in point was 82 against Warwickshire, which helped to achieve first innings lead just three hours from the end of a high scoring contest. Warwick had declared at the end of the first day on 411 for six. Northants eventually overhauled them and gained six points; if they'd declared behind and forced a victory, the reward was only eight points. Another short-lived system.

Where some days needed to be dour days of graft, others found him "going for his shots with spectacular results," (Fred Speakman). Among them, his 86 and 51 against Derbyshire (with Harold Rhodes), 55 against Sussex (with John Snow and Co.) and 53 against Gloucestershire (with John Mortimore and David Allen). His 76 against Leicestershire and 51 against Lancashire at Old Trafford (Statham again, six for 58) both came to nothing in the rain. No surprise, perhaps, that it rained in Manchester. Earlier in the year three consecutive three-day matches at Old Trafford were abandoned without a ball being bowled; the next match was switched to Southport. In the return fixture against Lancashire at Wellingborough, he top scored with 61 in a five wicket defeat, after Prid's declaration had proved a little generous. This time Ken Shuttleworth did the damage.

He had batted consistently in a season of Northamptonshire inconsistencies, often at his resolute best while others struggled. It is indisputable that he could smack it about with the best, but his technical excellence and commitment in difficult circumstances, is more meritorious. There is no self aggrandisement when he says: "As senior professional it was part of my responsibilities to set an example, never to throw it away."

Someone who would have appreciated that remark was Emmott Robinson, who died in 1969. Cardus described him as "richly endowed by native qualities of character, and gave himself, heart and soul with shrewd intelligence, to Yorkshire cricket. That's why he is remembered yet; that's why no statistics can get to the value of him." He might have said the same about Brian Reynolds, substituting the Tudor rose for the white. Cardus also tells an amusing tale that illustrates the art of understanding and coping with rain-affected wickets. On an occasion at Headingley, after heavy rain was replaced by hot sun, Emmott and Wilfred Rhodes went out to inspect the pitch. Rhodes pressed it with his finger, "It'll be sticky at four o'clock, Emmott." Then Robinson bent down and also pressed the wicket. "No, Wilfred," he said, "half past."

In his account of the Northamptonshire's victory at Cardiff in August 1965, Stephen Chalke described Brian as the "no-nonsense senior professional", quoting Keith Andrew as saying, "He was the sergeant-major for me. He made my job so much easier". Chalke also wrote that you would have "a great player, if you could combine Brian's determination with Micky Norman's stylish talent." An opinion that begs many questions.

Preferable to many is David Steele's linking of the three Brians: "Brian ('Tonker') Taylor, 'the Wad', and Closey." Now, what a player that combination would make. There'd be no doubts your platoon would make it through the jungle.

There are interesting comparisons between Messrs Reynolds and Close around this time. In 1968, the Yorkshireman played in twenty-two games, scoring 536 runs at an average of 24.36. 'The Wad' played in twenty Championship matches, scored 864 runs, average 28.80. Their careers coincided between 1949 and 1970, when Close appeared 536 times for Yorkshire. In 1971 he moved to Somerset, and a second prosperous period, playing and captaining until 1977, scoring another 7,567 runs (average 39.41) and taking 74 wickets on 142 matches. It is fanciful, of course, to push for too many clearcut parallels. For certain, however, both Brians were uncompromising, steadfast professionals, physically strong, in love with the game and its enduring principles, and wanted to play. True, Close played in twenty-two Tests, but many pundits believe that Brian at his peak might well have 'done a Steele' at international level, given the chance. Why then did Close have seven more prime years as a player than Brian? Was it simply because Close left his native Yorkshire, whereas it was impossible to imagine Brian playing for anyone else? Ironically, the same had been said about Close.

It's worth a glimpse at other details of player longevity among those who entered the first-class arena around the same time as Brian. Why not start with Brian Taylor, who played 539 games for Essex between 1949 and 1973. Don Shepherd of Glamorgan recorded an astonishing 647 from 1950 to 1972. Four Gloucestershire stalwarts continued beyond 1970: John Mortimore 594 appearances (1950-1975); Arthur Milton 585 (1948-1974); Ron Nicholls 534 (1951-1975), and David Allen 349 (1953-1972). Colin Cowdrey played 412 times for Kent (1950-1975) plus the pressures of Tests and touring. Similarly, Titmus, but he still managed 642 appearances for Middlesex (and one for Surrey) between 1949 and 1982 and Jim Parks 561 for Sussex (1949-1972). Among contemporaries whose playing careers were lengthier than Brian's are: Don Kenyon (1946-67), John Murray (52-75), Peter Sainsbury (54-76), Derek Shackleton (48-69), Terry Spencer (52-74), and Ken Suttle (49-71).

The list proves nothing, but it suggests support for Brian's feeling that he could have played a positive role in the side for at least another two years. As it was, 1968 was the first season he had not been an automatic choice since 1955, when he'd played eleven games. From 1956 to 1967, he had missed only four games, out of a possible 308, in the Championship, excluding, of course, the broken leg year.

The absurdity is that his achievements in 1968 were more than respectable. Two of his best performances were in August. An undefeated 95 (batting at seven) against Lancashire, on a slow Blackpool pitch, was followed by 120 against Surrey, which virtually won the game, with ten balls remaining. For one correspondent it was "brilliant hitting"; another described "Reynolds receiving a standing ovation from members for some of the most masterly batting of the season." His third-wicket stand with Mushtaq (72) produced 152 in an hour and a half and put their side within seven runs of victory. Both fell to Mike Selvey, who opened with Robin Jackman, backed by Pat Pocock, Graham Roope and Ken Barrington (all Test players). Also, in August, he had a not out 48 against Essex and 47 and 33 against Kent, (undone by Underwood, five for 54).

It was hardly the dying embers. In fact, he produced other commendable scores throughout the season. In May, his 57 against the Australians was Northamptonshire's top score in the second innings, as they lost by ten wickets. Ashley Mallett finished with seven for 75 and one report had it that "Reynolds alone mastered the attack." Another headline read, "Reynolds saves County's blushes."

That same month he opened with Milburn (53) and finished not out on 68, as Cheshire were overwhelmed at Macclesfield in the Gillette. In June, he produced 92 against Glamorgan and 60 against Warwickshire, then fifties in July - one of them in a thrashing by Lancashire, in which he was one of the few to offer any resistance to Shuttleworth, Ken Higgs, and Peter Lever. In the Gillette match against Sussex, in July, he received rave notices: his innings was called a "gem", full of "delightful shots". The local paper's reporter wrote: "his running between the wickets was good and he nursed along the impetuous Hylton Ackerman. Reynolds also made the Sussex fielders work all the time by offering to go for extra runs and then scampering back to the crease. It was an innings of great experience and professionalism. Unfortunately, this professionalism was wasted by the later batsmen." This was a player, remember, whom somebody, somewhere, had decided was about to become surplus to requirements. Had he been watching the cricket?

Some writers referred to 1968 as "tumultuous" for cricket: riots in Jamaica; the d'Oliveira affair that brought the cancellation of the MCC tour to South Africa; the introduction of overseas stars. At the Horton House Cricket Club dinner Tony

Nicholson, the Yorkshire bowler known as 'Uphill Nick' (he opened the bowling with Fred) lamented the introduction of overseas players to county cricket. He concluded, "If ever Yorkshire do away with a birthright qualification, county cricket will be dead." Doubtless Emmott, and Wilfred, Yorkshiremen personified, would have agreed. The implications of Nicholson's 'prophecy' are far reaching beyond what he could have imagined. As Sir Thomas Browne remarked, we should "study prophecies when they are become histories."

Yorkshiremen complaining about Northamptonshire being light on local-born players bring a wry smile to Brian's face. "It's always good to have locals if you can, but I remember, a long time ago, Dennis Brookes (a Yorkshireman) pointing out that the entire population of Northamptonshire was 100,000 fewer than Leeds."

Scattering the Aussies, 1968. Ashley Mallett is the bowler. The umpire is Hugo Yarnold, the former Worcestershire wicket-keeper who was killed in a road accident when driving home after officiating at Wellingborough in 1974

It's coincidental, if not ironic, that the 1969 Wisden included an article on the Kettering ground by Basil Easterbrook, while among its obituaries was that of Northamptonshire's Philip Wright who, in 1925, recorded his highest first-class score there. He was one of seven Kettering born Wrights who played for their county. In 1969, the Kettering fixture - Northamptonshire beat Middlesex by nine wickets in two days, on a wet wicket - was one of Brian's thirteen Championship appearances of the season. He scored 510 runs (average 26.84) and played several important knocks.

Among them top scores of 57 against Kent at Tunbridge Wells and 80 against Essex at Northampton. His forties included one in the Gloucestershire game, when Procter took eleven for 117. "Procky was a tremendous cricketer. The odd thing is that if you saw him as a young man, with his highly unorthodox action, you might have wondered about signing him." Later, Northamptonshire did sign him, but as 'Director of Cricket' for 1991.

In spite of half a dozen innings that proved Brian could still be a force in county cricket, it was clear the committee's black spot was on him. He had already been told he was no longer an automatic choice and of his replacement as senior professional by Brian Crump. No offence to Crump, but that must have hurt. "If people make their minds up, it doesn't matter what you do, " says Brian, before repeating a general truth, "you play better when you feel you're wanted and part of the set-up." It is not difficult to think of at least four Northamptonshire players who probably had similar thoughts at the end of the 1990s.

He was certainly "wanted" by supporters, former players, and the press, many of whom had criticised his omission since its first occurrence in 1968. Michael Tebbitt of 'The Chronicle and Echo' was bravely forthright on more than one occasion. In 1968 he had written: "Brian Reynolds should be found a regular first team place. A dedicated professional, he sets a perfect example to younger players, both on and off the field. He still has several years of first team cricket in him and it seems a pity that he should have lost his job as senior professional. Why, if Northamptonshire wanted to promote Crump, did they not appoint him vice-captain?" Keith Andrew was also supportive, talking of the "thought and endeavour" Brian put into his cricket. "One is urged to fight hard on the one hand and play shots on the other. If you play shots and get out, you are not fighting, and if you fight and don't play shots, you are not entertaining."

At a highly critical Annual General Meeting, one member praised Brian as "one of the most energetic, and if there were eleven fielders like him, the team would be higher." Arnold Payne, the Club's president, agreed: Reynolds "was the oldest member of the team and probably the fastest."

Indeed, there was universal agreement about his physical fitness and ability to be "the most forceful of batsmen" when the situation demanded, attributes invalidating the argument that he was unsuited to the feverish tempo of the John Player League's arrival in 1969. In the winter he played his golf and, when he worked for himself, would often fit in a quick round at the Wicksteed Park course with the green keeper, Fred Harrison. From the beginning of every January he embarked on a fitness programme, building to a peak in early April and pre-season training at the County Ground.

Someone else ideally suited to the Sunday League was Colin Milburn, but he only played in it thrice before losing an eye after a car accident. "It was tragic," says Brian, "obviously for Colin himself, but also for the game of cricket. A unique talent, he had the quickest reactions of any player I've ever seen." 'Ollie' made a comeback in 1973 but was never the same player. Occasionally he threatened to reproduce his old form. The crowd at Wellingborough for a John Player game was just getting excited when he was caught on the boundary. The catcher was his old opening partner, Roger Prideaux, then playing for Sussex under Tony Greig. Many present that day still maintain Prideaux was over the boundary. The game badly needed characters like Colin in 1969; in 2000 it is desperate for them.

"I'm not convinced everyone took the Sunday League seriously when it started", is Bronk's recollection of the early days of this competition. Starting at two o'clock and finishing at twenty to seven, it was designed to attract the family looking for an afternoon out, an aim seemingly forgotten as the matches have become longer and longer.

Pressed to reveal names, Brian remains tight-lipped, though "quite a few bowlers were unhappy about the run-up being restricted to fifteen yards. And quite a few weren't best pleased at having a restriction on the number of overs they could bowl."

At Northampton the early experience was rain. Nevertheless a 23 over thrash did produce a tight finish, though Glamorgan squeezed in by seven runs. At Trent Bridge, a nine wicket defeat, all out 132, had little to praise, though "the only occasion when the visitors showed any assurance was during a fifth-wicket partnership of 73 between Ackerman and Reynolds". Next on the agenda was Worcestershire, at Wantage Road, in front of the BBC2 cameras. Milburn retired ill, Brian perished near the end and Prideaux carried his bat for 68. Worcestershire made little attempt to get the 175 required. Tom Graveney came in at 42 for two; he was still there at the end of the 40 overs. Worcestershire were 108 for six, Graveney was on 18. "He doesn't understand the rules," was one of the politer comments from the West Stand, thwarted in their hope of seeing brighter cricket.

As Graveney led his side inexorably to defeat, a free-thinker in the West Stand predicted that one day someone would score a hundred in this League, a far-fetched vision which brought only derision to the soothsayer. In June Somerset's Greg Chappell, at Brislington, became the first. Five weeks later Somerset came to Northampton. Wicket-keeper Roy Virgin went for 1, Chappell for 0, both victims of David Larter who made a brief comeback, specifically for Sunday matches. But then, the West Stand watched it happen before their very eyes - the centurion, Tony Clarkson, later to become a first-class umpire.

There was no Reynolds in the opposition against Somerset, his last Sunday appearance of the season had been the previous week when his batting talents were not required in a nine wicket win at Hove. Ackerman and Peter Willey put on 162 in 98 minutes for the first wicket, an indication that players were beginning to get the drift of the John Player.

"One thing that was obvious early on," recalls Reynolds, "is that the travelling could be awkward. One Saturday we started a Championship game against Lancashire at Northampton. On the Sunday we went to Chesterfield and they went off somewhere. On the Monday morning we were all back at Northampton for the second day of the Championship match. The next week we played at Chelmsford on the Sunday, right in the middle of a Championship fixture at Lord's."

There had been a reduction of four Championship matches (twelve days) to accommodate the sixteen Sunday League matches but there were some lengthy spells without a day off. In the middle of July, Northamptonshire were scheduled to play on fifteen consecutive days, though the two-day victory over Middlesex at Kettering allowed them to rest on the fourteenth. Nowhere near the intensity of the

American baseball schedule but horrifying for the modern day "We don't want to play very often" brigade.

Tony Clarkson is at first slip as a lone admirer watches Reynolds on his way to 44 in the 1969 Championship fixture.

At the end of 1969, Haydn Sully and Malcolm Scott had left. at the end of 1969, Mike Kettle, Lightfoot and Prideaux in 1970. The side finished 1970 in fourteenth place in the Championship, thirteenth place in the John Player, fallen at the first hurdle in the Gillette Cup and lost £11,000 over the season. In the Chronicle & Echo, Michael Tebbitt was again strongly pro-Reynolds. Brian's first innings for the first team was not until May 31st. A week earlier, Tebbitt had written another courageous article urging the selectors to reinstate Brian in the side. Here is a flavour of it:

"Northamptonshire's fielding is among the most cumbersome of the seventeen first-class counties. In this department alone, the superfit Reynolds would set a fine example to youngsters such as Sarfraz Nawaz, Hylton Ackerman, and Peter Willey. Reynolds is still among the best half-dozen cover points in county cricket, and Northamptonshire clearly need a specialist in this position. In addition, Reynolds is a better runner between the wickets than a player half his age. His judgment of a run is almost uncanny. On past form alone, he looks capable of scoring more runs than the out-of-form David Steele and Peter Willey. Yet, above all, Northamptonshire need Reynolds for his sheer professionalism. As keen as the day he joined the groundstaff more than twenty years ago, he never gives less than 100 per cent.

Soccer and rugby selectors take physical fitness into consideration when picking teams. If cricket did the same, Reynolds would have been in the side from the start of the season. In pre-season training sessions under 'Sergeant Major' Jack Jennings, Reynolds gave maximum effort while many of his colleagues merely went through the motions during exercises.

Brian Reynolds will be thirty-eight next month, but he is still far from being a back number. Before anyone revives the 'too old' tag, let me remind them that Dennis Brookes was on the wrong side of forty when leading Northamptonshire to second place in the Championship table in 1957. Reynolds is clearly worth his place on merit and in terms of morale alone, his regular presence in the first team would be nothing short of a godsend."

In Brian's concluding ten first-class matches he made 358 runs. He had played especially well in his 83 against Nottinghamshire (coincidentally also his highest score for the seconds that year). At the end of June, he played his final games on his home-town ground ("dear to my heart"), a Championship match against Sussex sandwiching the John Player fixture. A painting of the old Kettering pavilion, by local artist Ralph Hartley, hangs in the Reynolds' family home. The pavilion had been built after the 1927 Yorkshire side complained about the facilities; part of the funds came from raffling a motorcycle.

Brian played for the County in seventeen Championship matches on the Kettering ground, fifteen at Peterborough and Wellingborough, and eight at Rushden. He always enjoyed out-ground fixtures and thinks his colleagues felt the same way. The wickets were better than they hinted to the opposition, though changing and abluting facilities could be cramped and idiosyncratic.

At Rushden, for example, the umpires shared space with the players. This didn't matter, particularly with umpires like Alec Skelding, whom Colin Cowdrey describes as having the players on his side, and "could be relied upon to bring humour to brighten the dullest day." Brian remembers his doing just that at Rushden. Alec was short sighted and wore thick-lensed spectacles, of the style favoured by Samuel Beckett, whose university had once played at Rushden's Short Stocks ground. Skelding's eyesight necessitated an elaborate pre-match ritual with restorative drops. He duly carried this out over the minute wash basin, turned to retrieve his glasses, and went into spectacular freefall over a cricket bag. Like Frank Tyson, Alec was given to reciting poetry during a match. Most literary buffs can tell you that Beckett played in a first-class fixture against Northamptonshire, but few are aware that the novelist HE Bates's insights into the human condition stem from his experiences in the Rushden Cricket Club's changing rooms.

Brian has a fund of stories involving Skelding, who officiated in his debut game. A favourite is Trueman's appealing for lbw against Jock Livingston in a game at Sheffield. "I'm afraid, Jock, I shall have to give that one out." To which Jock replied, "Fair enough, but if you've got to give me out, there's no need to make a speech about it. Mind you, I reckon it might have missed leg stump." "That's as maybe, Jock, but it's far better to please ten thousand Yorkshiremen than one bloody Aussie."

His Championship farewell was against Leicestershire, almost twenty years to the day of his debut against Sussex. He was lbw to Jack Birkenshaw for 0 (our little world is ended with an 0). The umpire was John Langridge, who had played for the opposition in August 1950. To compound the coincidences, he was run out in his final innings (in the John Player) just as in his first. And that was that. Or as Chaucer put it, "Some time an end there is of every deed,"

If the deeds had ended, the words had not. On September 3, 1970 Arnold Payne, the Club's President, wrote to Brian.

Northamptonshire County Cricket Club

A. C. PAYNE Esq., President

SECRETARY
K. C. TURNER
———
HON. TREASURER
B. A. SCHANSCHIEF, Esq.

County Cricket Ground
Northampton NNI 4TJ
PHONE: 32917
Pavilion Phone 32697

September 3 1970.

Dear Brian,

    Now that you are no longer on the staff, I write to thank you for your many years of loyal service to Northampton-shire County Cricket Club.

    With your entertaining batting and excellent fielding you have given many people a lot of pleasure, and I hope you have enjoyed your time with us.

    I hope you will often visit us at the County Ground where you will be most welcome.

    My kindest regards to your wife and yourself, and I hope the twins are well.

                Yours sincerely,

                Arnold Payne

                A.C. Payne,
                President.

There were letters in the local press, after reports that Brian's contract was not to be renewed. This one, from Len Smith of Kettering, typified the feelings of many.

"I was most surprised and disappointed when I read that Brian Reynolds' contract with Northamptonshire was not to be renewed. I know there is no sentiment in sport these days, but one wonders if we are too ready to forget the unstinted service men like Brian Reynolds give to cricket. After all, knowing his physical fitness, I would have thought that he could have been found a job helping the Colts or playing for the second eleven. 38 is no age, considering the age of some cricketers who are representing the MCC this winter."

Then it went quiet, until the start of the next season. In early May, Brian was interviewed for an article by Paul Webb. "When you see the sun shining," he said, "and you're not out in it, it comes a little hard. But after a while you adapt to it. I'd do it all again. I enjoyed every moment of it and have played with and against some great players." The article ended: "I felt I had a couple of years left of first-class cricket, but the committee decided otherwise."

He was right, and someone in the Club's hierarchy agreed. In November 1971, speaking at the Kettering Club's dinner, Northamptonshire's skipper Jim Watts said, "I think the County know they have made a mistake." He then suggested that Brian should be in charge of the second team, to give young players the "schooling" they need.

"Schooling in the second team last season was not hard enough," said Watts, "so the young players were not ready to go through into the first team. I think Brian would have been ideal to give them that training."

It was a credit to Watts's perspicacity and integrity that he said what he did. The rest of the hierarchy took note.

I L Reynolds c Butler b Watkinson 42

Worksop, 1989

"On the green they watched their sons, playing till too dark to see,
As their father watched them once, as my father once watched me,
While the bat and beetle flew, on the warm air webbed with dew."

Edmund Blunden
'Forefathers'

The Fuller

Lord's and Highbury

Van Man

Twin success

"Take my motor."

Angela Reynolds made her first visit to the County Ground in 1953. Aged fourteen, she was among a party of pupils from Kettering Central School. Although she had grown up just a short walk from Kettering's North Park and had occasionally joined the ranks of casual spectators sprawled on the park's grassy bank on sunny summer Sunday afternoons, she had little interest in cricket. Most of the players taking the field that morning were just names on the scorecard, although she had heard of Frank 'Typhoon' Tyson, the ferocious fast bowler who was about to open the Northants attack. She watched expectantly as he paced out his run almost as far as the sightscreen, turned, and thundered in to deliver his first ball. The ball whistled through the air, pitched, leapt, and thudded viciously into the keeper's outstretched gloves. Turning to a friend she remarked, 'I feel sorry for the wicket-keeper'. The object of her compassion was Brian Reynolds.

Four years passed before the couple met socially. A regular church-goer, Brian had struck up a friendship with the Rev. Ronald Goulding, the minister at Kettering's Fuller Baptist Church who, much later, would officiate at the wedding of Angela and Brian's son, Ian, to Selina. The two shared an occasional round of golf and, when invited by the minister to join him for a game of badminton at the church youth club, Brian readily accepted. Kettering's Fuller Institute was the congenial location for these Friday night meetings. The fifties - Elvis Presley, drainpipe pants and frothy coffee - might be sliding inexorably down the slippery slope towards the sixties but inside the 'Stute, badminton, table-tennis, American cream soda and the occasional barn-dance still held sway. It was then a typical setting for romance.

Brian and Angela met, the relationship flourished, and after Sunday evening church services Angela and half a dozen friends would pile into Brian's barrel-shaped Ford motor car, registration number AJF 276, to visit each other's homes for supper. Brian's culinary expertise made the journey to the house he still shared with his father in The Oval well worth the crush.

Brian, and the girl from Wordsworth Road were now, in modern parlance, an item. Angela became fully immersed in Brian's sporting life. There were Saturday trips to the Rockingham Road ground, accompanied by her mother, a blanket, a flask of hot soup and the hope that a Poppies victory would bring a win bonus to fund dinner at Wellingborough's Hind Hotel that evening. There were visits to pre-season cricket matches at British Timken with fellow 'willow-widows' Glenys (later Mrs John Wild) and Marion (later Mrs Stan Leadbetter), and charity games at Newmarket hosted by Neil Durden-Smith. When Northamptonshire played at Edgbaston, Angela would occasionally stay with aunt Jessica, one of Brian's mother's several sisters. Aunt Jessica had originally shared a flat with another sister, Beattie, in Kettering's Hampden Crescent before marrying somewhat late in life and moving to Birmingham, where her husband was the advertising manager for BSA.

An outstanding memory from those early days is of excursions to the Scarborough Festivals in 1957 and 1958. "The teams, relatives and friends stayed at the Chatsworth Hotel in The Crescent and were made honorary 'Freemen of the Borough' for the duration of the festival, meaning we could both visit the theatre and park the car free of charge. The highlights of the 1957 game were Bronk's 75 runs, of course, and sitting in the pavilion alongside the great Wilfred Rhodes. He was blind, but knew exactly the direction the ball was placed by its sound on the bat."

Included in the Reynolds entourage that year were brother Jack, sister-in-law, Pauline, and Brian's father, Len. When removed from the cricketing action, the family spent their time basking in the September sunshine. Here, on the North Bay sands, in contrasting attire are Len and Angela.

There was to be no return to Scarborough in the summer of 1959. Angela learned the devastating news of Brian's footballing injury at Clacton in March from a neighbour. "By the time I saw him, he had already come to terms with the break and was typically single-minded, saying how he intended to be playing cricket again by the end of June. Although I knew how sad it was for him to lose a season, looking at him plastered from hip to toe, I probably shared his captain, Raman Subba Row's sentiments, expressed in a letter some days before, "What a clot you are!"

Recovery was no doubt aided by Brian's determination not to allow his injury to impair his life-style. "Bronk carried on exactly as before. He played golf and continued driving his car, despite the huge plaster on his accelerator foot." His initial target for recovery proved unrealistic but, fully restored to fitness and back in the County side, he played a vital part in Northamptonshire's unlikely victory over the touring South Africans the following May.

Len Reynolds died in January 1962, just two months before Angela and Brian married. The wedding took place at the Fuller Baptist Church in Gold Street on Thursday March 29th, the Reverend CJW Doble officiating, and after a reception at the Central Hall the pair set off for a honeymoon in London. True to type, Brian had booked a room at the Portland Hotel in St John's Wood, Northamptonshire's usual venue when playing at Lord's. The next morning the groom met Donald Carr, one of the hotel's other guests, in the foyer and proudly introduced Angela with the words, 'I don't believe you've met my wife?' Coincidentally, the couple were en-route for the headquarters of the MCC. First day of a honeymoon or not, Brian had arranged for Roy Harrington, the ground's general factotum, to take them on a tour of his spiritual home. Roy even allowed Angela to enter the hallowed Long Room, confiding, "The only other woman to set foot in here was the Queen." We can only guess what Donald Carr would have said. The sporting theme continued the following day with a visit to Highbury. Knowing Brian's honeymoon destination, team-mate Colin Milburn had contacted Laurie Brown, the former Cobblers player who had joined Arsenal for a record £30,000 fee the previous year, and acquired tickets for Saturday's game.

The couple spent the first four months of their married life in The Oval before moving to the house in St Peter's Avenue where they have lived for the past 38 years. "'We were on our way to visit one of Bronk's aunts in Durban Road when we saw the 'For Sale' sign. I liked the house, he liked the garden, so we decided to buy." 'To buy', of course, stretches the truth somewhat. In those days, few County cricketers could afford to pay for their houses outright. Three years later, however, proceeds from a well-earned benefit enabled the Reynolds to clear their outstanding mortgage.

New wife, new house, new car. Recalling Brian's purchase of a brand new Ford Anglia earlier in the year, Jack Reynolds' tale of fraternal affection speaks volumes for the strength of the brothers' relationship. Jack and his wife were looking forward to their summer holiday in Falmouth. They had planned to travel by train, necessitating a journey across London from St Pancras Station to Paddington. One evening, a few days before they were due to leave, Jack was working on the roof of the garage he was building at his house in Windermere Road, when an argument with an electric saw resulted in a nasty cut across the palm of his right hand.

"The wound was so deep it required clamping with special metal clips. There was no way I could have carried our suitcases. The holiday seemed doomed." When Brian heard of the problem he was quick to suggest a solution. "Take my motor," he said. Jack was without a car at that time, a moped providing his normal means of transport. He was tempted but cautious on two counts. "Brian had only had the car a few weeks, but my biggest worry was his cricket. How would he get to Northampton on match days?"

For the fortnight Jack was away, Brian travelled to the County Ground on the moped. No wonder he smiles wryly when observing the ranks of sponsored cars that fill the Wantage Road car-park today.

When addressing a meeting of the Kettering Fuller Men's Fellowship, Brian once described the two essentials for success in cricket as a high degree of physical fitness and an understanding wife. His lengthy playing career is testimony to the first, while an appreciation of Angela's vital contribution to their partnership is readily apparent. For her part, it is obvious that she was abundantly suited to the role. "People talk of cricket widows and it is true that the wives are on their own for a large part of the season, but there is also a plus side. Some of the friendships I made in the early days are still in existence. Only recently Lyn Crump, Carol

Steele and I joined other wives for a re-union evening, which was so successful we're making it an annual event. Lyn and I always used to sit at matches with Mrs Bertha Milburn, Colin's mum. Before Colin came out to bat, Bertha would disappear to Abington Park. However, when she learned that he was in, she would return to the ground and sit completely motionless throughout his innings. I think she had her eyes shut."

As Angela recalls, friendships were not confined to the Northamptonshire players and their wives. "I would occasionally travel to an away game and would stay with a friend from the opposition, such as Derek Morgan and his family in Derby."

Brian sometimes brought his work home. "Occasionally he would sit and talk through the day's play, going over the key moments. However, nothing compares with the time he went 'sleep-walking'. All cricketers were a little superstitious in the old days – perhaps they still are. Bronk always had to brush his cap before going out to bat, (no helmets then, of course). One night after he had scored a 'ton' during the day he got out of bed, stood at the dressing table and began moving things about. When I asked, 'What are you looking for?' he replied, 'My cap', before getting back into bed and dropping straight off to sleep again. When I challenged him about it the next morning, he explained that he must have been re-living his innings in a dream and had to find his cap before he went out to bat."

In August 1963, Brian played in the Hastings Festival against the touring West Indians. While he recalls an innings ended prematurely by Joe Solomon's marvellous pick-up and throw, following Mick Norman's confident but ill-advised call for a quick single, it is the tourists' elegance, charm and sheer talent that live on in Angela's memory. "Their captain, Frank Worrell, was a gentleman and the players were great fun to be with. Indeed, the West Indians' enjoyment extended far beyond the field of play. When the hotel bar closed that evening, Rohan Kanhai drew Brian to one side and whispered conspiratorially, 'Come to my private bar.' Sauntering over to a nearby window, he slid back the curtains to reveal an impressive array of drinks secreted on the sill."

Memories of touring sides bring recollections of the summer of 1965, his benefit season, when Brian came so close to realising a boyhood ambition. 'Bronk was chosen as twelfth-man for England in the final Test match of the series. What a thrill, the Oval in Kettering to the Oval in Kennington, although he was convinced it was a wind-up when he first heard the news. He actually checked twice to make sure they'd got the right person. Sadly, he didn't fulfil his dream and take to the field although he came very close. He was denied only by Brian Statham's determination to continue, despite a nasty foot injury and Bronk's insistence that he should rest." Apparently the great bowler dashed the substitute's hopes with a simple explanation. "I can't let the lads down, Brian".

On Saturday April 27th 1968 the Reynolds' life was changed dramatically. On the previous day, five weeks before their first baby was due, Angela was admitted to St Mary's Hospital suffering from high blood pressure. Brian had been selected to play in an inter-club match at Kettering Golf Club on the Saturday afternoon and shortly before leaving, decided to ring the hospital for news of his wife's condition. "It was out of courtesy really. When I got through, the doctor said, 'Are you sitting down?' He then broke the news that Angela had had a baby boy. I replied, 'She can't have. I only brought her in for blood pressure.' But the doctor wasn't finished. 'If you wait a minute, there's another one coming,' he said. And he was right. Ten minutes after Ian was born, Sue arrived. Undiagnosed twins. They told me there was no point in visiting so I rang the Golf Club and dropped out of the team but decided to fill the time by playing a less competitive round with David and George Buckby instead. I was still in such a state of shock I played the worst golf of my life that afternoon."

Two years after the birth of the twins, the family was dealt a massive blow when Brian's contract with Northamptonshire was not renewed. Every winter since 1952 he had been technically out of work but had filled his time between cricket seasons in a variety of occupations. One such was at Kettering's Labour Exchange where he was responsible for finding work for the town's unemployed. The manager of the exchange, Ted Durham, had described Brian as, "ideal for the job. Being well-known in the county and knowing so many people himself he knows just where to go to find the jobs."

But now the boot was on the other foot. Angela remembers the hurt, the damage to his professional reputation and pride and his warranted sense of injustice. She also recalls his fortitude. "It was just like when he suffered the broken leg. Life had to go on. He now had a young family to support and he couldn't do that on self-pity."

Jack Tebbutt, an old cricketing colleague from his Kettering Town days, came to the rescue. "He knew I'd had a fair bit of experience in the shoe trade over the years. I'd started at J W Towell's, of course, and later when I worked for myself I'd done good quality outwork for Charles East's. I'd even made ski boots for PA Wright's factory in Durban Road, making the whole boot from scratch. Jack put me in touch with Jim Mann, manager of the bottom-stock buying office at the Lotus shoe factory on The Mounts in Northampton. There was a vacancy, I was interviewed and got the job. I had a firm's van and spent some of my time picking up and delivering accessories, like soles, heels, uppers, welts, laces and adhesives to factory units around the county. Jim Mann was a logistical genius who knew the state of play in every department in the factory and ensured they never ran out of materials."

In 1973 Brian was offered the post of Second Eleven captain and coach at the County Ground. There was never any doubt that he would accept. As Angela says, "His heart was in his cricket. It had been his whole life and I was pleased for him."

John Draper, the boyhood acquaintance from The Oval and astute observer of life's vagaries, expressed his thoughts in typically metaphysical fashion. "One door closes, Brian, and another one opens."

As Brian is well aware, the support of his family had been crucial during the most difficult period of his adult life. The experience would shape his attitude to his new post and bring him closer to youngsters who failed to make the grade. "When I saw players struggling to come to terms with rejection, I could say, hand on heart, 'I've been through it'. I had a fair idea how they felt!"

Following Brian's return to Wantage Road, the Reynolds renewed their devotion to the County's cause. There were many good times, particularly in one-day competitions, and Angela visited Lord's on each of the occasions that Northants reached a final, starting with the Gillette Cup game against Lancashire in 1976. "I've held the NatWest Trophy and the Benson and Hedges Cup, and even drank wine from it when we won in 1982."

In 1977, Brian's interest in the development of young cricketing talent came closer to home. 'Young Waddy', as he was later dubbed at Kettering Boys School by aficionado Anthony 'Fred' Barker, made his debut at the age of nine for Norman Lake's Broughton Youth side at Thorpe Malsor. As Angela recalls, "Ian wore a pair of pads so big he couldn't run in them." There was almost no need. As the batting prodigy himself remembers, he was rolled over first ball by David Billing - off a no-ball. After surviving a few overs, he returned to the pavilion, only to be chastised by his father for missing chances to take quick singles by not backing up. "You were too busy looking around to run."

Within a year, Ian had played his first game at Kettering Town. Brian had visited Northampton Road on the Friday evening and discovered that the club's third team, the Wanderers, were depleted for the match the following day. "They're a bit short, so I've got you a game." No doubt Brian was thinking back to those immediate post-war days and his own cricketing baptism.

Ian won the club's single-wicket competition, beating Brian Mitchum in the final, and in 1981 made his County League debut for the second team at Desborough. By 1983, he had won a place in the first team and was selected for the NCA county squad. The following year he hit his maiden century, scoring 113 not out against Isham. As Brian was prone to remark, "The not outs, I like."

1st XI 1983
Standing: M Bettles (Scorer), P Bates, I Reynolds, B White, P Fellows, D Billing, S Ashby.
Sitting: D J Ingham, B T Sanders, S A Leadbetter (Capt), G R Abbott, N Crabb.
Absent: D Carruthers.

Taken from the Kettering Town Centenary book, this team group shows young Waddy as a member of the team led by Stan Leadbetter, twenty-nine years after Stan and Brian had played together in the County Seconds.

157

Ian never resented his father's advice. "I didn't feel as if he was forcing me. I'd been brought up with sport and loved every minute. I suppose his expectations were high, but I wanted to do well. As a professional coach, Dad was used to watching and evaluating players and it was only natural that he passed on his observations to me. Sometimes it seemed a bit hard. If I scored a hundred he'd say, 'Why did you get out?' But I understood what he meant."

As Ian's prowess grew and his batting scores were recorded in the local press, reports were often prefaced with, 'son of Brian'. Hence the family nick-name. "We used to say, 'Dad's got his name in the paper again and he hasn't done anything'." With Brian involved in his County duties, it was Angela who often supported 'son of' during school matches. A point much appreciated by teacher, Kim Davis, who always acknowledged her with, "Thank you, Mrs Reynolds for coming to watch." When she was unable to attend, Ian was quick to take advantage of her absence by indulging in a gentle wind-up. "How many did you get today then?" she'd ask when he got home. "Only nine," he'd reply, shamefacedly, later repeating the story when his father returned. "Nine", Brian would say in disgust. "Is that all?" It was hours later before they discovered that he'd really hit 109 or some similar big score.

As Brian recalls, his presence at school football matches was a source of embarrassment to his son. "I remember one game when his team were beating Latimer School by a bucketful, the referee gave Latimer a consolation gift goal and I couldn't resist shouting from the touchline, 'Miles off-side ref!' He looked across and shouted back, 'Do you think you can do any better?' and offered the whistle. 'I think I can, but I don't want to,' I replied. 'Well, shut up then!' the ref retorted. As the match progressed, the teacher approached Ian and asked him, 'Who's that shouting on the touchline?' He replied, 'I'm sorry to say that's my dad.' When he got home, he approached his mother and begged her not to let me go to any more matches. I was banned."

After taking 'A' levels, in 1986 Ian moved on to Loughborough University where he obtained a First Class BSc degree in Materials Engineering. During his career at Loughborough, he quickly became established in the University cricket team. In 1987 he hit 214 not out for the seconds against Leicester but the highlight came in 1989, his final year, when he opened the batting in the side which won the UAU Championship, beating Durham by four wickets in the final. The two finalists contained a number of players who would eventually make their marks in the national side, including Ian's fellow opener, Nick Knight and Durham's captain, Nasser Hussain, though the man of the match was Chris Tolley, then at Worcestershire and later with Nottinghamshire.

The 'Daily Telegraph' said that "Reynolds punished anything short and hit a stylish 42"; The 'Times' described the innings as "rapid". Wisden's review of the 1989 UAU competition carries one other mention of young Waddy. "In their League matches, Loughborough easily overcame Leicester, and aided by a dominating 136 from Stephen Reynolds, they swept past Warwick by nine wickets." At least he wasn't referred to as "son of BC" (or BG or BR).

UAU CHAMPIONSHIP FINAL, 1989

DURHAM v LOUGHBOROUGH at Worksop College on June 21

DURHAM

RSM Morris	c Folland	b Tolley	55	Wedderburn	16	2	64	3
TJG O'Gorman	c Gillgrass	b Bostock	61	Tolley	29.4	8	80	5
N Hussain		b Tolley	3	McCartney	3	1	21	0
JI Longley	c Bostock	b Wedderburn	14	Bostock	11	1	35	1
+MP Speight	c Sheppard	b Wedderburn	9					
*SG Foster		lbw b Tolley	0					
PJ Butler	c McCartney	b Wedderburn	21					
MT Boobbyer	c Gillgrass	b Tolley	4					
SJ Watkinson		run out	2					
J Boiling	not out		12					
C Ridley		b Tolley	13					
		l11, w3, n3	17					
			211					

LOUGHBOROUGH

IL Reynolds	c Butler	b Watkinson	42	Boobbyer	13	0	45	1
NV Knight		lbw b Boiling	37	Ridley	4	2	10	0
N Folland	c Speight	b Watkinson	15	Boiling	25	5	79	2
S Hooper	c Speight	b Watkinson	17	Watkinson	16	2	70	3
CM Tolley	not out		48					
MDI Sheppard	c and	b Boobbyer	9					
*MC Abberley		b Boiling	19					
+AAD Gillgrass	not out		14					
R Bostock								
A McCartney								
M Wedderburn								
		l11, w2, n1	14					
		(6 wkts)	**215**					

LOUGHBOROUGH won by four wickets

On Ian's return to Northamptonshire that summer, to take up a post with the prestigious local firm, Cosworth Engineering, he played for the County Colts side which won the County League, alongside Tony Penberthy, John Hughes, Andy Roberts, Jeremy Snape and Duncan Wild. Coincidentally, Andy Roberts' father, David, had attended county trials with Brian Reynolds back in 1949, while John Wild had been a team-mate in the early sixties.

Over the next eight years, Ian acquired a deserved reputation as a prolific run-getter with the Colts, Kettering and Old Northamptonians. In May 1993, he won the 'Evening Telegraph' Player of the Month award after scoring 119 against Irthlingborough, but was already suffering the serious back problem which was to bring his cricketing career to an untimely end four years later. At least he had the satisfaction of scoring 71 in his final game against the County Colts at Wantage Road – the setting for so many of his father's fine innings.

Ian with the Evening Telegraph 'Cricketer of the Month' award for May 1993. "After much deliberation," went the citation, "we found it impossible to ignore the claims of Old Northamptonians batsman Ian Reynolds after his outstanding start to the summer. The former County Colt scored two unbeaten centuries while notching up 379 runs in seven innings during April and May at a healthy average of 94.75."

The presentation took place at the Northamptonshire Cricket Association's match against their Hertfordshire counterparts. Ian's colleagues, from left, were: Sam Gascoyne, Robert Pack, Mark Barrett, Richard Ashton, Jim Hawkins, Andy Trott, Richard Dalton, Gareth Smith, Richard Coulson and Gavin Hughes-Rowlands.

One Sunday at the Fuller, the visiting minister surveyed the massed ranks at the church parade and asked for a volunteer to assist him with his address. Sue Reynolds, then aged twelve and a member of the Fuller Girl Guides, stepped forward somewhat reluctantly. As she approached the pulpit, the minister held up an object, the visual aid with which he obviously intended to engage the interest of the younger element in his congregation. "I don't suppose you know what this is, do you?" he asked, rhetorically. The church erupted. The object was a cricket bat.

Sue was no less affected by the Reynolds family's main pre-occupation than her brother. Gender was no barrier to her interest in sport and from a very early age she joined enthusiastically in a range of ball games. "If dad got home early enough in the evening he would bowl us a few balls in the back garden although I always got the impression that he thought cricket was really a man's game". There were crises when the ball was struck into neighbouring gardens, but a delicate incident closer to home necessitated an ingenious response. "Dad and I are both keen gardeners. I'm flowers, he's vegetables. One day Ian and I were playing football in the garden when the ball struck one of his runner bean stalks and snapped it in half. I hastily stuck the two parts together with sellotape, the plant continued to flourish and dad was none the wiser until he pulled up the canes in the autumn."

When Ian began playing cricket in the local mid-week league, Sue took up the role of scorer, graduating along with her brother to Kettering Town. After, came the dizzy heights of responsibility when substituting for County regular Tony Kingston in a Northants Second Eleven fixture.

The love of sport extended to a range of games, including tennis, rounders and netball but it was her hockey skills which brought early recognition. She made her debut for Kettering's first team at Warboys when only twelve, benefiting from the advice and encouragement of experienced players like Val Chamberlain and Fran Davis. Her parents were immensely supportive – "Mum was a great taxi-driver" – but, like Ian, she occasionally found her father's presence at matches somewhat embarrassing. "He understood how the game should be played and stood on the touchline making critical comments. I remember him bellowing, 'Where are the halves, the team's attacking, they should be up there!' Fran Davis looked across at him and shouted, 'You can have my stick if you can do any better!' I had to apologise for him after the game." Son and daughter were treated with a similarity that would delight the Equal Opportunities Commission.

Equality in 1986 came for the 17 year old twins with a most unusual double; Sue was selected as Head Girl at Southfield School, Ian as Head Boy at Kettering Boys School.

161

At Southfield School for Girls, Sue developed her sporting expertise, winning County honours at netball and hockey. Here the advantages of expert coaching were graphically demonstrated when inspirational teacher, Gill Snelson, joined the staff. "She was a great influence, improving my game enormously and encouraging me in my choice of career." Another Southfield teacher, Jean Smith, was instrumental in encouraging Sue to join Kettering Ladies Hockey Club.

When Sue moved to Bedford College of Physical Education in 1986 she had an opportunity to play organised cricket for the first time. As an opening bat and first change bowler, she maintained the family tradition for match-winning performances although her displays were often received with scepticism by her father. After graduating in 1990 and taking a teaching post at Northampton's Ryelands Middle School, Sue was quick to get Brian involved in cricket coaching. "Despite all his experience, he couldn't believe that some children didn't know which way up to wear their pads. I told him that when I'd started they didn't even know which end of the bat to hold."

In 1995 Sue married Giles Ferguson, an RAF policeman. "We decided on a July wedding as Giles was due to be posted to Cyprus later in the summer and we wanted to be married before we left England. Dad said, 'It's in the cricket season. I don't know if I'll be there.' But of course he was."

Today, the Fergusons are living near Kettering. Sue teaches at the local school, Giles has joined the police force and their first child, Scott Leonard, arrived on September 22nd, 2000.

Her brother is also a family man. 'Young Waddy' and wife Selina, whose father Brian Bambridge was himself an accomplished sportsman, have a daughter, Charlotte. Another generation of Reynolds. Newspaper editors would be advised to prepare space in the sports pages in anticipation.

Among the pictures which line the walls of Brian and Angela's house in St Peter's Avenue are a number of evocative paintings by local artist Ralph Hartley, all reminders of Brian's early sporting days. A portrait, painted by Hartley in the Reynolds back garden but set against a background of the County Ground, was donated to the club on permanent loan and now hangs in the bar of the new indoor cricket school at Northampton. Other illustrations depict some of the cricketing greats who shared the stage with Brian during his long first-class career. But while these mementoes of his sporting life are an obvious source of satisfaction, it is the family photographs which have pride of place.

Coach and Second XI Captain

1973 - 1985

"So sweetly they bade me adieu,
I thought that they bade me return.
William Shenstone

Going back

Stern but benevolent

A4

Observe those principles

"Never mind the fancy thirties, let's see a not out hundred."

"Never go back," they say. Professional cricketers are a superstitious lot, but Northamptonshire's have often ignored this adage, as they returned to the County Ground in various roles. One thinks of Jim Watts, David Steele, Neil Mallender, Alan Hodgson, Nigel Felton, Ray Bailey and Bob Carter. When the opportunity arose, Brian Reynolds didn't hesitate.

In October 1973 he received his letter of appointment from Ken Turner.

Northamptonshire County Cricket Club

N. D. BARRATT Esq., President

SECRETARY
K. C. TURNER

HON. TREASURER
L. McGIBBON, Esq.

County Cricket Ground

Northampton NN1 4TJ

PHONE: 32917

Pavilion Phone 32697

9th October 1973

B. Reynolds Esq.,
202 St. Peters Avenue,
Kettering
Northants.

Dear Brian,

The Executive Committee last night, confirmed the decision to offer you post of Coach which would cover the duties of the training and discipline of uncapped players, the Captaincy of the 2nd X1, Scouting and arranging Teams for 2nd X1 Matches.

The Contract to be of a 5 year period in the first place, with an annual review of the Terms.

Would you be good enough to let me have your acceptance in writing. I shall not announce the appointment to the Press for a week or so, as I have one or two people to inform before making it public.

I think perhaps you will need a blazer and some sweaters which should be ordered before the turn of the year.

I would like to take this opportunity of wishing you luck and I do express my pleasure that you will be joining the Club.

Yours sincerely,

K. C. TURNER
Secretary.

Accepted
12/10/73.

The offer arrived on October 11; a letter of acceptance was sent the next day. The appointment was welcomed in the press. Locally, Fred Speakman wrote that it would be "popular throughout the county and many people think he is the type of man to develop the young players on the right lines." There had been earlier suggestions that the Club needed a manager and that Brian "would have been the ideal man for the job."

He was the first full-time coach since Dennis Brookes had vacated the post, two years previously, to become assistant secretary. In the meantime, coaching had been carried out at different times by Bob Cottam and Roy Virgin, while they were qualifying, along with Roy Wills and Percy Davis. Roy Wills had done a valuable job as Second Eleven captain, but was now training to become a schoolteacher.

There were various reappraisals of cricket's structure in 1974, but none was then questioning the very existence of county second elevens, as was the case at the turn of the century. Brian defends their raison d'etre as still important in training youngsters with playing potential to become first-class cricketers, not least through competitive matches. His disagreement with current practice is the urge to make the second eleven competition a mirror image of the County Championship, with respect to four-day games. He favours returning to two-day games, the norm until the switch to three days in 1979. Two-day games, he argues, provide young players in particular with more opportunities to practise their craft each week, whether in the Championship, friendlies, or other training programmes. "My suspicion is that with four-day games there's a tendency to be sitting on the balcony for too long, rather than playing, in whatever form. Especially in your formative years, you want to be batting and bowling as often as you can."

It is difficult to draw conclusions as to how much cricket young professionals now play by comparison with their counterparts of yesteryear. For example, over the years no one has logged hours spent in the nets, in fielding practices, or even friendlies. Another thought: where does the learning process start and end? The greatest batsman of them all, Sir Donald Bradman, not only practised unremittingly on his own, but also talked of coaching himself by watching and analysing. It's an approach that adds credibility to Brian's belief that the Second Eleven coach should be on the field, analysing and advising as things happen, and encouraging his players to do likewise. He remembers Jim Griffiths as someone who needed reminding about analysing his field placing. "I once said to Jim that I could send all his side off the field and he wouldn't notice. To be fair, he did listen and learn." Brian continued to play until 1982. He made 105 appearances for the seconds between 1961 and 1982, mostly in an advisory capacity when coach. The batting skills were still there when needed. In 1977 he top scored in a match against Worcestershire with an unbeaten 63. In 1975, he captured five wickets (for 128). Sadly, those were the only five of his coaching career; his final figures were five for 193 off 52 overs. The explanation is that he sacrificed himself as an attacking spinner to take on the role of declaration bowler. At least, that's one explanation.

Brian rejects current thinking that emerging players are necessarily better prepared for Championship cricket if they've experienced four day games in the seconds. "It's foolish to ignore the lessons of the past. How is it that players of previous generations coped with the switch to longer games in the first team or, come to that, from County cricket to Test matches? Some went from half-day games in the leagues to first-class cricket. I think Dennis (Brookes) did just that."

He believes a staff of twenty full-time professionals is about right. Part of his job specification was to arrange second eleven selection. This could be influenced by injuries, space for trialists, and out-of-form first teamers. Once school and university terms had ended, there might well be superfluous players to keep busy, whereas earlier in the season it could be necessary to use a player from a local club to fill a vacancy. That was no bad thing; not least it helped to establish, or strengthen, links between county and clubs. Brian has been a long standing promoter of this liaison, well before similar ECB initiatives, as numerous speeches at club dinners suggest and the 'also batted' lists in the averages confirm. In an article written soon after he took up his coaching post, he stressed his intention of giving local talent the opportunity to play for the second eleven and urged clubs to help in this by recommending players with potential. "I cannot be everywhere at once", he said, "so I rely on recommendations that I can follow up."

The end product, therefore, was generally a side consisting of a regular nucleus of full-time professionals, plus a flexible mix. The number of players representing the seconds during Brian's period in charge averaged around thirty per season (in 1979 it was thirty-six) and this is but one reason, he feels, why final positions in the Second Eleven Championship were of limited significance. There are several others. For instance, why bring a young leg spinner down from Carlisle for a trial, let's say, and then not give him an extended bowl, even if the match circumstances are inappropriate. It may be that loss of form requires a dropped, 'capped' player to be given a lengthy spell to help regain it. In short, says Brian, the needs and results of a second team must sometimes be secondary to the Club's longer term gains. The popular jargon about "teams developing the winning habit" is less important than individuals developing winning habits.

For what it's worth, the team's average position was twelfth during Brian's time as coach, but let's consider its composition in 1979, 1980 and 1981, when Northamptonshire finished last in successive seasons. Bottom maybe, yet it was nurturing the likes of Robert Bailey and David Capel ("both good listeners," says Brian), Duncan Wild and Neil Mallender. Robin Boyd-Moss and Bob Carter also played a number of games. Others such as Peter Mills, Chris Booden, Ian Peck, Robert Tindall, Ian Richards, and Vince Flynn made first eleven appearances; regulars Neil Priestley and Grant Forster played one game each, David Eland not at all. Andy Pearson and Ray Swann were among the local amateurs who featured occasionally.

Three other interesting names appear in the averages in these years: David East (later of Essex), Richard Illingworth (Worcestershire and England) and the West Indian Test player Franklyn Dacosta Stephenson, who headed the bowling averages in 1981 with fourteen wickets at a cost of 16.42. Rob Bailey came second, also with fourteen wickets, at 24.28.

Rob became a professional cricketer in 1980. In his article, 'Bailers moves on', in the County handbook for 2000, Chief Executive Stephen Coverdale wrote: "The first few years provided a tough and unglamorous cricketing education as he served his 'apprenticeship' under the stern but benevolent Chief Coach, Brian Reynolds. Rob said: 'People think that it's a recent trend for cricketers to train hard, but Brian most definitely put us through our paces. There were no days off. He was a very tough task master, but he was the one who gave me all the opportunities and had faith in me'." In the annual publication, 'The Cricketers' Who's Who', a large number of players list Brian among 'cricketers particularly learnt from'. Those tributes are the surest sign of his achievement as a coach.

There were many outstanding individual performances during Brian's years at the helm. Nine players had scores of over 150 (Martin Bamber had two). Richard Williams took prime spot with an unbeaten 208, Rob Bailey had a 193, Duncan Wild 176, Alan Tait 168 not out. Interestingly, each of those players was aged twenty when making those scores. Brian liked a greedy batsman. "Never mind the fancy thirties, let's see a not out hundred." Yet another of cricket's quaint statistics is that no fewer than seven bowlers took seven wickets in an innings: Jim Griffiths, Alan Hodgson, Wayne Larkins, Neil Mallender, Sarfraz Nawaz, John Tilley, and Alan Walker. Neil Mallender, then aged twenty, had the best figures, with seven for 28. Of those seven, only Tilley never made the first team; he opted for an alternative career. The team's highest total was 463 against Derbyshire at Heanor; their lowest, 48 against Lancashire at Horton House.

Some other statistics catch the eye, relating to the number of appearances for the seconds and progression from second to first team. Wayne Larkins played a surprising 101 matches for the seconds (168 innings, average 31.10) and Richard Williams 78 matches (134 innings, average 40.62). A partial explanation in Larkins' case was the difficulty in transferring his lustrous talent between levels, so that initially he see-sawed frustratingly. It's extraordinary to be reminded that at one point there were doubts about his chances of success at the higher level. Richard Williams' first-class debut was 1974, as a seventeen year old, and he continued until 1992. Larkins played from 1972 to 1991, before switching to Durham. Like Brian, he scored 1,000 runs in a season ten times.

Just as Brian and Wayne are very different characters, so with cricket coaches. Look no further than David Lloyd and Duncan Fletcher or, for that matter, Keith Fletcher. Brian would probably agree that Stephen Coverdale's description "stern but benevolent", and Rob Bailey's "a very tough task master" is apt for his style of coaching. Players were treated firmly but fairly, whatever their status, for the benefit of Northamptonshire cricket. In one season the experienced John Dye was having a problem over running down the wicket. His selection for the seconds was an opportunity to rectify it. John said to Brian that he would bowl off his short run; Brian made it clear he would bowl off his usual run, for obvious reasons. After the ensuing "difference of opinion", John bowled off his long run. Background, schooling, National Service, and his own apprenticeship under Freddie Brown, doubtless combined to determine his approach. Brian Radford's 1985 book, 'From the Nursery End', contained the views of all seventeen county coaches and Don Wilson, then chief coach at Lord's indoor school, on various aspects of the game. Alongside his opinions about 'non-walkers' and inadequate pitches, Brian Reynolds criticised the lack of discipline and dedication among players. He is not alone in believing that discipline, on and off the field, should be paramount in professional sport, from the ascetic Wilson of 'The Wizard', via Stanley Matthews and GA Gooch, to the (almost) successful 2000 Munster XV. All around Munster's dressing room were pinned A4 sheets of paper bearing the one word 'discipline'.

In idle moments, imagine Douglas Jardine (or Captain Bolton) pinning up A4 sheets of paper carrying motivational slogans.

Once upon a time, perhaps a more surprising believer in the 'discipline' philosophy was Graeme Fowler, now himself an authoritative coach at Durham University. In August 1985, he said this: "And if you are in a situation where there is no discipline, you exploit it. Everyone gets away with things when they can, especially sportsmen, because in the main they are like mischievous lads at school who, if they can take advantage of things, do. Not everyone, but that is generally the sort of characters they are - sharp, alert, the types who manipulate people." He expressed those thoughts during the course of a second eleven game between Northamptonshire and Lancashire at Wantage Road.

Brian also believes that principles (cricketing or otherwise) should not be compromised to accommodate changing patterns of behaviour. Cricket's hierarchy, like politicians, have often talked of principle, while their actions smack of self-interest. For example, in Radford's book, Brian had also been critical of the 'rebels' who toured South Africa, supporting the three year ban, "They got what they deserved. All of them." He could be equally unwavering about shoddy play, scruffy appearance, or disrespect for umpires, or spectators. He expected players to acknowledge applause in a gracious manner, or to sign autographs in a similar fashion. Like Brian Close, he finds much of the incessant on-field shouting not inspirational or bonding, but inane. John Woodcock, the distinguished writer on cricket, draws an interesting comparison: "When, say from third man, a fielder, under no particular pressure, returns the ball to the top of the stumps, was he always applauded by the rest of his side? Actors are not, by their fellow actors, when they get their lines right." Worse, is when a sloppy return on the half-volley is greeted with the daft cry of "Great arm", when the 'motivator' was without satirical intent.

Anyone inclined to criticise Brian's unbending attitude to principle should consider the slippery slope that leads from seventies petulance to reports in February 2000 that the Northern Premier League, one of Britain's top competitions, is trying to curb growing dissent and shabby behaviour by introducing a football style yellow card system for players. The move is a consequence of several seasons of indiscipline, including that of a current Test-playing professional.

In the year Brian returned to County cricket, Wisden commented on the incident involving Rohan Kanhai, captain of the West Indies, and Arthur Fagg, the umpire, in the Edgbaston Test. Kanhai had shown dissent when Fagg rejected an appeal against Boycott, and the umpire needed persuading to resume. Fagg was criticised, yet his stand focused attention on a growing problem, as Wisden's editor pointed out: "For too long, and not only in this country, players from junior to senior standing have been reflecting their dislike at umpires' decisions, almost with disdain." He added that the TCCB had taken a firm stance by declaring that umpires would receive full support in reporting, as was their duty, any pressurising on the field. Captains, he wrote, more than anyone, held the key to clearing up a bad habit which had no place in cricket.

That was 1974. Does anyone in cricket deny that pressurising umpires has not only continued, but intensified? How far is that the result of compromising principles to suit changing behaviour? A preference for acquiescence over action.

Perhaps we need more "stern" captains and coaches, like Brian Reynolds, before we see yellow cards in the first-class game. Fanciful? Then try to imagine a Brookes or Reynolds leaping all over FR Brown after he had taken a wicket. In 1950, would anyone have predicted that on-field kissing and hugging would be *de rigeur* in 2000? It is said that Tony Lock was one of the first captains to encourage this 'bonding' during his years at Leicestershire. On one occasion Maurice Hallam dropped a straightforward catch. Asked at the tea interval how he managed to do such a thing, he replied that he didn't want to be kissed by Tony Lock.

"Sergeant major" (to Keith Andrew's captain) he might have been, but there was no lack of "benevolence" or humour during the Reynolds' regime. A net was a serious business, but cricket and slapstick are never far apart. In 1979, David Eland was having trouble in bowling from close to the stumps. During one net practice, Brian hit on the idea of placing a large metal waste bin on the edge of the crease, thus forcing David to deliver the ball from the required spot. All went well and Waddy moved to net two. Shortly after, there was an enormous clatter: the bin was half way down the wicket, with Eland under it and rubbish everywhere. "Sorry coach, I forgot what I was doing." Brian had more luck with another improvised coaching aid, using the boundary rope to help Neil Mallender adjust his angle of delivery. It should be stressed that the rope was on the ground, (not Neil's neck) as a low-tech version of Channel 4's red line.

At some point in their emerging careers, most players enjoyed the hospitality at St Peter's Avenue in Kettering. One thinks of Brian as the Duke in 'As You Like It': "Sit down and feed, and welcome to our table." Angela recalls that he would invite the whole squad in for a curry. "On one occasion," she recalls, "they were travelling from Marske-by-the-sea to play in London the next day and a fifty-two seater coach pulled up outside our house while twelve players, the scorer, and coach driver called in for refreshments." Brian's men, like an army, marched on its stomach. It says much for Angela and Brian's generous nature that these invitations, to their home and table, were so freely issued.

The prospect of a Reynolds' curry was another argument in favour of the team's travelling together by coach. Brian thinks it helped team morale and avoided cliques. The many could show concern for the individual. This was so in his early playing career, when a respectful silence fell between 6.45 and 7.00 pm, while Dennis Brookes listened to 'The Archers'.

Life isn't all roses, Tudor or otherwise. In 1983, Brian lived through many miserable days after the sacked groundsman, Les Bentley, took the County Club to an industrial tribunal. It was the only occasion, in nearly fifty years, when he had thought of resigning. "I seriously considered giving the job up. I'd had enough." Those words, spoken at the tribunal, show the extent of his unhappiness. This was a job he enjoyed, at a club he loved. Moreover, it is not in Brian's character to opt out of his difficulties.

Cricket often mirrors life (the other way round, some would say). Central to his coaching philosophy is the importance of confronting weaknesses and mastering them through diligence. Nothing new or unique in that. Brian's namesake, Sir Joshua Reynolds, told students at the Royal Academy: "If you have great talents, industry will improve them: if you have but moderate abilities, industry will supply their deficiency." Brian had little time for the dilettante and the self-absorbed maverick, with inflated opinions of their ordinary ability. He believes that in every department of the game there are enduring playing principles, which all the greats have observed far more than they have ever disregarded. His role was to train young players, in particular, to "observe those principles", achieved above all through their own dedication and professionalism. Fads will come and go, like new balls. Timeless technique, and the sheer will to succeed, are unkept secrets. Brian wanted players to succeed, for their own benefit and that of Northamptonshire County Cricket Club. That meant he was never content with less than the best, whether in his own efforts or his players'. "There is no teaching," wrote Emerson, "until the pupil is brought into the same state or principle in which you are."

When Stephen Coverdale properly described Brian as "stern but benevolent", he wouldn't have known that he echoed some lines of a poem learnt by the young Reynolds almost sixty years earlier.

> "A man severe he was, and stern to view;
> Yet he was kind; or if severe in aught,
> The love he bore to learning was in fault."

Goldsmith wouldn't mind if you substituted "cricket" for "learning".

Cricket Development Officer

1986 - 1997

"And gladly wolde he lerne,
and gladly teche."
> Geoffrey Chaucer,
> 'The Canterbury Tales'

Back to school

Kwikly

Curtly

Responsibility and respect

"The character-building aspects of cricket still make it unique."

When Bob Carter took over as coach in 1986, Northamptonshire broke new ground by appointing Brian Reynolds as the county's initial Cricket Development Officer. It was a pioneering appointment and one of the first anywhere in the country. Brian still regards the change as a 'sideways' move, "They wanted to keep me, and at the same time get me out of the way," but no-one on the staff was better qualified or more suited to the challenge.

He was given little guidance on what the job entailed but, as his 'end of term' report for 1986-87 reveals, Brian had soon devised a busy schedule which included scouting for new talent, coaching in secondary schools, establishing a Centre of Excellence and fulfilling a variety of public relations duties on the County's behalf.

Among the young players to catch the eye during the first year were wicket-keepers, Wayne Noon and Russell Warren and bowlers Andy Roberts and John Hughes, all of whom went on to gain professional contracts with the club.

Brian was quick to recognise the ever-increasing importance of promoting cricket in schools. As winter employment during his playing career he had once spent time working in Northampton's Delapre and Bective Secondary schools. Both headteachers were particularly helpful, Bective's Len West underpinning his support by promising to administer "six of the best to anyone who gives you any nonsense." It was an offer Brian never had cause to accept.

With support from the County Education Inspectorate, a programme of visits was arranged covering schools as far apart as Thrapston and Towcester, Deanshanger and Daventry. Brian's comments at the end of the first year make interesting reading. He expresses general satisfaction with the pupils' progress, delight at their enthusiasm, surprise that most seemed a little scared of catching a hard ball and disappointment at the length of grass on the outfields.

His new position also afforded opportunities to promote the game by providing support at grassroots level throughout the county. He could build on the foundations long established at the club's indoor cricket school where Brian, the holder of an MCC advanced coaching certificate since 1956, had been employed to help his former team-mate and mentor, Dennis Brookes.

"Dennis watched me at work in the nets and then gave me a piece of advice which became my guiding principle. 'You're trying to make them all into world beaters,' he said. 'Concentrate on those that are receptive. Let the others enjoy themselves'." With support from the Northamptonshire Cricket Association, and particularly its chairman, Doug Lucas, in 1987 five indoor centres were set up around the county. Throughout the winter, Brian maintained a demanding schedule, dividing his time between school-children and club players. Every weekday evening, from about four o'clock until late, he provided advice and encouragement to the hundreds of enthusiasts who attended the sessions. Remembering Dennis Brookes' maxim, he concentrated on achieving a balance between finesse and fun while remaining conscious of the need to make provision for individual levels of ability.

"Sportsmen are born not made. They're like diamonds in the ground, created by nature, and all you need to make them sparkle is to knock off the rough edges. The most natural ball-player I ever saw was Colin Milburn. Imagine flat-batting a bouncer from Wes Hall back over the bowler's head for six. What co-ordination!

You can't teach that. Fielding at short leg, he could catch balls off the meat of the bat, not bat and pad dollies. At sixteen stones, he caught them in his hands, at eighteen he took them against his body. Natural talent – and a coach's nightmare!"

The value of this individualistic approach is apparent in the following example. "There was a promising lad at Deanshanger called Robert Ford who always tended to fall to the right when playing anything on his leg stump. I concentrated on that specific weakness, getting him to keep his head up on middle and leg. His game improved and he's still getting runs for Wolverton."

Of course, not everyone responded so positively to Brian's advice. Sometimes there were fundamental problems with communication. "One boy from Corby just couldn't get his bowling action right. I tried everything I knew to help but in the end suggested he practise his run-up and delivery on the way to school. 'When you approach a lamp-post or a tree, pretend it's the wickets, line yourself up and bowl an imaginary ball at the imaginary stumps.' The boy looked at me for a moment and then started to laugh. 'I can't do that,' he said. I was a bit miffed. 'Why ever not?' I asked. His reply was devastating. 'I go to school on my bike,' he said."

● Best foot forward . . . 12-year-old Chris Stott gets a helping hand with his forward defensive stroke from former Northants star Brian Reynolds, who is conducting a series of coaching sessions for promising local youngsters at Kettering's Recreation Centre.

On other occasions, there were difficulties in persuading players to abandon old habits. "The Wellingborough Indians used to come to my Tuesday sessions at the Drill Hall in Kettering. They were smashing lads, really keen, and came as regular as clockwork. One of them, whose name was Umesh, always insisted on batting with his watch on. I told him, week in, week out, that he'd be sensible to take it off but he always said the same thing – 'no matter Mr Reynolds' – and carried on wearing it. The mat at the Drill Hall was pretty uneven and not the best of surfaces for batting. One evening Umesh got a really nasty delivery which pitched where two sections of the mat joined. The ball flew up and hit him viciously on his wrist scattering bits of watch all over the floor. I looked across and said, rather smugly, 'I warned you that would happen.' He just smiled ruefully and replied, 'No matter, Mr Reynolds, it's my brother's watch'."

The success of the county-wide network led to a remarkable innovation which has widened cricket's appeal amongst primary school children. In the summer of 1991, initial discussions took place at the County Ground between Northamptonshire's Steve Coverdale and Jim Harker, clerk to the Kettering Old Grammar School Foundation, with regard to coaching for young people in the area. Following a further meeting in September, involving Jim Harker, Bob Denney, the KOGSF chairman, the Headteacher of Kettering Boys School, representatives of the town's primary schools and Brian Reynolds, the Foundation Governors agreed to support the ambitious scheme to enhance the position of cricket in schools. Its primary aims were to introduce cricket to as wide a range as possible and later offer extra coaching for gifted children. Eighteen groups were to be established around the Borough of Kettering with Brian Reynolds providing weekly coaching during the winter months. Sessions would be based around the Kwik Cricket format, which offered an exciting introduction to the game, ensured full involvement and could be played equally successfully indoors, or outside when the weather was favourable. To increase interest among primary school teachers a demonstration of the game, with Brian Reynolds and Rob Bailey in attendance, was held at the Boys School.

The Foundation generously agreed to meet both the costs of coaching and the provision of Kwik Cricket kits for all participating schools and it was estimated that some 1,800 children aged between eight and eleven would benefit from the scheme. Immediately after the official launch in October, contacts were established with interested schools, equipment purchased and Brian's exhausting timetable got underway.

While most of the larger town schools had a hall large enough to accommodate coaching sessions, there were often constraints in more rural areas. "The teacher at Rushton was very keen and I always enjoyed going there. One visit coincided with the school's Ofsted inspection and I was certain they wouldn't want me but, 'Come along as usual,' the teacher said. I'd planned to be outside on the playground, but unfortunately it was raining and we had to use the tiny church hall which was far too cramped. Halfway through the session this inspector arrived with a clipboard and began taking notes. When the report was published he'd written, "Accommodation rather crowded for cricket. Enjoyment factor high.' Praise indeed!"

Unsurprisingly, Brian is very positive about the Kwik version of the game which he sees as a worthwhile introduction to the real thing. He always ensured that the children were fully involved by using a rotational format, so that all the children had opportunities to bat, bowl, field and keep wicket in sequence. "They loved the competitive element of the game and I used to promote their keenness by giving rewards – posters of county players and the like – to those whose skills showed the biggest improvement."

The introduction of a Kwik Cricket competition in 1992 gave children an opportunity to pit their skills against opposition from other schools. As Brian recalls, "I can't remember who suggested it would be a good idea, but I know they said, 'Can you organise it?' I might not have agreed so happily if I'd known how many sleepless nights it would bring."

The inaugural tournament was held on the Kettering Boys School field and attracted entries from eleven local schools. Barton Seagrave Primary School defeated Geddington Primary by seventeen runs to become the first winners of the competition, which was so successful it was decided to make it an annual event.

Barton Seagrave's class of '92. Back (l to r): Chris Randle, Danny Marinovic, Adam Flawn, Chris Shaw. Front (l to r): Scott Davidson, Chris Donovan, Ryan Dudfield, Dean Whitwell.

Brian received assistance from Boys School games teacher, Kim Davis, who recalls the major organisational problems caused by the unpredictable British weather. "If rain seemed imminent, there were often difficulties in alerting all the participating schools and, inevitably, there were times we got it wrong – postponement brought sunshine, continuation a downpour. However, the biggest concern was over the refreshments. These were prepared in advance by staff at Jim Harker's office in the Headlands and a late postponement resulted in mountains of unwanted sandwiches."

1993 saw two such postponements before the competition eventually took place, Barton Seagrave retaining the trophy. The following year, the venue moved to the County Ground, Northampton, giving large numbers of children an opportunity to perform on a big stage. Indeed, just days after Barton Seagrave had completed a hat-trick of victories in the final, Brian Lara also performed there, hitting 197 for Warwickshire in the County Championship.

The Grammar School Foundation scheme grew to include over twenty local schools, eventually becoming too onerous a job for one man alone, and David Ripley was appointed to share the load. Reference to the wicket-keeper provoked a cautionary tale from Brian's days in charge of the Second Eleven. "On the morning before we were due to play a three-day game at Wellingborough School, the trialist we'd included as wicket-keeper rang in to say he'd broken his finger and couldn't play. The first team was playing away, Ken Turner had left me in charge and I was desperate for a replacement. One of the youngsters we'd got down for trials at the time was a lad named Pickles, inevitably dubbed 'Wilf'. When he heard we were short of a wicket-keeper, he mentioned his mate David Ripley, who just happened to be playing for the Yorkshire under 15 schools side against Northamptonshire at Wellingborough Town that afternoon. I rushed over to take a look, discovered he'd made ninety not out so he could bat a bit, and had a word with the team manager about his wicket-keeping skills. Apparently he hadn't intended to play him there but, when I explained the situation, kindly gave him a few overs behind the stumps. He was good enough for me, so after the game I approached him about the possibility of playing in the three-day match. He rang his parents for permission and duly turned out the next day.

At the weekend David turned up to play for Farsley, his local side, understandably full of his experiences playing for Northants seconds. The following Monday I was summoned into Ken Turner's office. He was holding the telephone, one hand over the mouthpiece, and breathing fire. 'What's all this about you playing a lad called Ripley at Wellingborough?' he asked. I explained that I'd simply had no option. He wasn't appeased. 'Well, you better speak to this fellow from Farsley,' he said. 'He's far from pleased about you poaching schoolkids. By the way, his name's Raymond Illingworth!' I just turned round and pointed to my shoulders. 'They're broad enough,' I said."

Ken Turner was eventually pacified, but it resulted in a trip to Lord's. Brian was hauled over the coals, received a severe warning from the powers-that-be, and the incident led to a change in the rules making it illegal for counties to approach schoolboys under the age of sixteen. Some time later, of course, when fourth in line for the wicket-keeper's job with his home county, David Ripley moved to Northamptonshire.

Within the remit of Cricket Development Officer, Brian retained responsibility for following up leads from members of the club's scouting network, watching recommended prospects and organising trials where appropriate. When he first spotted the precociously talented David Sales at the English Schools Cricket Association's Under-15 Festival at Lincoln, Brian was suitably cautious about making an approach. "I remember thinking 'he's the best player I've seen since Peter May', but getting him was another story. He was a Surrey lad and had been all through their coaching schemes. Funnily enough, although he hit the ball harder than anyone I'd seen for years and could bowl a bit too, Surrey didn't seem very interested in him. However, after the Ripley incident, I had to be very careful. I picked out his mother, who was keeping score, and then his father who was sitting watching on the boundary. I cultivated him for a couple of days but, rather than risk a direct approach, I just offered him my phone number. To my surprise, and against all the odds, Mr Sales eventually made contact and David came to Northamptonshire. Mind you, there was no shortage of doubters at the County ground either. Even when he became the youngest to score a Sunday League fifty and the County Championship's youngest double centurion, there were those who wondered if he would make a first-class cricketer."

According to Brian, unearthing genuine young talent has become far more difficult in recent years. "There are problems getting on to other people's territory, most counties are really strapped for quality, there are national coaches by the dozen and what talent there is has been picked up through the ESCA courses. Any promising youngsters have already been seen by a host of people, and, of course, we can't tap Durham's rich seam any more since their elevation to the County Championship. There was a time when I'd go to an Under-15 schools festival and spot half a dozen lads who stood head and shoulders above the rest. Now there are just a couple and the rest are much of a muchness."

The Schools Cricket Festivals not only proved an important source of young talent, but also provided Brian with an excuse to travel the country and enjoy many of its more picturesque locations. Cornwall was a particularly favoured venue. "I'd drive through the quiet lanes and backwaters with no sign of a village let alone a cricket ground. Then suddenly, with no warning, one would appear like an oasis in the middle of nowhere. I often used to take a tent in those days, find a camp-site and nip about between the grounds."

It was on one such occasion that Brian enjoyed a most bizarre experience that might have come straight from the script of the farce, 'Outside Edge'. After a long and tedious journey down to Cornwall, Brian arrived at the camp-site late into the night, pitched his tent in the dark and slept rather longer than intended. When he eventually awoke he began to panic. He realised he had no idea just how far away he was from the cricket ground where he was supposed to watch the morning's play. To his considerable surprise and delight a glance over the camp-site wall into the next field revealed a wooden pavilion, sightscreens and the wicket all marked out in readiness for the match. There was only one problem. Water lay in pools all over the pitch. It had rained all night and was still drizzling. There was no way they could possibly play cricket that day. After watching for some time under his umbrella, Brian was astounded to see a coach pull up and two teams of youngsters clamber off. However, no sooner had they reached the pavilion door than they were smartly turned around again by the teachers in charge, ushered back on to the coach and driven away. Someone must have pinned a notice to the outside cancelling play for the day. Sensible decision he thought. Some time later the reason for their hasty departure became apparent. Apparently the groundsman, after his strenuous efforts to prepare the wicket, had suffered a heart attack, collapsed and lay dead behind the door blocking the entrance into the pavilion. Eventually an ambulance arrived and the body was taken away, but the drama didn't end there.

As the teams were recalled and crowds began to gather more in hope than expectation of the game going ahead, a rather forthright Oxford headmaster named Proctor, but always referred to as 'Procky', exerted his considerable authority. He was determined that the match should take place despite the waterlogged pitch. Brian's old friend Mike Rowson, a teacher with the Midlands Schools side, reported that 'Procky' had telephoned the Station Commander at RAF Culdrose suggesting a useful training exercise for a helicopter pilot. Minutes later the watchers observed a Sea King air-to-sea rescue machine in the distance. It approached the cricket ground, proceeded to hover just above the square, and within a matter of half-an-hour or so the wicket was dry enough to play on and the match took place after all.

A similar excursion to Cornwall had alerted Brian to the talent of Tony Penberthy, and he followed up his interest when the all-rounder appeared in a county schools game at Towcestrians. "He swung the ball around a fair bit and then went out and knocked up a quick fifty. John Malfait, of the Northants Cricket Association, knew Tony and we got lucky."

A rare 'one that got away' was Nottinghamshire and England batsman, Tim Robinson. His family had moved from Nottingham to Dunstable and the boy turned out for Bedfordshire in a schools match at Finedon. While appreciating the lad's batting potential, it was a gesture reminiscent of his own youth that particularly impressed Brian Reynolds. "The first thing he did when he got back to the pavilion after knocking up a good score was to rub down his bat with a bit of wire wool. I remember thinking, 'looking after the most important tool of his trade – he's got the right attitude'." Robinson made a single appearance for Northamptonshire II and although he didn't score many runs, defied the opposition's best efforts to get him out. Unfortunately, when the family returned to Nottingham shortly afterwards, Tim joined his home county.

Alan Fordham was another to benefit from Brian's continuing interest over a period of time. He too had played in the Bedfordshire schools side but it was while playing for Bedford Town that he eventually progressed to the Northamptonshire staff. "When I went to watch him play at Wolverton he was out without scoring. Nevertheless, I sought him out, had a chat and discovered that he was intending to take a year out before going on to Durham University. I thought both he and the club would benefit from his spending a summer on the staff and reported this to Ken Turner. Ken's first question was inevitable. 'How many did he get?' I replied somewhat sheepishly, 'I hoped you wouldn't ask. Nought.' But at least it gave me the chance to talk to him!"

As Brian's initial contact with Michael 'Dickie' Davies demonstrates, no matter how meticulous the long-term planning, good fortune can often prove the most important factor in unearthing star quality. He had gone to the final of the UAU competition between Bristol University and Loughborough at Luton, with the intention of watching a Bristol spinner who'd taken seven wickets in the semi-final. On an early circuit of the ground he met the father of a boy he'd recently coached at the County's centre of excellence and briefly explained his interest in the fixture.

The other man was unimpressed. "I watched that semi-final," he said. "The wicket was so bad, you'd have taken seven wickets! The lad Davies is a far better proposition. He's already had the odd game for Leicestershire seconds."

Brian sought out Toby Bailey, the Loughborough wicket keeper. "I knew he'd give me an honest opinion and when he confirmed that Davies could really turn the ball I set about getting him." As with David Sales, Brian was successful in gaining the confidence of kith and kin. He got into conversation with Michael's mother, learned of her son's interest in making a career in cricket, and set the wheels in motion.

It's perhaps no surprise that the arrival of Jason Brown from the Potteries was largely due to Brian Crump. "Jason came down to Northampton for us to have a look at. He is one of the most accurate off-spinners I've ever seen. His first-team chances have, apparently, been restricted due to his poor batting. If that's so, then the next step is fairly obvious."

By far the biggest stroke of luck saw one of post-war cricket's greatest names take up residence at Wantage Road. "I was chatting to Jack Simmons one afternoon at the County Ground. We go back a long way, he and I. I played in Jack's first game for Lancashire when he was a pro at Blackpool. Anyway, I asked him if there were any useful fast bowlers about in the northern leagues. He replied that he'd had reports of one lad but couldn't remember his name. However, he promised to tell me the following day after ringing home that evening for the details. He was as good as his word. 'His name's Ambrose, Curtly Ambrose,' he reported. 'He's the young pro at Heywood, and they're at home this weekend'."

That Saturday, Brian drove up north and watched the game. It was forty-eight overs a side and Curtly bowled half of his side's allocation, taking four wickets. At the end of each over bowled, the beanpole simply loped to gully. Brian was greatly impressed. "The following weekend, Roy Wills and I went to watch him again. The weather was dreadful as we drove up the M6 and getting worse. There were radio reports of thunderstorms moving east. The sky was as black as night. Fortunately Heywood fielded first and Curtly got in a couple of overs before the heavens opened and play was abandoned. Within ten minutes you could have boated across the field, but we'd seen enough. A few days later I took Steve Coverdale to watch him play for a League XI in a 'swank' match. They talked and Curtly came down to Northampton later in the summer to bowl in the nets. That winter he went back to the West Indies, got into the Test team and was taking wickets. By the time he joined the County side at the start of the following season he'd progressed from being a relative unknown to being a Test match star. That's luck for you!"

Chief Executive Coverdale, though, was not always as receptive to Brian's recommendations. "I remember suggesting that a bowling machine with an automatic feed would be most useful. It would take a lot of the drudgery out of net practice and save my arm getting tired at the same time. They were on the market for about £250. His reply was unequivocal. 'What do we need a bowling machine for? We've got you'."

Brian's request for a Sharp Viewcam video recorder for taking on scouting missions received similar short shrift. "It was light to carry, very discreet, would have been particularly useful for reviewing batting and bowling technique and cost around £550. They decided it was too expensive – that is until John Emburey arrived and then they bought two!"

He is uncompromising regarding the importance of the exemplary nature of the coach's role. "In my early days, I was hugely influenced by Jack Mercer, Percy Davis and Dennis Brookes. They were gentlemen with the high standards and principles which have governed my own approach to working with young players."

Trialists received particularly sensitive treatment. No youngster ever left Northampton without receiving a private word from Brian, 'letting the lad down gently', if his spell at the County Ground proved unsuccessful. Not that he was a lenient taskmaster. Ken Turner's instruction when Brian took over the seconds, "I want those lads so tired by the time you've finished with them that they'll have no inclination to go night-clubbing," was taken to heart.

His lengthy experience working with promising young players at the County Ground, visiting schools and coaching in the local community gives additional credibility to his thoughts about the present state of cricket at grass roots level. Many of his views correspond closely to those expressed by the likes of Matthew Engel, who point to significant changes in life-style having a detrimental effect upon the game.

"These days there is so much competition with other activities. You rarely see anyone playing the kind of impromptu games that were part and parcel of my life as a child. The streets are too busy, many parents think the parks are not safe and lots of children would rather be indoors on their computers anyway."

He regards the decline in school cricket as another important factor. "Lots of secondary schools have lost their playing fields, Games and PE lessons have become optional extras rather than an essential part of the curriculum and fewer teachers are involved in promoting the sport. I've discovered how enthusiastic primary children can be, but there is no guarantee that this interest will be developed when they move on to their next school. Quality of provision is arbitrary and often depends so much upon the interest of individual teachers."

The difference that such commitment can make is illustrated by Brian's recollection of a sports-loving teacher from Pytchley village school. "As soon as the children arrived in school at the age of four she gave them each a tennis ball to play with. They learned to bounce and throw and catch from an early age. It became second nature. No wonder Pytchley beat lots of bigger schools in the catching competition I organised at our centre of excellence, held in my old school, Stamford Road, or the William Knibb Centre as it's now known."

He is less complimentary about the large urban school he visited where, despite the wickets painted on walls encouraging the children to practise, tennis balls and cricket bats were banned during playtimes. "It's all rather pointless unless there's continuity. I sometimes felt that the moment I left the school site they'd be out playing rounders."

Another major constraint is the exorbitant cost of equipment. "A parent told me recently that it cost around £300 to kit out his son to play for the Northamptonshire Board XI. What with flannels, sweaters, pads, bat, gloves, 'coffin', and the now mandatory helmet alone costing £30, it's an expensive business."

Another important breeding ground for young talent is experiencing similar problems to the schools. "'At club level it's often a case of too much falling to the same few to organise. In many clubs it's the same people doing the work now that were there thirty or more years ago. Will anyone else step into their shoes when that generation has gone? I know that many local cricket clubs give a high priority to developing young players and youth cricket is flourishing but the wastage is enormous when they reach their late teens. Too often promising youngsters are denied the chance to break through into the adult sides. Gone are the Kettering Town League and the days when three matches were played simultaneously on grounds like the North Park or Recreation Field. And have you seen the state of the pitches or the changing facilities? There's little Sunday cricket either. Wives and partners are much more influential these days. You might be allowed to play once at the weekend, but twice is out of the question."

In the face of all these problems, it's pertinent to ask if cricket remains a worthwhile activity for young people. Brian has no doubts. "The character-building aspects of cricket still make it unique, despite these match-fixing revelations. You need to learn how to cope with success and failure. Technique is crucial and requires hours of practice. The individual contest between bowler and batsman makes it a game within a game. Ninety-nine times out of a hundred you can play for yourself and still play for the team, but there comes the occasion when the interests of the side come first. Good batsmen shouldn't use their skill to avoid the better bowlers and preserve their skins or batting averages. You soon lose credibility in those circumstances if you're seen to be playing for yourself."

Fenner's holds many happy memories. Brian's century in 1950 (before the pavilion in the background was built) was followed by a ton for Ian in the 1987 under 19 Cambridge Festival. It's a venue still visited annually as Brian continues to search for new talent.

Brian and Angela still worship regularly at the Fuller Baptist Church and, as friends and relatives are quick to point out, they act out their faith in a practical way. However, it is easy to see why the strong principles which have dominated Brian's life since boyhood have occasionally resulted in conflict. It is not only fools that are suffered less than gladly.

Like so many of his generation, he found it difficult to accept the decline of the overt discipline and formality that had both shaped his formative years and laid the corner-stone on which he built his professional life. During school, work, National Service and his cricketing apprenticeship he had learned to respect those from whom he could learn. Men like Arthur Weatherall, Joe Buckby, the Rev Beach, Edgar Towell, Freddie Brown and Dennis Brookes. But this was far from blind subservience. If they were his 'betters' it was only because they could do things better than he could, be it making shoes or making runs.

He has never tired of learning. When the time came to pass on his own expertise it was only to be expected that he would demand the same response from his 'pupils'. For some, his occasionally uncompromising approach to discipline smacked of the 'sergeant–major', but to Brian responsibility and respect were not negotiable.

BIBLIOGRAPHY

The most important source of information was undoubtedly local newspapers: the **Kettering Leader**, the **Northamptonshire Evening Telegraph** and the **Northampton Chronicle & Echo**. National dailies have also been used extensively.

This publication would not have been possible without access to the following annuals and series.

MCC Yearbooks	MCC	Annual
News Chronicle Cricket Annual	News Chronicle	Annual
Northamptonshire CCC Year Books	Northamptonshire CCC	Annual
Playfair Cricket Annual	Headline	Annual
Wisden Cricketers' Almanack	Wisden	Annual
County First-Class Records	Limlow	Series
First-Class Cricket: A Complete Record 19XX	Limlow	Series

Books consulted and/or mentioned include:

Addis, Ian		
A Passing Game, Part 1 1945-1970	Jema	1995
Bailey, Thorn & Wynne-Thomas		
Who's Who of Cricketers	Newnes / ACS	1984
Bell, Bert		
Still Seeing Red	Glasgow City Libraries	1996
Benaud, Richie		
On Reflection	Willow	1984
Bird, Dickie		
Not Out	Arthur Barker	1978
Birley, Derek		
A Social History of English Cricket	Aurum	1999
Brown, Freddie		
Cricket Musketeer	Nicholas Kaye	1954
Carr, JL		
Carr's Dictionary of extra-ordinary English Cricketers	Quince Tree	1981
Chalke, Stephen		
Caught in the Memory	Fairfield	1999
Runs in the Memory	Fairfield	1997
Coldham, James D		
Northamptonshire Cricket: A History	Heinemann	1959
Cowdrey, Colin		
MCC	Hodder & Stoughton	1976
Engel, Matthew & Radd, Andrew		
The History of Northamptonshire CCC	Helm	1993
Foot, David		
Harold Gimblett	Heinemann	1982

Francis, Lionel		
75 Years of Southern League Football	Pelham	1969
Grande, Frank		
Northampton Town FC Centenary History	Yore	1997
Graveney, Tom & Seabrook, Mike		
Bloody Lucky	Simon & Schuster	1990
Groom, Andy & Robinson, Mick		
The Posh	Yore	1992
Hill, Alan		
Bill Edrich	Andre Deutsch	1994
Holt, Richard		
Sport and the British	OUP	1989
Hughes, Simon		
A Lot of Hard Yakka	Headline	1997
Lemmon, David		
The Great Wicket-keepers	Stanley Paul	1984
Martin-Jenkins, Christopher		
The Complete Who's Who of Test Cricketers	Orbis	1980
The Spirit of Cricket	Faber & Faber	1994
The Wisden Book of County Cricket	Queen Ann	1981
McDonald, Trevor		
Clive Lloyd	Grafton	1986
McIntosh, PC		
Sport in Society	Alden & Mowbray	1963
Mosey, Don		
Fred Then and Now	Kingswood	1991
Laker	Queen Anne	1989
Pawson, Tony		
Runs and Catches	Faber	1980
Peebles, Ian		
Denis Compton	Macmillan	1971
Robertson-Glasgow, RC		
Cricket Prints	Sportsman's Book Club	1951
Ross, Alan		
The Penguin Cricketer's Companion	Penguin	1960
Williams, Marcus		
The Way to Lord's	Willow	1983
Wright, Graeme		
Betrayal	Witherby	1993

Larter, JDF	111, 113, 119, 121, 122, 125, 130, 131, 135, 140, 146	Mann, FG	57
		Mann, J	156
		Manning, JS	88
Lawton, T	76-8, 96	Mansfield, A	78, 97
Laxton, K	28	Marinovic, D	175
Lay, RS	108, 123	Marks, VJ	105
Leadbetter, M	153	Marlar, RG	111
Leadbetter, SA	84, 153, 157	Marner, PT	127, 132
Lee, Fs	67	Marshall, P	110
Lee, G	6	Marshall, RE	131
Lee, L	23	Marston, M	97
Lee, PG	140	Martin-Jenkins, C	42
Lenham, LJ	112	Mason, A	10
Lever, P	143	Mason, JM	114
Lewis, AR	112	Mather, H	96, 97
Lewis, F	126	Matthews, KPA	41
Liddell, AWG	8	Matthews, S	167
Lightfoot, A	64, 106, 113, 114, 118, 119, 124, 130, 147	Matthews, TJ	43
		May, PBH	10, 82, 83, 177
		Medhurst, H	38
Lilford, Lord	40	Melford, M	105, 116
Lillee, DK	116	Melluish, MEL	81, 93
Lilley, R	22	Mence, MD	129
Lindwall, RR	24, 25, 112	Mercer, J	180
Livingston, L	8, 10, 36, 40, 41, 62, 64, 67, 71, 80, 88, 90, 104, 116, 148	Meunier, A	29
		Meyer, BJ	117
		Milburn, B	155
Lloyd, CH	123	Milburn, C	10, 66, 113, 114, 118, 120, 122, 125, 128, 129, 131, 135, 138, 140, 141, 143, 145, 146, 154, 155, 172
Lloyd, D	167		
Loader, PJ	65, 88		
Loasby, B	14		
Lock, GAR	82, 83, 88, 138, 169		
Logie, J	77	Miller, KR	24
Lomax, JG	108	Miller, S	29
Long, A	91	Mills, JM	52
Longley, JI	159	Mills, JPC	40, 166
Lowson, FA	9, 40	Milton, CA	117, 118, 131, 143
Loye, MB	63, 64, 106	Milton, J	44, 73, 139
Lucas, D	172	Minney, JH	59, 114, 140
Lynn, V	12	Mitchum, BA	157
Macaulay, A	77	Montgomerie, RR	64
McAuley, P	51	Moore, HD	27
McCartney, A	159	Moore, R	75
McConnon, JE	65	Morgan, DC	155
McDonald, CC	72	Morris, A	24, 25
McDonald, H	78	Morris, RSM	159
McGlew, DJ	110	Morrow, HJE	96, 98
McIntosh, PC	94	Mortimore, JB	118, 141, 142
McIntyre, TF	114	Mosey, D	59
McKenzie, GD	114, 125	Moss, AE	66, 67, 122
McLaurin, Lord	43 , 94, 140	Moss, Amos	78
McNamee, P	75	Munton, B	102
Mabelson, D	28	Murray, JT	143
Maguire, P	28	Mushtaq Mohammad	137, 138, 140, 141, 143
Malfait, J	126, 178		
Mallender, NA	164, 166, 167, 169	Nashe, T	140
Mallett, AA	143, 144	Neale, PA	51
Mandeville, C	27	Nelson, A	75
Mandeville, C	106, 107	Newsom, DJ	114